Technician Class

FCC License Preparation
for
Element 2
Technician Class Theory

BY
GORDON WEST
WB6NOA

FOURTH EDITION

Master Publishing, Inc.

Also by Gordon West, WB6NOA

General Class
FCC License Preparation for
Element 3 General Class Theory

Extra Class
FCC License Preparation for
Element 4 Extra Class Theory

GROL-Plus
General Radiotelephone Operator License
Plus Ship Radar Endorsement

(*with* Fred Maia, W5YI)

FCC Commercial Radio License Preparations for
Element 1, Element 3, and Element 8 Question Pools

This book was developed and published by:
Master Publishing, Inc.
Lincolnwood, Illinois

Editing by:
Pete Trotter, KB9SMG
Gerald Luecke, KB5TZY

> *Thanks to Fred Maia, W5YI Group, for technical review of the RF safety and FCC material contained in this book.*

Printing by:
Arby Graphic Service
Lincolnwood, Illinois

Photograph Credit:
All photographs that do not have a source identification are either courtesy of Radio Shack, the author, or Master Publishing, Inc. originals.
Cover photo by Julian Frost, N3JF.

Fourth Edition
   9   8   7   6   5   4   3   2   1

Table of Contents

QUESTION POOL NOMENCLATURE

The latest nomenclature changes and question pool numbering system recommended by the Volunteer Examiner Coordinator's question pool committee (QPC) for question pools have been incorporated in this book. The Technician Class (Element 2) question pool has been rewritten at junior-high-school and high-school reading levels, respectively. This question pool is valid from April 15, 2000 until June 30, 2003.

FCC RULES, REGULATIONS AND POLICIES

The NCVEC QPC releases revised question pools on a regular cycle, and deletions as necessary. The FCC releases changes to FCC rules, regulations and policies as they are implemented. This book includes the most recent information released by the FCC at the time this copy was printed.

Preface

Welcome to the fabulous, fun hobby of Amateur Radio! It has never been easier to enter the amateur radio service than now!

Changes to Amateur Radio regulations announced by the Federal Communications Commission on December 30, 1999, that became effective April 15, 2000, have made it easier than every to obtain your entry-level Technician Class ham radio license — and to move up through all the license classes to earn the top Extra Class license.

And when I say "made it easier than ever" I really mean it! The Technician Class examination question pool has been reduced from 943 Q&A's down to 384. The new Element 2 written examination that you will take now has just 35 total questions on it, down from 65. *Absolutely no knowledge of Morse code is required for your entry-level ham license.* And there aren't many math skills required, either.

In just one exam session, you can satisfy all of the requirements to earn your Technician Class amateur radio license. Within days of passing your written exam (you need to answer 26 of the 35 questions correctly — that's just 74%) you can be on the air talking through repeaters, transmitting via satellites to work other stations thousands of miles away, and even getting a taste of some ionospheric skywave worldwide contacts.

And once you get started, you won't want to stop at Technician! Everyone will want the General Class license that gives you worldwide privileges on every single ham band. To study for your Element 3 exam, use my *General Class* book. And it's very easy to learn Morse code using my tapes, CDs, or computer software. The FCC has reduced the required code speed to just 5-words-per-minute. It's the only code test required for the General, and that qualifies you for the top ham radio ticket — the Extra Class license. Hey, *even you* can learn the code at 5-wpm in just one weekend!

Extra Class is the top Amateur Radio license. When you're ready to move up to that level, I have a book to help you study for that written exam as well — *Extra Class.*

Three license classes. One Morse code speed. It couldn't be easier to get involved in one of the most fascinating and fun hobbies in the world!

Ready to get started? Hurry up — I am regularly on the airwaves and I hope to make contact with you very soon with your new Technician Class call sign.

73

Gordon West, WB6NOA

About This Book

This book provides you with all of the study materials you need to prepare yourself to take and pass the Element 2 written examination to obtain your Technician Class amateur radio license. Technician Class is the entry-level amateur operator/primary station license issued by the Federal Communications Commission — the FCC. *Absolutely no Morse code test is required* for the Technician Class license, which will give you unlimited VHF and UHF ham band privileges.

Our book also provides you with valuable information you need to be an active participant in the amateur ranks. To help you get the most out of *Technician Class,* here's a look at how our book is organized:

- *Chapter 1* provides an overview of the amateur service, and gives a brief history of ham radio regulations. It contains details on the December, 1999 FCC Report & Order that greatly simplified the FCC's Amateur Radio service licensing structure, which streamlined the number of examination elements and reduced the emphasis on Morse code for all classes of ham radio licenses. It's your introduction and orientation to ham radio.

- *Chapter 2* tells you about all of the ham radio operating privileges you will have with your new Technician Class license — including those additional privileges you can earn if you decide to take and pass the *optional* 5-wpm Morse code test.

- *Chapter 3* describes the Element 2, Technician Class written examination, and contains all 384 questions that comprise the Element 2 question pool. 35 of these questions will be on your written examination. If you answer 26 of them correctly (74%) you'll pass the exam and receive your FCC license. Along the way, as you study these questions, you'll be learning important things you need to know to get started on the air as a licensed ham.

- *Chapter 4* focuses on Morse code. Even though you don't need the code to become a Technician Class operator, it has never been easier to move up through the ranks of amateur radio knowing the code at just 5-words-per-minute. We urge you to learn the code!

- *Chapter 5* will tell you what to expect when you take your Element 2 written exam, where to find an exam session, how you will apply for and receive your new FCC license, and more — all the details you need to know to get your license and get on the air.

- The *Appendix* has valuable lists and reference information. And reading the *Glossary* will get you up to speed on some of the amateur radio "lingo" that you might not understand as you begin studying our book.

So let's begin with your orientation to the exciting world of ham radio!

THE AMATEUR SERVICE

ABOUT THIS CHAPTER

As a person who is about to be a new member of the amateur service, we think it's important to tell you a little bit about the nature of our hobby, its history, and give you an overview of how you will progress through the amateur ranks from your first, entry-level Technician Class license to the top amateur ticket — the Extra Class license.

In this chapter you'll also learn all of the licensing requirements under the new rules that became effective April 15, 2000. And you'll learn about the six classes of license that were in effect prior to that rules change. That way, when you run into a Novice or Advanced operator on the air, you'll have some understanding of their skill level, experience, and frequency privileges.

We know this background knowledge will make you a better ham!

WHAT IS THE AMATEUR SERVICE?

More than 750,000 Americans are licensed amateur radio operators. According to our Federal Communications Commission, the U.S. Government agency responsible for licensing amateur operators: "The amateur service is for qualified persons of all ages who are interested in radio technique solely with a personal aim and without pecuniary interest." Ham radio — as it also is known — is first and foremost a fun hobby! In addition, it is a *service*.

The amateur service exists under international treaty and is authorized in practically every country around the world. Each government has its own rules for admission to the ham ranks. Numerous frequency bands throughout the radio spectrum are allocated to the amateur service on an international basis, making it possible for amateur operators to communicate with each other in all parts of the world — even in space. Astronaut Owen Garriott, W5LFL, became the first ham operator to communicate from space during the Columbia/Spacelab mission in 1983. He stood at the window of the Spacelab and used a hand-held radio and an antenna to talk to fellow hams here on Earth. Gordon West, your author, was among the first hams to communicate with W5LFL in the Spacelab.

More than 2,000,000 operators exchange ham radio greetings and messages by voice, teleprinting, telegraphy, facsimile, and television worldwide. Japan, which also has a no-code license, has over one million hams alone! It is very commonplace for U.S. amateurs to communicate with Russian amateurs, while China is just getting started with its amateur service. Being a ham operator is a very good way to promote international good will.

AMATEUR SERVICE BENEFITS

The benefits of ham radio are countless! There is something for everyone. Ham operators are probably known best for their contributions during times of disaster. When all else fails, the ham operator traditionally gets messages through. In addition, over the years, amateurs have contributed much to electronic technology. They have even designed and built their own orbiting communications satellites.

On the other hand, the amateur service isn't just for the technically inclined. It is for everyone of all ages. There are ham radio operators under eight years old — and many over 80! Most hams are just plain folks, but many famous celebrities are amateur operators. Arizona's U.S. Senator Barry Goldwater was K7UGA, ex-pro baseball player Joe Rudi is NK7U, guitarist Chet Atkins is WA4CZD, and singer Ronnie Milsap is WB4KCG. Other famous amateurs are Bill Halligan (who founded Hallicrafters), Arthur Godfrey, Andy Devine, Pee Wee Hunt, Alvino Rey, General Curtis LeMay, Walter Cronkite, Jon Bongiovi, Patti Loveless, Gary Shandling... and recent Gordon West Radio School graduates Priscilla Presley, Marlon Brando, and Shari Belafonte.

For the handicapped, ham radio is a godsend! It is a great equalizer, since everyone is the same behind a microphone or a packet radio computer keyboard. Being an amateur service ham operator can take the disabled to the far flung corners of the world. Recent FCC rules for the disabled now allow special examination techniques to be offered to anyone with a handicap.

The ham fraternity knows no geographic, political or social barrier. And if you stick to your guns and make the effort, you are going to be part of our fraternity. Probably the primary prerequisite for passing any amateur radio license examination is the will to do it. If you follow the suggestions in this book, your chances of passing the written exam are excellent. If you are fascinated by radio communication, learning will be easy and fun!

Before we go into the exam requirements, we want to give you a perspective on how ham radio has grown since its inception.

A BRIEF HISTORY OF AMATEUR RADIO LICENSING

Amateur radio really got started around the turn of the last century when Italian inventor Guglielmo Marconi flashed his first wireless signal across the English Channel in 1899. Two years later, he telegraphed the letter "s" from England to Newfoundland. This was the first successful trans-Atlantic radio transmission. *Marconi considered himself an amateur* and he inspired hundreds of others to experiment with radio communications.

Before government licensing of amateur operators and stations was instituted in 1912, radio amateurs could operate on any wavelength they chose and could even select their own call letters. The Radio Act of 1912 mandated the first Federal licensing of radio stations and banished amateurs to the short wavelengths of less than 200 meters. But these requirements didn't stop them.

Marconi in 1896
(Courtesy Marconi Co. Archives)

Within a few short years, there were thousands of licensed ham operators in the United States.

Since radio signals do not respect national boundaries, it is international in scope. National governments enact and enforce radio laws within a framework of international agreements which are overseen by the International Telecommunications Union. The ITU is a worldwide United Nations agency headquartered in Geneva, Switzerland. The ITU divides the radio spectrum into a number of segments or frequency bands. Each band is reserved for a particular use. Amateur radio is fortunate to have many bands allocated to it all across the radio spectrum.

In the United States, the Federal Communications Commission is the Federal agency responsible for the regulation of wire and radio communications. The FCC further allocates frequency bands to the various services in accordance with the ITU plan — including the Amateur Service — and regulates stations and operators.

By international agreement, in 1927 the alphabet was apportioned among various nations for basic call sign use. The prefix letters K, N and W were assigned to the United States, which also shares the letter A with some other countries.

The Early Years of Amateur Radio Licensing

In the early years of amateur radio licensing in the U.S., the classes of licenses were designated by the letters "A," "B," and "C." The highest license class with the most privileges was "A."

In 1951, the FCC dropped the letter designations and gave the license classes names. They also added a new Novice Class — a one-year, non-renewable license for beginners that required a 5-wpm Morse code speed proficiency and a 20-question written examination on elementary theory and regulations, with both tests taken before one licensed ham.

In 1967, the Advanced Class was added to the Novice, Technician, General and Extra classes. The General exam required 13-wpm code speed, and the Extra Class required 20-wpm. Each of the five written examinations were progressively more comprehensive and formed what came to be known as the *Incentive Licensing System*. The idea was to get General Class amateurs to upgrade their license. Advanced and Extra Class amateurs were awarded tiny slivers of voice and CW spectrum — the "incentive" to upgrade — in exchange for increased telegraphy skill and electronic knowledge. Many General Class amateurs were furious that they had lost some spectrum privileges and had to pass more examinations to get them back. Some are still angry to this day!

In the '70s, the Technician Class license became very popular because of the number of repeater stations appearing on the air that extended the range of VHF and UHF mobile stations and some very-large, hand-held equipment. It also was very fashionable to be able to patch your mobile radio into the telephone system, a practice which allowed hams to make telephone calls from their automobiles.

In 1979, the international Amateur Service regulations were changed to permit all countries to waive the manual Morse code proficiency requirement for "...stations making use exclusively of frequencies above 30 MHz." This set the stage for the Technician "no-code" license.

Self-Testing In The Amateur Service

Among the things that happened in the '80s that encouraged the growth of ham radio was the advent of the volunteer examination program that occurred when the FCC turned over responsibility for the actual test giving to the amateur community. Until 1983, all amateur radio operator examinations were administered by FCC personnel at various FCC Field Offices around the country. The following year, the FCC adopted a two-tier system beneath it called the VEC System to handle license examinations in the amateur service. It also increased the length of the term of amateur radio licenses from five to ten years.

The VEC (Volunteer Examiner Coordinator) System was formed after Congress passed laws that allowed the FCC to accept the services of Volunteer Examiners (or VEs) to prepare and administer amateur service license examinations. The testing activity of VEs is managed by Volunteer Examiner Coordinators (or VECs). A VEC acts as the administrative liaison between the VEs who administer the various ham examinations and the FCC, which grants the license.

A team of three VEs, who must be approved by a VEC, is needed to conduct amateur radio examinations. General Class amateurs may serve as examiners for the Technician Class and the 5-wpm code test. Advanced Class amateurs may administer exam Elements 1, 2 and 3; that is, all except Element 4. The Extra Class written Element 4 may only be administered by a VE who holds an Extra Class license.

For the first couple of years of the VEC System, the FCC handled the development and revision of the examination questions. The questions supposedly were "secret," but word eventually got around as to their content. To combat this situation, the FCC changed to a question pool system that had been successfully used by the Federal Aviation Administration for its written examinations: henceforth, all exam questions would be selected from lists of publicly-available question pools.

In 1986, the FCC turned over responsibility for maintenance of the exam questions to the National Conference of VECs, which appointed a Question Pool Committee (QPC) to develop and revise the various question pools according to a schedule. The QPC is required by the FCC to have at least ten times as many questions in each of the pools as may appear on an examination. As a rule, one question pool is changed annually. The QPC and the question pool system still continues in operation today.

Since the inception of the VE system in 1984, more than one million examinations have been administered to applicants for amateur radio operator licenses under the VEC System at essentially no cost to the government or taxpayer.

Novice Enhancement

In 1987, there was a new program to generate additional enthusiasm among entry-level amateurs. The "Novice Enhancement" proceeding allowed beginners to operate on the 220-MHz and 1270-MHz bands at reduced power, and the sub-band on 10 meters for Novices and Technicians was enlarged to 28.1 to 28.5 MHz (CW) and 28.3 to 28.5 MHz (CW and SSB). This provided an incentive for Novices to pass the 13-wpm code test and other written theory exams so they could obtain access to still more worldwide frequencies. The plan worked well.

The Novice written Element 2 was increased from 20 to 30 questions, and written Element 3 was split into two parts with the Technician (VHF-oriented) questions being placed into the Element 3-A pool and the General (HF-oriented) questions into the Element 3-B pool. These so-called "old Techs" would ultimately be granted complete credit for the new General Class license since they had been examined on code and HF operation. The new RF safety standards introduced in 1998 further increased the Novice exam questions from 30 to 35, and the Technician and General from 25 to 30 questions each.

By this time, the number of Amateur Service examinations had been increased to eight. Five different license classes could now be obtained by passing combinations of five written and three telegraphy examinations.

A major boost to the hobby occurred in 1991, when the 5-wpm Morse code requirement for the Technician Class was the eliminated. New licensees were now permitted to operate on all amateur bands above 30 MHz. Applicants for the no-code Technician license had to pass the 35-question Novice and 30-question Technician class written examinations but, for the first time, not a Morse code test. Those two written examinations provided the basis for the new Element 2 exam, the requirement for the new Technician Class license that is the subject of our book.

Technician Class amateurs who also passed a 5-wpm code test were awarded a Technician-Plus license, now creating a total of six Amateur Service license classes. Besides their 30 MHz and higher no-code frequency privileges, they gained the Novice CW privileges and a sliver of the 10 meter voice spectrum. It was during this time of upgrading in the late '80s and '90s that there were all sorts of different Technician Class categories — "Old Techs," "Classic" Technicians, Technician "No-Coders," "Tech Plus" code, and Technicians with code credit that didn't show up on their older Tech licenses. Much of this confusion continues to this day as Volunteer Examiners try to sort out who passed the original 5-wpm Morse code test, and when!

The Amateur Service Is Restructured

As we approached the end of the 1990s, the majority of licensed amateur operators realized there was a lot more to HF operation than just passing a Morse code test. In 1998, the FCC began a review of the amateur radio service with the objective of streamlining the licensing process, eliminating unnecessary and duplicated rules, and to possibly reduce the emphasis on the Morse code tests. The result of this review was a complete restructuring of the U.S. amateur service that became effective April 15, 2000. Henceforth, applicants for amateur service licenses will only be examined for three license classes:

- Technician Class — the VHF/UHF entry level license;
- General Class — the HF entry level license, and
- Amateur Extra Class — a technically-oriented senior license.

In addition, there now is only one Morse code test speed at 5 words-per-minute (now called Element 1), which is required for the General Class and Extra Class licenses.

Individuals with licenses issued before April 15, 2000, have been "grandfathered" under the new rules. This means that current Novice and Advanced Class amateurs will be able to modify and renew their licenses indefinitely. Technician-Plus amateur licenses will be renewed as Technician Class, but these licensees will retain their HF operating privileges indefinitely. The FCC elected not to change the operating privileges of any class. The previously-mandated ten written exam topics were eliminated and the VECs' Question Pool Committee (QPC) will now decide the content of each the three written examinations. Both the Technician Class Element 2 and General Class Element 3 written examinations contain 35 multiple-choice questions. The Extra Class Element 4 written examination has 50 questions.

Finally, there were no automatic upgrades. Technicians (pre-1987) with 5-wpm code and Element 3B credit qualify immediately for the General Class license, but must apply at VE session showing evidence of having held a Technician license prior to 1987.

That completes your history lesson. Now let's turn our attention to the privileges you'll earn as new Technician Class operator.

LICENSE PRIVILEGES

An amateur operator license conveys many privileges. As the control operator of an amateur radio station, a ham operator is responsible for the quality of the station's transmissions. Most radio equipment must be authorized by the government before it can be widely used by the public but, for the most part, this is not true for amateur equipment! Unlike the citizen's band service, amateurs may design, construct, modify and repair their own equipment. But you must have a license, and even though it is easier than ever, there are certain things you must know before you can obtain the needed license from the FCC.

Everything you need to know is covered in this book.

OPERATOR LICENSE REQUIREMENTS

To qualify for an amateur operator/primary station license, a person must pass an examination according to FCC guidelines. The degree of skill and knowledge that the candidate demonstrates to the examiners determines the class of operator license for which the person is qualified.

There is a big difference between CB and amateur operation. The amateur service is both a public service and a hobby. CB exists for short-distance, low-power, personal and business communications only. There is no 150-mile distance limitation in ham radio as there is using CB. Using higher-output power levels, you can talk around the world — limited only by radio propagation conditions. Hams are licensed with call signs and don't use "handles." Licensing and call signs were discontinued for CB many years ago. CBers are prohibited from experimenting, which is the cornerstone and one of the fun activities of Amateur Radio. You'll find that ham radio offers you far more capabilities — more frequencies, higher power, more emissions, more modes — and lots of fun, too. Hams can even interconnect their radios with the telephone system.

Anyone is eligible to become a U.S. licensed amateur operator (including foreign nationals, if they are not a representative of a foreign government). There is no age limitation. If you can pass the examinations, you can become a ham!

One of the reasons for the existence of the amateur service is to provide communications in times of emergency. Although hardly ever used on the ham bands during an emergency anymore, CW (Morse code) is one way to pierce through interference when other modes cannot get through. Packet radio is another very special type of emergency communications that uses your personal computer over the airwaves. As an amateur operator Technician Class licensee, you can concentrate on packet communications without ever having to worry about learning the Morse code for emergency communications.

Why Morse Code?

By the way, Morse code is *required* under the terms of international radio regulations (Article S25 of the International Telecommunications Union's International Radio Regulations) for operation on those worldwide frequencies shared by other amateur radio operators throughout the globe. Passing the simple 5-wpm Morse code test will meet these requirements.

If you learned Morse code in the Scouts or military, or you just like the intrigue of translating short and long sounds into letters and words, you can go ahead and request the 5-wpm code test at the same session when you take your entry-level Technician Class license examination.

Again, a Morse code test is *not* required for the entry level Technician Class. But if you do decide to take and successfully pass the simple 5-wpm code test (Element 1), you will get a Certificate of Successful Completion of Examination (CSCE) certificate good for 365 days, during which time you will want to take and pass the General Class written exam (Element 3). In addition, even if you never upgrade to General Class, once you pass the 5-wpm test you get to operate forever on the Technician portion of the worldwide high-frequency 80-, 40-, and 15-meter bands reserved for CW, and on the segment of the 10-meter band reserved for CW/SSB.

Remember: *exam credit* is good for 365 days. The *operating authority* you earn by passing the code test remains valid as long as you hold and renew your Technician Class license. If you fail to pass the General Class Element 3 written exam and want to upgrade later, you'll have to retake the 5-wpm code test after one year to regain your exam credit. The 5-wpm test is the only Morse code test you will have to pass, since it is a requirement for both the General and Extra Class. And if you decide to stay a Technician for the rest of your life, you can do that, too — just renew your license (without any test required) every 10 years.

OPERATOR LICENSE CLASSES & EXAM REQUIREMENTS

There are now three official, successive levels of amateur operator licenses issued by the FCC. Each license requires progressively higher levels of learning and proficiency, and each gives you additional operating privileges. This is known as *incentive licensing* — a method of strengthening the amateur service by offering more radio spectrum privileges in exchange for more electronic knowledge. There is no waiting time required to upgrade from one amateur license class to another, nor any required waiting time to retake a failed examination. You can even take all three examinations and the Morse code test at one sitting if you're really brave!

Table 1-1 details the new amateur service license structure and required examinations with three license classes and one Morse code test. *Table 1-2* details the *former* license structure, which had six classes of license and three Morse code tests. Individuals who hold these former licenses have been "grandfathered" under the new rules and may continue to enjoy their present radio frequency privileges, holding that specific license indefinitely as long as they renew it every 10 years. Comparing the two charts will give you an excellent idea of how much easier the FCC has made it to get to the top ham radio license.

Table 1-1: Current Amateur License Classes and Exam Requirements
(Effective April 15, 2000)

License Class	Exam Element	Type of Examination
Technician Class	2	35-question, multiple-choice written examination. Minimum passing score is 26 questions answered correctly (74%).
General Class	3	35-question, multiple-choice written examination. Minimum passing score is 26 questions answered correctly (74%). Also requires passing Element 1 Morse code test.
Extra Class	4	50-question, multiple-choice written examination. Minimum passing score is 37 questions answered correctly (74%).
Morse Code	1	Demonstrate ability to receive Morse code at a 5-word-per-minute rate. (See Chapter 4 for more information and an example test.)

Table 1-2. Previous Amateur License Classes and Exam Requirements
(Prior to April 15, 2000)

Grandfathered License Class	Exam/Test Elements	Type of Examination
Novice	Element 2 and Element 1A	35-question written examination 5-wpm code test
Technician	Element 2 and 3A	65-question written examination in 2 parts (35 Element 2 plus 30 Element 3A questions) (No Morse code requirement)
Technician-Plus	Element 2 and Element 3A and Element 1A	35-question written examination, and 30-question written examination, and 5-wpm code test
General	Element 3B and Element 1B	30-question written examination 13-wpm code test
Advanced	Element 4A	50-question written examination (No additional Morse code requirement)
Extra	Element 4B and Element 1C	40-question written examination 20-wpm code test

ABOUT THE WRITTEN EXAMINATIONS

What is the focus of each of the new written examinations, and how does it relate to gaining expanding amateur radio privileges as you move up the ladder toward your Extra Class license? *Table 1-3* summarizes the subjects covered in each written examination element. *Table 1-4* shows the examination subelement topics, total number of questions within each pool, and the number of questions taken from the various subelements for each of the three written examinations.

Table 1-3. Question Element Subjects

Exam Element	License Class	Subjects
Element 2	Technician	Elementary operating procedures, radio regulations, and a smattering of beginning electronics. Emphasis will be on VHF and UHF operating.
Element 3	General	HF (high-frequency) operating privileges, amateur practices, radio regulations, and a little more electronics. Emphasis is on HF bands.
Element 4	Extra	Basically a technical examination. Covers specialized operating procedures, more radio regulations, formulas and heavy math. Also covers the specifics on amateur testing procedures.

Table 1-4. Examination Topic Distribution Over License Classes

Written Examination Subelement	Element 2 — Technician Class		Element 3 — General Class		Element 4 — Extra Class	
	Pool	Exam	Pool	Exam	Pool	Exam
1 Commission's Rules	102	9	66	6	99	7
2 Operating Procedures	55	5	66	6	46	4
3 Radio Wave Propagation	33	3	33	3	34	3
4 Amateur Radio Practices	44	4	55	5	68	5
5 Electrical Principles	33	3	22	2	111	9
6 Circuit Components	22	2	11	1	72	5
7 Practical Circuits	22	2	11	1	95	7
8 Signals and Emissions	20	2	22	2	69	5
9 Antennas and Feed Lines	22	2	44	4	71	5
0 RF Safety	31	3	55	5	0	0
Total Questions	384	35	385	35	665	50

No Jumping Allowed

All written examinations for an amateur radio license are additive. You *cannot* skip over a license class or by-pass a required examination as you upgrade from Technician to General to Extra. For example, to obtain a General Class license, you must first take and pass the Element 2 written examination for the Technician Class license, plus the Element 3 written examination and the required 5-wpm Element 1 code test. To obtain the Extra Class license, you must first pass the Element 2 (Technician) and Element 3 (General) written examinations, and the 5-wpm Element 1 code test, and then successfully pass the Element 4 (Extra) written examination. Again, you only need to pass the 5-wpm Morse Code test once.

THE ELEMENT 2 EXAM

Now that you have an overview of the history and current status of ham radio, as well as all of the required written examinations and the one Morse code test, it's time to turn our attention to the heart of our book — the Element 2 written examination that will earn you your Technician Class license.

Study Time

The Technician Class question pool has been cut by more than half, so it will probably take you no more than three weeks to study for Technician Element 2 exam (and an additional couple of weeks to prepare for the 5-wpm code test, if you decide to go that route). Remember, you can't skip over Technician and take the General written test first — you must take the written examinations in order: Element 2 Technician, Element 3 General, and Element 4 Extra.

The Element 2 Question Pool

The Element 2, multiple-choice Technician Class question pool contains a total of 384 questions and multiple-choice answers and distracters (the false answers are called *distracters*). 35 of these questions will appear on your up-coming Technician Class, Element 2, written examination. All of these examination questions, plus the precise multiple-choice answers — one of which is the correct answer — *are identical to those included in this book.*

The Volunteer Examiners who will administer your exam are not permitted to reword the questions, nor are they be permitted to change any of the right or wrong answers (but they can change the A B C D *order* of the answers). This is good news for you — there are no secret questions, no strange answers, and absolutely no surprises on your written exam once you have completely studied this book. EVERY QUESTION IN THIS BOOK, LETTER FOR LETTER, WORD FOR WORD, NUMBER FOR NUMBER, AND EVERY RIGHT AND WRONG ANSWER, WILL BE EXACTLY THE SAME ON YOUR UP-COMING 35-QUESTION TECHNICIAN, ELEMENT 2, TEST.

The new question pool for Technician Element 2 in this book went into effect on April 15, 2000, and will remain valid until June 30, 2003. During this three-year period, the questions and answers are frozen and may not be altered on your upcoming test. If FCC rules change or advancements in technology cause any questions to become obsolete, those questions will simply be eliminated from your up-coming test and there will be absolutely no surprises in the exam room.

Your Element 2 written examination will have 35 questions. A score of 26 or more correct (74%) will earn you a passing grade. The right and wrong answers are so obviously different that there should be no hesitation on your part in determining the correct answer. Again, there will be absolutely no changes in the question and answer wording from the question pool that appears in Chapter 3 of this book. The only thing you *won't find* on your upcoming exam will be the author's descriptions of why the right answer is the correct one, or why the wrong answers are ridiculously incorrect.

Table 1-6 shows you the subelement topics, the total number of questions in the pool, and the number of questions from each subelement that will appear on your Element 2 written examination.

Table 1-6. Question Distribution for the Technician Class Element 2 Exam

Subelement Number	Subelement Topic	No. of Questions in Pool	No. of Questions on Exam
T1	Commission's Rules (FCC rules for the Amateur Radio services)	102	9
T2	Operating Procedures (Amateur station operating procedures)	55	5
T3	Radio Wave Propagation (Radio wave propagation characteristics of amateur service frequency bands)	33	3
T4	Amateur Radio Practices (Amateur Radio practices)	44	4
T5	Electrical Principles (Electrical principles as applied to amateur station equipment)	33	3
T6	Circuit Components (Amateur station equipment circuit components)	22	2
T7	Practical Circuits (Practical circuits employed in amateur station equipment)	22	2
T8	Signals and Emissions (Signals and emissions transmitted by amateur stations)	20	2
T9	Antennas and Feed Lines (Amateur station antennas and feed lines)	22	2
T0	RF Safety (Radiofrequency environmental safety practices at an amateur station)	31	3
Total		384	35

(Titles in parentheses are the subelement titles on which you will be examined.)

TAKING THE ELEMENT 2 EXAM

Here's a summary of what you can expect when you go to the exam session in your area to take the Element 2 written examination for your Technician Class license. Detailed information about how to find an exam session, what to expect at the session, what to bring to the session, and more, is included in Chapter 5.

Examination Administration

As mentioned previously, all amateur radio examinations are administered by three-person teams of Volunteer Examiners (VEs) who have been accredited by a Volunteer Examiner Coordinator (VEC). The VEs are licensed hams.

How to Find an Exam Session

Examination sessions are organized under the auspices of an approved VEC. A list of VECs is located in the Appendix of this book. The W5YI-VEC and the ARRL-VEC are the 2 largest examination groups in the country, and they test in all 50 states. Their 3-member, accredited examination teams are just about *everywhere*. So when you call the VEC, you can be assured they probably have an examination team only a few miles from where you are reading this book right now!

Want to find a test site fast?
Visit the W5YI-VEC website at www.w5yi.org, or call them at 817-461-6443.

Taking the Exam

The Element 2 written exam is a multiple-choice format. The VEs will give you a test paper that contains the 35 questions and multiple choice answers, and an answer sheet for you to complete. Take your time! Make sure you read each question carefully and select the correct answer. Once you're finished, double check your work before handing in your test papers.

The VEs will score you test immediately, and you'll know before you leave the exam site whether you've passed. Chances are very good that, if you've studied hard, you'll get that passing grade!

GETTING YOUR FIRST CALL SIGN

Once the VE team scores your test, and you've passed, the process of getting your official FCC Amateur Radio License will begin — usually that same day.

At the exam site, you will complete NCVEC Form 605, which is your application to the FCC for your license. If you pass the exam, the VE team will send on the required paperwork to their VEC. The VEC, in turn, will file your application with the FCC. This filing is done electronically, and your license will be granted and your call sign posted on the FCC's website within a few days. As soon as you see your new call sign, you are permitted to go on the air as a licensed amateur. See Chapter 5 for more details on this process.

Vanity Call Signs

Your first call sign is assigned by the FCC's computer, and you have no choice of letters. However, once you have that call sign, you can apply for a Vanity Call Sign. Again, see Chapter 5 for details.

HOW MANY CLASSES OF LICENSES?

Once you've passed your Element 2 exam and go on the air as a new Technician

Class operator, you'll be talking to fellow hams throughout the U.S. and around the world. Here's a summary of the new and "grandfathered" licenses that these fellow amateurs may hold, and a recap of the level of expertise they have demonstrated in order to gain their licenses.

New License Classes

As mentioned previously, for new examinations taken after April 15, 2000, there are just three written exams and three license classes — Technician, General, and Extra. There is only one Morse code test, and that is 5 wpm. But persons who hold licenses issued prior to April 15, 2000, may continue to hold onto their license class and *continue* to renew it every 10 years for as long as they wish.

Technician Class (Element 2 written exam)

Your first written exam for your ham radio license will be Element 2 for Technician Class theory. This is the examination for which this book will help you prepare. As you will see, this exam is a cinch to pass with just a few weeks of studying the relatively easy questions and answers, along with the author's explanation of why an answer is the correct one. With just a little dedicated effort and study time, you'll be able to "ace" this written exam!

General Class (Element 3 written exam)

The second ham radio license is General Class, and this gives you access to *all* of the worldwide bands plus your existing Technician Class privileges on VHF and UHF. And on *all* of the worldwide bands, you get a large amount of voice and data frequencies along with the CW sub-bands. As a new General Class operator, you'll probably find yourself operating most of the time either on single-sideband (SSB) voice talking around the world, or jumping on your computer and doing a lot of worldwide digital contacts. Best of all, the General Class requires you to only pass the 5-wpm code test. As of April 15, 2000, the old 13- and 20-wpm code tests have been discontinued, and the 5-wpm code test is all that is necessary to satisfy the CW requirements of Element 1.

The study material for the General Class written examination is found in our second book, *General Class,* which contains the Element 3 question pool of 385 total questions, of which just 35 will be on your written exam.

General Class licensees can serve as accredited Volunteer Examiners to give the Element 1 code test and the Element 2 written exam for the Technician Class license.

Extra Class (Element 4 written exam)

The new top license is the Extra Class. This license allows you unlimited privileges on *all* of the ham bands. This is part of incentive licensing — when you get to the top, you get more frequency privileges!

Our third book, *Extra Class,* is the study guide you'll want to use to get through the Extra Class exam. It contains more than 665 very heavy technical questions in the Element 4 question pool. 50 of these questions will appear on your Extra Class examination. But the good news — no further code requirements beyond the 5-wpm code test you successfully passed for General. And you don't even need to re-take the 5-wpm code test again for Extra Class!

Extra Class licensees can serve as accredited Volunteer Examiners to administer *all* amateur radio exams. (Grandfathered Advanced Class licensees can serve as accredited VEs to administer the Element 1 code test, the Element 2 Technician, and the element 3 General examinations.)

"Grandfathered" Licensees

As mentioned previously, individuals licensed prior to April 15, 2000, will continue to enjoy band privileges based on their licenses. So, once you get on the air with your new Technician Class privileges, every now and then you might meet a Novice operator while yakking on 10 meters, or sending CW on 15, 40, or 80 meters.

And you'll see some older licenses saying "Technician Plus," which belong to grandfathered Technician Class operators licensed prior to April 15, 2000, who passed their 5-wpm code test and who get to keep their code credit indefinitely as long as they renew their license. Technician Plus operators will have their licenses renewed as Technician Class with permanent code operating credit.

And then there are the Advanced Class operators who may continue to hold onto their license class designation until they finally decide to move up to Extra Class — without any further code requirement.

When you look at the Frequency Charts in this book that tell you the various band privileges, you will continue to see designated sub-bands for Extra, Advanced, General, Tech Plus, Tech, and Novice. These sub-bands won't change — any ham licensed prior to April 15, 2000, is automatically "grandfathered" to their original frequency privileges and will not lose a single kilohertz of operating room. But they'll get more privileges if they upgrade to the top — the new Extra Class!

NOW, ABOUT THAT CODE TEST

In order to upgrade to General Class you'll have to take and pass the 5-wpm Element 1 Morse code test. And you need to be a General Class licensee to upgrade to Extra Class.

As explained previously, if you are a new Technician Class operator after April 15, 2000, and pass the 5-wpm code test, your license will still say "Technician." You'll be given a Certificate of Successful Completion of Examination (CSCE) by the VE team that gives you the test. The CSCE is only good for 365 days for your General Class upgrade, and you'll need to re-take the code test again if you don't upgrade before the CSCE expires. While the CSCE only allows *exam credit* for 365 days, it does convey *permanent* HF operating privileges on four worldwide band segments at 80, 40, 15, and 10 meters.

Now, if you wish, you can decide to take the Element 1 code test at the same time as your Element 2 Technician written examination. All the better — you will have satisfied the one and only code test required for the next two higher grades of ham radio license. And if you never upgrade, you'll enjoy additional HF privileges for years.

If you don't know the Morse code, it's easy to learn! Your author has developed fun, educational, and very unique audio cassette tapes for learning the dots and dashes by sound. By using the tapes along with the code information included in Chapter 4 that will help you memorize the characters, it shouldn't take you more than a couple of weeks to get the feel of the code. If you're musical, you might have it down in just 10 days. Chances are you can pick up a set of the author's code tapes at RadioShack or the same place where you purchased this book. And while you're at it, go ahead and look at the *General Class* Element 3 book and see how easy that test is, too.

IT'S EASY!

Probably the primary pre-requisite for passing any amateur radio operator license exam is the *will* to do it. If you follow the author's suggestions in this book, your chances of passing the Technician exam are excellent. And once you pass, then it's on to our *General Class* book.

Yes, indeed, the year 2000 brought some big changes to ham radio, and everyone comes out a winner! This is incentive licensing at its best, and there has never been a better time to join the ranks of ham radio hobbyists. So study hard! We hope to hear you on the air very soon.

AN IMPORTANT WORD ABOUT SHARED AND PROTECTED FREQUENCIES

In Chapter 2, we will be discussing the Amateur Radio frequency privileges you will receive when you pass your exam and receive your license and call letters from the FCC. It is important, however, that you know that every ham band above 225 MHz is shared on a secondary basis with other services. This means that the primary users get first claim to the frequency!

For example, Government radiolocation (radar) is a primary user of some bands. And a multitude of industrial, scientific and medical services have access to the 902-928 MHz band. Just because the frequency is allocated to the amateur service does not mean that others do not have prior right or an equal right to the spectrum. You must not interfere with other users of the band.

There also are instances where amateurs *must not* cause interference to other stations, such as foreign stations operating along the Mexican and Canadian borders, military stations near military bases, and FCC monitoring stations. Also, amateur operators must not cause interference in the so-called *National Radio Quiet Zones* which are near radio astronomy locations. The astronomy locations are protected by law from Amateur Radio interference. Operation aboard ships and aircraft also is restricted. The FCC also can curtail the hours of your operation if you cause general interference to the reception of telephone or radio/TV broadcasting by your neighbors.

Every amateur should have a copy of the Amateur Radio Service Part 97 Rules and Regulations. It would be good for you to especially read Part 97.303 on frequency sharing requirements.

> You can obtain a copy of the current Part 97 Rules
> from the W5YI Group by calling 1-800-669-9594.

2

Technician Class Privileges

ABOUT THIS CHAPTER

There is plenty of excitement out there on the amateur VHF and UHF bands with just the Technician Class license. You don't need to learn Morse code to get all of the "radio real estate" described in *Table 2-1*. But if you do learn the code and pass the CW test at the same time you take the Element 2 written examination for your Technician license, you'll earn privileges on some "bonus" CW and voice frequencies that you'll be allowed to use as a Technician Class operator.

TECHNICIAN CLASS PRIVILEGES

The Technician Class license is now the most popular way to get started in the amateur service. The question pool has just been slashed by more than half, so it's now easier than ever to enter the amateur radio service as a Technician Class operator — with or without the code.

If you're not going to take the code test as a Technician Class operator, you will still have plenty of excitement on radio frequencies above 30 MHz. You will have full operating privileges on all of the exciting VHF, UHF, SHF, and microwave bands shown in *Table 2-1*. You can work skywaves on 6 meters to communicate all over the country; on the 2-meter band, you'll operate through repeaters and orbiting satellites. On the 222 MHz band, you may operate through linked repeaters; on the

Table 2-1. Technician Class No-Code Operating Privileges

Wavelength Band	Frequency	Emissions	Comments
6 Meters	50.0–54.0 MHz	All modes	Sideband voice, radio control, FM repeater, digital computer, remote bases, and autopatches. Even CW. (1500 watts PEP output)
2 Meters	144–148 MHz	All modes	All types of operation including satellite and owning repeater and remote bases. (1500 watt PEP output)
1¼ Meters	222–225 MHz	All modes	All band privileges. (1500 watt PEP output)
70 cm	420–450 MHz	All modes	All band privileges, including amateur television, packet, RTTY, FAX, and FM voice repeaters. (1500 watt PEP output.)
33 cm	902–928 MHz	All modes	All band privileges. Plenty of room! (1500 watt PEP output.)
23 cm	1240–1300 MHz	All modes	All band privileges. (1500 watt PEP output)

440 MHz band, you might try amateur television, satellite, and remote base operation; and on 1270 MHz there are more frequencies for amateur television, satellites, repeater linking, and data point-to-point systems. And then there are the microwave bands where dish and loop Yagi antennas will beam out signals a lot further than you might think.

Even without the worldwide CW and voice privileges earned by passing the 5 wpm code test, the Technician Class without code has plenty of worldwide excitement on 6 meters, and our new satellites may carry your signals thousands of miles away. Let's explore the different bands for the Technician Class operator without the Morse code Element 1 certificate.

6-METER WAVELENGTH BAND, 50.0-54.0 MHZ

The Technician Class operator will enjoy all amateur service privileges and maximum output power of 1500 watts on this worldwide band. Are you into radio control (R/C) and want to escape the interference between 72 and 76 MHz? On 6 meters, your Technician Class license allows you to operate on exclusive radio control channels at 50 MHz and 53 MHz, just for licensed hams. *Table 2-2* shows the ARRL 6-meter wavelength band plan.

Table 2-2. 6-Meter Wavelength Band Plan, 50.0-54.0 MHz

MHz	Use
50.000–50.100	CW weak signal
50.060–50.080	CW Beacon FM
50.100–50.300	SSB, CW
50.100–50.200	DX window & SSB DX calling
50.225	Domestic SSB calling frequency and QSO each side
50.300–50.600	Non-voice communications
50.620	Digital/Packet calling frequency
50.800–50.980	Radio control
	20 kHz channels
51.000–51.100	Pacific DX window
51.120–51.480	Repeater inputs (19)
51.120–51.180	Digital repeater inputs
51.620–51.980	Repeater outputs (19)
51.620–51.680	Digital repeater outputs
52.000–52.480	Repeater inputs (23)
52.020, 52.040	FM simplex
52.500–52.980	Repeater outputs (23)
52.525, 52.540	FM simplex
53.000–54.480	Repeater inputs (19)
53.000, 53.020	FM simplex
53.1/53.2/53.3/53.4	Radio control
53.500–53.980	Repeater outputs (19)
53.5/53.6/53.7/53.8	Radio control
53.520	Simplex
53.900	Simplex

On 6 meters, the Technician Class operator can get a real taste of long-range skywave skip communications. During the summer months, and during selected days and weeks out of the year, 50-54 MHz, 6-meter signals are refracted by the ionosphere, giving you incredible long-range communication excitement. It's almost a daily phenomena during the summer months for 6 meters to skip all over the country. This is the big band for the Technician Class no-code operator because of this type of ionospheric, long-range, skip excitement. There are even repeaters on 6 meters. So make 6 meters "a must" at your future operating station.

2-METER WAVELENGTH BAND, 144-148 MHZ

The 2-meter band is the world's most popular spot for staying in touch through repeaters. Here is where most all of those hand-held transceivers operate, and the Technician Class operator receives unlimited 2-meter privileges! *Table 2-3* gives the 2-meter wavelength band plan proposed by the ARRL VHF/UHF advisory committee.

The United States, and many parts of the world, are blanketed with clear, 2-meter, repeater coverage. They say there is nowhere in the United States you can't reach at least one or two repeaters with a little hand-held transceiver. 2-meters has you covered! Here are examples:

Handie-talkie channels	Simplex autopatch	Rag-chewing
Transmitter hunts	Contests	Radio teleprinter
Autopatch	Traffic handling	Radio facsimile
Moon bounce	Satellite downlink	Emergency nets
Meteor bursts	Satellite uplink	Sporadic-E DX
Packet radio	Remote base	Aurora
Tropo-DX-ducting	Simplex operation	

The Technician Class license allows 1500 watts maximum power output for specialized 2-meter communications, and also permits you to own and control a 2-meter repeater.

Table 2-3. ARRL 2-Meter Repeater frequency pairs (input/output):

144.61/145.21	144.83/145.43	146.22/146.82	147.75/147.15
144.63/145.23	144.85/145.45	146.25/146.85	147.78/147.18
144.65/145.25	144.87/145.47	146.28/146.88	147.81/147.21
144.67/145.27	144.89/145.49	146.31/146.91	147.84/147.24
144.69/145.29	146.01/145.61	146.34/146.94	147.87/147.27
144.71/145.31	146.04/146.64	146.37/146.97	147.90/147.30
144.73/145.33	146.07/146.67	146.40 or 146.60/147.00*	147.93/147.33
144.75/145.35	146.10/146.70	146.43 or 146.63/147.03*	147.96/147.36
144.77/145.37	146.13/146.73	146.46 or 146.66/147.06*	147.99/147.39
144.79/145.39	146.16/146.76	147.69/147.09	
144.81/145.41	146.19/146.79	147.72/147.12	

Some states use a different band plan. Additional channels available in large cities when 15 kHz and 20 kHz "splinter channels," interspersed between regular channels, are used.
*local option

Table 2-3. ARRL 2-Meter Wavelength Band Plan, 144-148 MHz

MHz	Use
144.00–144.05	EME (CW)
144.05–144.06	Propagation beacons (old band plan)
144.06–144.10	General CW and weak signals
144.10–144.20	EME and weak-signal SSB
144.20	National SSB calling frequency
144.20–144.275	General SSB operation, upper sideband
144.275–144.30	New beacon band
144.30–144.50	New OSCAR subband plus simplex
144.50–144.60	Linear translator inputs
144.60–144.90	FM repeater inputs
144.90–145.10	Weak signal and FM simplex
145.10–145.20	Linear translator outputs plus packet
145.20–145.50	FM repeater outputs
145.50–145.80	Miscellaneous and experimental modes
145.80–146.00	OSCAR subband—satellite use only
146.01–146.37	Repeater inputs
146.40–146.58	Simplex
146.61–146.97	Repeater outputs
147.00–147.39	Repeater outputs
147.42–147.57	Simplex
147.60–147.99	Repeater inputs

1 ¼-METER WAVELENGTH BAND, 219-220 MHZ

On the 222 MHz band, the frequencies 219 MHz to 220 MHz may be used by point-to-point digital message forwarding stations operated by Technician Class licensees or higher. These stations must register with the American Radio Relay League 30 days prior to activation, and these stations must not interfere with primary marine users near the Mississippi River, or any other primary user of this band. Remember, before you turn on a point-to-point digital message forwarding station, you must first register your operation with the American Radio Relay League 30 days before going on the air on 219 to 220 MHz.

The 100 kHz channels for point-to-point fixed digital message forwarding stations, 50 watts PEP limit, are shown in *Table 2-4*.

Table 2-4. ARRL 1 ¼-Meter Wavelength Band Plan, 219-220 MHz

MHz	Use			
219–220	Point-to-point fixed digital message forwarding systems. Must be coordinated through ARRL. 100 kHz Channels. 50W PEP limit.			
	Channel	**Freq. (MHz)**	**Channel**	**Freq. (MHz)**
	A	219.05	F	219.550
	B	219.150	G	219.650
	C	219.250	H	219.750
	D	219.350	I	219.850
	E	219.450	J	219.950
220–222	No longer available			

Due to inactivity, the Federal Communications Commission has reallocated two MHz of this band, 220-222 MHz, to the land mobile commercial radio service. The 220-222-MHz band is a shared band and narrow-band business radio is not compatible with amateur transmissions. The frequencies 220 MHz to 222 MHz might be found on older hand-held and mobile equipment, but are no longer authorized to the amateur service. It is hoped that the Technician Class license will fill all the VHF and UHF bands with activity so we don't ever lose more frequencies due to inactivity!

1¼-METER WAVELENGTH BAND, 222-225 MHZ

Table 2-5 shows the proposed usage for this band. It is filled with activity by Novice Class operators transmitting from 222.0 MHz to 225.0 MHz. The Technician Class license also permits you to use the entire band at 1500 watts maximum output power, instead of the 25 watts for Novice Class licensees. If you need some relief from the activity on 2 meters, the 222-225 MHz band is similar in propagation and use. 222 MHz to 225 MHz is now exclusively assigned to our Amateur Radio service.

Table 2-5. ARRL 1¼-Meter Wavelength Band Plan, 222-225 MHz

MHz	Use
222.00–222.15	Weak-signal modes (FM only)
222.00–222.05	EME
222.05–222.06	Propagation beacons
222.10	SSB and CW calling frequency
222.10–222.15	Weak signal CW and SSB
222.15–222.25	Local coordinator's option: Weak signal, ACSB, repeater inputs, control points
222.25–223.38	FM repeater inputs only
223.40–223.52	FM simplex
223.50	Simplex calling frequency
223.52–223.64	Digital, packet
223.64–223.70	Links, control
223.71–223.85	Local coordinator's option: FM simplex, packet, repeater outputs
223.85–224.98	Repeater outputs only

Simplex frequencies (MHz):

223.42	223.52	223.62	223.72	223.82
223.44	223.54	223.64	223.74	223.84
223.46	223.56	223.66	223.76	223.86
223.48	223.58	223.68	223.78	223.88
223.50*	223.60	223.70	223.80	223.90

*National simplex frequency

Repeater frequency pairs (input/output):

222.32/223.92	222.54/224.14	222.76/224.36	222.98/224.58	223.20/224.80
222.34/223.94	222.56/224.16	222.78/224.38	223.00/224.60	223.22/224.82
222.36/223.96	222.58/224.18	222.80/224.40	223.02/224.62	223.24/224.84
222.38/223.98	222.60/224.20	222.82/224.42	223.04/224.64	223.26/224.86
222.40/224.00	222.62/224.22	222.84/224.44	223.06/224.66	223.28/224.88
222.42/224.02	222.64/224.24	222.86/224.46	223.08/224.68	223.30/224.90
222.44/224.04	222.66/224.26	222.88/224.48	223.10/224.70	223.32/224.92
222.46/224.06	222.68/224.28	222.90/224.50	223.12/224.72	223.34/224.94
222.48/224.08	222.70/224.30	222.92/224.52	223.14/224.74	223.36/224.96
222.50/224.10	222.72/224.32	222.94/224.54	223.16/224.76	223.38/224.98
222.52/224.12	222.74/224.34	222.96/224.56	223.18/224.78	

70-CM WAVELENGTH BAND, 420-450 MHZ

As you gain more experience on the VHF and UHF bands, you will soon be invited to the upper echelon of specialty clubs and organizations. The 450-MHz band is where the experts hang out. *Table 2-6* presents the ARRL 70-cm (centimeter) wavelength band plan. Amateur television (ATV) is very popular, so there's no telling who you may see as well as hear. This band also has the frequencies for controlling repeater stations and base stations on other bands, plus satellite activity. With a Technician Class license, you may even be able to operate on General Class worldwide frequencies if a General Class or higher control operator is on duty at the base control point. You would be able to talk on your 450-MHz hand-held transceiver and end up in the DX portion of the 20-meter band. As long as the control operator is on duty at the control point, your operation on General Class frequencies is completely legal!

The 450 MHz band is also full of packet communications, RTTY, FAX, and all those fascinating FM voice repeaters. If you are heavy into electronics, you'll hear fascinating topics discussed and digitized on the 450-MHz band. A Technician Class operator has full power privileges as well as unrestricted emission privileges.

Table 2-6. ARRL 70-cm Wavelength Band Plan, 420-450 MHz

MHz	Use
420.00–426.00	ATV repeater or simplex with 421.25-MHz video carrier control links and experimental
426.00–432.00	ATV simplex with 427.250-MHz video carrier frequency
432.00–432.07	EME (Earth-Moon-Earth)
432.07-432.08	Propagation beacons (old band plan)
432.08–432.10	Weak-signal CW
432.10	70-cm calling frequency
432.10–433.00	Mixed-mode and weak-signal work
432.30-432.40	New beacon band
433.00–435.00	Auxiliary/repeater links
435.00–438.00	Satellite only (internationally)
438.00–444.00	ATV repeater input with 439.250-MHz video carrier frequency and repeater links
442.00–445.00	Repeater inputs and outputs (local option)
445.00–447.00	Shared by auxiliary and control links, repeaters and simplex (local option); (446.0-MHz national simplex frequency)
447.00–450.00	Repeater inputs and outputs

Repeater frequency pairs (input/output is local option):

442.000/447.000	442.600/447.600	443.200/448.200	443.800/448.800	444.400/449.400
442.025/447.025	442.625/447.625	443.225/448.225	443.825/448.825	444.425/449.425
442.050/447.050	442.650/447.650	443.250/448.250	443.850/448.850	444.450/449.450
442.075/447.075	442.675/447.675	443.275/448.275	443.875/448.875	444.475/449.475
442.100/447.100	442.700/447.700	443.300/448.300	443.900/448.900	444.500/449.500
442.125/447.125	442.725/447.725	443.325/448.325	443.925/448.925	444.525/449.525
442.150/447.150	442.750/447.750	443.350/448.350	443.950/448.950	444.550/449.550
442.175/447.175	442.775/447.775	443.375/448.375	443.975/448.975	444.575/449.575
442.200/447.200	442.800/447.800	443.400/448.400	444.000/449.000	444.600/449.600
442.225/447.225	442.825/447.825	443.425/448.425	444.025/449.025	444.625/449.625
442.250/447.250	442.850/447.850	443.450/448.450	444.050/449.050	444.650/449.650
442.275/447.275	442.875/447/875	443.475/448.475	444.075/449.075	444.675/449.675
442.300/447.300	442.900/447.900	443.500/448.500	444.100/449.100	444.700/449.700
442.325/447.325	442.925/447.925	443.525/448.525	444.125/449.125	444.725/449.725
442.350/447.350	442.950/447.950	443.550/448.550	444.150/449.150	444.750/449.750
442.375/447.375	442.975/447.975	443.575/448.575	444.175/449.175	444.775/449.775
442.400/447.400	443.000/448.000	443.600/448.600	444.200/449.200	444.800/449.800
442.425/447.425	443.025/448.025	443.625/448.625	444.225/449.225	444.825/449.825
442.450/447.450	443.050/448.050	443.650/448.650	444.250/449.250	444.850/449.850
442.475/447.475	443.075/448.075	443.675/448.675	444.275/449.275	444.875/449.875
442.500/447.500	443.100/448.100	443.700/448.700	444.300/449.300	444.900/449.900
442.525/447.525	443.125/448.125	443.725/448.725	444.325/449.325	444.925/449.925
442.550/447.550	443.150/448.150	443.750/448.750	444.350/449.350	444.950/449.950
442.575/447.575	443.175/448.175	443.775/448.775	444.375/449.375	444.975/449.975

33-CM WAVELENGTH BAND, 902-928 MHZ

Radio equipment manufacturers are just beginning to market equipment for this band. Many hams are already on the air using home-brew equipment for a variety of activities. If you are looking for a band with the ultimate in elbow room, this is it!

Table 2-7 shows the 33-cm wavelength band plan adopted by the ARRL Board of Directors in July, 1989.

Table 2-7. ARRL 33-cm Wavelength Band Plan, 902-928 MHz

MHz	Use
902.0–903.0	Weak signal (902.1 calling frequency)
903.0–906.0	Digital Communications (903.1 alternate calling frequency)
906.0–909.0	FM repeater inputs
909.0–915.0	ATV
915.0–918.0	Digital Communications
918.0–921.0	FM repeater outputs
921.0–927.0	ATV
927.0–928.0	FM simplex and links

23-CM WAVELENGTH BAND, 1240-1300 MHZ

There is plenty of over-the-counter radio equipment for this band, thanks to Novice Class operators getting onto the frequencies and exploring how far microwave signals go. Although the Novice Class operator is allowed only 5 watts, the

Technician Class operator may run any amount of power—with 20 watts about the maximum limit.

Technician Class operators, and higher, are allowed the entire band, 1240 MHz to 1300 MHz without restrictions. Novice operators are allowed 1270 MHz to 1295 MHz, with a 5-watt power output restriction.

The frequencies are in the microwave region, and this band is excellent to use with local repeaters in major cities.

Like the 450-MHz band and the 2-meter band, this band is sliced into many specialized operating areas. You can work orbiting satellites, operate amateur television, or own your own repeater with your Technician Class license. *Table 2-8* presents the 23-cm wavelength band plan adopted by the ARRL Board of Directors in January, 1985.

Table 2-8. ARRL 23-cm Wavelength Band Plan, 1240-1300 MHz

MHz	Use
1240–1246	ATV #1
1246–1248	Narrow-bandwidth FM point-to-point links and digital, duplexed with 1258-1260 MHz
1248–1252	Digital communications
1252–1258	ATV #2
1258–1260	Narrow-bandwidth FM point-to-point links and digital, duplexed with 1246-1252 MHz
1260–1270	Satellite uplinks, reference WARC '79
1260–1270	Wide-bandwidth experimental, simplex ATV
1270–1276	Repeater inputs, FM and linear, paired with 1282-1288 MHz, 239 pairs every 25 kHz, e.g., 1270.025, 1270.050, 1270.075, etc. 1271.0-1283.0 MHz uncoordinated test pair
1276–1282	ATV #3
1282–1288	Repeater outputs, paired with 1270-1276 MHz
1288–1294	Wide-bandwidth experimental, simplex ATV
1294–1295	Narrow-bandwidth FM simplex services, 25-kHz channels
1294.5	National FM simplex calling frequency
1295–1297	Narrow bandwidth weak-signal communications (no FM)
1295.0–1295.8	SSTV, FAX, ACSB, experimental
1295.8–1296.0	Reserved for EME, CW expansion
1296.0–1296.05	EME exclusive
1296.07–1296.08	CW beacons
1296.1	CW, SSB calling frequency
1296.4–1296.6	Crossband linear translator input
1296.6–1296.8	Crossband linear translator output
1296.8–1297.0	Experimental beacons (exclusive)
1297–1300	Digital communications

10-GHZ (10,000 MHZ!) BANDS AND MORE

There are several manufacturers of ham microwave transceivers and converters for this range, so activity is excellent. Gunnplexers are the popular transmitter. Using horn and dish antennas, 10 GHz is frequently used by hams to establish voice communications for controlling repeaters over paths from 20 miles to 100 miles. Output power levels are usually less than one-eighth of a watt! It's really fascinating to see how directional the microwave signals are. If you live on a mountain-top, 10 GHz is for you.

Table 2-9. Gigahertz Bands

2.30–2.31 GHz	10.0–10.50 GHz*	119.98-120.02 GHz
2.39–2.45 GHz	24.0–24.25 GHz	142.0-149.0 GHz
3.30–3.50 GHz	47.0–47.20 GHz	241.0-250.0 GHz
5.65–5.925 GHz	75.50-81.0 GHz	All above 300 GHz

*Pulse not permitted

All modes and licensees except Novices are authorized on the bands shown in *Table 2-9*. There is much Amateur Radio experimentation on these bands.

EARN ADDED TECHNICIAN CLASS PRIVILEGES WITH YOUR MORSE CODE CERTIFICATE

In the previous sections of this Chapter, we described in detail all of your Technician Class privileges above 30 MHz without having to know anything about Morse code dots and dashes. Now we want to tell you about the additional band priviliges you will have as a Technician if you just make up your mind to learn the code and pass that simple, 5-wpm test.

80-METER WAVELENGTH BAND, 3500-4000 KHZ

Your valid code certificate gives you privileges on the 80-meter band for CW only from 3675 to 3725 kHz.

40-METER WAVELENGTH BAND, 7000-7300 KHZ

Passing a 5 wpm code test gives you Morse-code-only privileges on this band from 7100 to 7150 kHz. This is a popular night-time and early morning band because signals in code can reach up to 5,000 miles away!

15-METER WAVELENGTH BAND, 21,000-21,450 KHZ

Technician Class operators holding the code certificate for 5 wpm may operate CW from 21.1 MHz to 21.2 MHz in this portion of the worldwide band. You can expect daytime range in excess of 10,000 miles using CW.

10-METER WAVELENGTH BAND, 28,000-29,700 KHZ

Passing a code test at 5 wpm allows you to operate on sub-bands available to grandfathered Novice class operators and grandfathered Technician-plus operators. You may operate code and digital computer communications from 28.1 MHz to 28.3 MHz, and monitor 28.2 MHz to 28.3 MHz for low-power propagation beacons. Now here's the good news — you may operate single-sideband voice between 28.3

MHz to 28.5 MHz, and literally work the world during band openings during daylight hours.

Table 2-10 summarizes the additional operating priviliges you will have as a Technician Class operator who holds a Morse code certificate – as well as the VHF/UHF privileges discussed earlier.

See, it really is worth the little bit of extra effort needed to learn the code so you can pass that Element 1, 5-wpm code test. Even if you never upgrade, you will always retain these operating priviliges as a Technician Class operator. And as soon as you pass the test, you'll have exam credit for 365 days, making it even easier to upgrade to General Class.

Table 2-10. Technician Class Operating Privileges with Morse Code Certificate

Wavelength Band	Frequency	Emissions	Comments
80 Meters	3675–3725 kHz	Code only	Limited to Morse code (200 watt PEP output limitation)
40 Meters	*7100–7150 kHz	Code only	Limited to Morse code (200 watt PEP output limitation)
15 Meters	21,100–21,200 kHz	Code only	Limited to Morse code (200 watt PEP output limitation)
10 Meters	28,100–28,500 kHz	Code	Morse code (200 watt PEP output code limitation)
	28,100–28,300 kHz	Data and code	
	28,300–28,500 kHz	Phone and code	Sideband voice (200 watt code PEP output limitation)
Plus These Existing VHF/UHF Frequencies			
6 Meters	50.0–54.0 MHz	All modes	Morse code, sideband voice, radio control, FM repeater, digital computer, remote bases, and autopatches (1500 watts PEP output)
2 Meters	144–148 MHz	All modes	All types of operation including satellite and owning repeater and remote bases. (1500 watt PEP output)
1¼ Meters	219–220 MHz	Data	Point-to-Point digital message forwarding
	222–225 MHz	All modes	All band privileges. (1500 watt PEP output)
70 cm	420–450 MHz	All modes	All band privileges, including amateur television, packet, RTTY, FAX, and FM voice repeaters. (1500 watt PEP output)
35 cm	902–928 MHz	All modes	All band privileges. Plenty of room! (1500 watt PEP output)
23 cm	1240–1300 MHz	All modes	All band privileges. (1500 watt PEP output)

* U.S. licensed operators in other than our hemisphere (ITU Region 2) are authorized 7050-7075 kHz due to shortwave broadcast interference.

So once you pass Technician, don't stop! Go onto General class, and ride the worldwide airwaves of excitement, and still have all of your Technician class privileges on VHF and UHF, too.

After you pass your Technician written Element 2 exam, your next step is our second book, *General Class*. The General Class license opens up all of the worldwide bands for long-range communications. Code speed is just 5 wpm. If you pass your code test during the Tech test, you have 365 days to cash in on this CW certificate for General Class.

SUMMARY

Enjoy the excitement of being a ham radio operator and communicate worldwide with other amateur operators without a code test. Your Technician Class operator license allows you all ham operator privileges on all bands with frequencies greater than 50 MHz. You have operating privileges on the worldwide 6-meter band, on the world's popular 2-meter and 222-MHz repeater bands, on the amateur television, satellite communications, and repeater-linking 440-MHz and 1270-MHz bands, and on the line-of-sight microwave bands at 10 GHz and above.

Remember, you may enter the amateur service as a Technician Class operator, passing Element 2, without a code test. You will receive full privileges on all of the VHF/UHF bands we have just described.

If you decide to take the 5-wpm Element 1 code test and pass it, you'll also receive the additional privileges on 10-, 15-, 40-, and 80-meters to join in with grandfathered Novice operators and higher class operators using these portions of the band.

But more important, taking and passing Element 1, the simple 5-wpm code test, will satisfy the requirements for code for General Class worldwide communications, provided you pass the General Class, Element 3 written examination within 365 days of passing the Element 1 test. If not, you'll have to re-take the Element 1 code test for your General Class upgrade.

But let's not get ahead of ourselves. It's time now to take a look at those test questions and answers!

3

GETTING READY FOR THE EXAMINATION

ABOUT THIS CHAPTER

Your Technician Cass, Element 2, written examination will consist of 35 multiple-choice questions taken from a total of 384 questions in the pool. Each question on your examination and the multiple-choice answer will be *identical* to what is contained in this chapter. Sorry, but the author's explanations — and an indication of the correct answer — will not appear on you examination papers as they do in our book.

This chapter contains the official, complete 384-question question pool from which your examination will be taken. Again, your exam will contain 35 of these questions, and you must get 74% of the questions correct — which means you must answer 26 questions correctly in order to pass.

If you're also going to take the Element 1, 5-wpm Morse Code test, you can do it at the same test session, or schedule it later. Or, you can schedule the Code test before your written examination, and receive a 365-day credit for passing the test.

What? Not into dots and dashes? Then forget about the code, and just go for Technician Class, Element 2. If you decide to do the Code 5 years from now, no problem! There is absolutely no time limit on when you must take the Code test when you hold the Technician Class license.

Your examination will be administered by a team of 3 or more Volunteer Examiners (VEs) — amateur radio operators who are accredited by an area or national Volunteer Examiner Coordinator (VEC). You will receive a Certificate of Successful Completion of Examination (CSCE) for passing any of the examination elements. This is official proof that you have passed the test when you walk out of the exam room. In just a few days, you will find your call letters on the worldwide web; and as soon as you know them you are licensed to go on the air!

NEW APRIL 15, 2000 QUESTION POOL

The NCVEC Question Pool Committee had a scant 30-day window to develop the new Element 2 Technician Class question pool. The new question pool was prepared using the old Technician Class question pool, along with some questions from the old Novice Class question pool. In addition, some new questions were written to reflect the changes made to the rules by the FCC's Report & Order of December 30, 1999. Every member of the ham radio community should be grateful to the dedicated members of the QPC for their fine efforts in pulling this new question pool together in a very short time frame.

This new Technician Class question pool was carefully developed by the National Conference of Volunteer Exam Coordinators' Question Pool Committee. Committee members are Ray Adams, W4CPA, Fred Maia, W5YI, Bart Jahnke, W9JJ, and Scotty Neustadter, W4WW. If you ever hear any one of these fine gentlemen on the air, tell them how much you appreciate the hard work they put in on pulling this question pool together.

The QPC members invite your comments and any corrections to the question pool. Please send them to your author, Gordon West, at the address included in the Appendix of this book. He will pass them on to the Question Pool Committee for its consideration the next time the question pool is revised and updated.

WHAT THE EXAMINATION CONTAINS

The examination questions and the multiple-choice answers (one correct answer and three "distracters") for all license class levels are public information. They are widely published and are identical to those in this book. FCC rules prohibit any examiner or examination team from making any changes to any questions, including any numerical values. No numbers, words, letters, or punctuation marks can be altered from the published question pool. By studying the Element 2 question pool in this book, you will be reading the same exact questions that will appear on your 35-question Element 2 written examination.

Table 3-1 shows how the Element 2, 35-question examination will be constructed. The question pool is divided into 10 sub-elements. Each sub-element covers a different subject. For example, for the Element 2 examination, 9 questions of the 35 total questions will be taken from sub-element T1 on the Federal Communications Commission's rules. On operating procedures, you will find 5 questions; and on radio wave propagation, just 3 questions. While it is up to the Volunteer Examination Coordinator's Question Pool Committee to develop the examination mixes, you'll find that your question topics and question mix will follow the sub-element examples in *Table 3-1*.

Table 3-1. FCC Element 2 Technician Class Question Pool

Subelement	Topic	Page	Total Questions	Exam Questions
T1	Commission's Rules	34	102	9
T2	Operating Procedures	64	55	5
T3	Radio Wave Propagation	80	33	3
T4	Amateur Radio Practices	91	44	4
T5	Electrical Principles	103	33	3
T6	Circuit Components	114	22	2
T7	Practical Circuits	121	22	2
T8	Signals and Emissions	128	20	2
T9	Antennas and Feed Lines	135	22	2
T0	RF Safety	143	31	3
TOTALS			384	35

All Volunteer Examination teams use the same question pool and multiple-choice answers. This uniformity in study material ensures common examinations throughout the country. Most exams are computer-generated, and the computer selects the correct number of questions from each sub-element for your upcoming Element 2 exam.

Trust me — trust me, every question on your upcoming Element 2 exam will look very familiar to you by the time you finish studying this book.

QUESTION CODING

Each and every question of the 384 Element 2, Technician Class question pool is numbered using a **code.** *The coded numbers and letters reveal important facts about each question!*

And if you know what the code means, its a "secret" way of finding out how many questions on specific topics may be on your upcoming Element 2, Technician class exam. This also works for Element 3, General Class, as well as Element 4, Extra Class.

The numbering code always contains 5 alphanumeric characters to identify each question. Here's how to read the question number so you know exactly how the examination computer will select one question out of each group. Once you know this information, you can increase your odds of achieving a passing score on the exam, especially if there is a specific group of questions which seems impossible for you to memorize or understand. When you get to Element 4, Extra Class — a very tough exam — this trick will really come in handy!

Close your eyes and pick a typical Element 2, Technician Class question — question number T0A02, as shown in *Figure 3-1.* Here's what the numbers and letters mean:

- The first character "T" identifies the license class question pool from which the question is taken. "T" is for Technician. "G" would be for General, and "E" would be for Extra.
- The second digit, a zero, identifies the sub-element number, 1 through 0. Technician sub-element "zero" deals with RF Safety. These are some of the questions in last sub-element of the Element 2 Technician question pool.
- The third character, "A," indicates the topic within the sub-element. Topic "A" deals with RF Safety Fundamentals.
- The fourth and fifth digits indicate the question number within the sub-element topic's group. The "02" indicates this is the second question about RF Safety Fundamentals. Note that the question numbers in a specific group always have 2 digits, with a leading "0" required for questions 1 through 9.

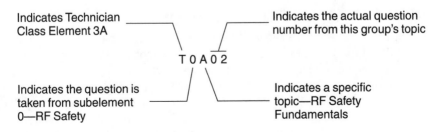

Figure 3-1. Examination Question Coding

Here's the Secret Study Hint

Only one exam question will be taken from any single group! A computer-generated test is set up to take one question from one single topic group. It cannot skip any one group, nor can it take any more than one question from that group.

Since sub-element 0 for Technician has 3 groups about RF safety, and since there will be only 1 question out of each group, the total number of questions out of the Technician sub-element T0 (RF Safety) is exactly 3.

When you're studying, if you get stuck on any one group within a subelement, skip it for later! The maximum number of questions that can come from this group is exactly one!

Your upcoming Element 2, Technician Class, written exam is relatively easy with no bone-crusher math formulas. The same thing is true for the Element 3 exam, General, found in our second book, *General Class*. But when you get to the *Extra Class* book, there may be one or two groups that have formulas so complicated that you may want to wait until the very end to digest them. And if you decide to skip them completely, guess what — how many questions out of any one group? That's right, only one per group. This means you are not going to get hammered on any upcoming test with a whole bunch of questions dealing with a specific group item. Great secret, huh?

A QUICK LOOK AT ELEMENT 2 EXAM QUESTIONS

In just a couple more pages we are going to look at the Technician Class, Element 2, examination question pool. First, scan through 10 or 15 pages, and remember the secret we just talked about on sub-element groups. Also see where we have indicated the number of examination questions to be taken from the sub-element.

You will quickly see that there is about one test question that could appear on your exam for about every 1 or 2 pages of the question pool.

Also note that there is only one correct answer. Hey, makes sense to me! You will see that the correct answer is identified, and then we give you a fun explanation on why the answer is indeed correct, and why some of the distracters are indeed wrong. You'll also be learning how each question relates to the real world of amateur radio.

Believe it or not, memorization of the correct answers to the question pool will indeed come in handy when you are ready to go on the airwaves. The Question Pool Committee has done a fabulous job of choosing those questions that will really play an important part as you begin to enjoy the ham radio service.

MARK THE HECK OUT OF THIS BOOK

Your author can always tell when one of his weekend amateur radio class students has prepared well for the exam — all he needs to do is look at their book. If he sees a lot of highlighted questions, check marks, circles, exclamation points, and question marks, this tells him the student has really been working the book.

Now, the way you "work the book" before the Element 2 examination is to put a check mark beside those questions that are so easy that you may think it's ridiculous that they even ask them. Circle those questions that require a little more study, and maybe highlight those questions if you really want to go back and review just before you take the exam.

Work the heck out of this book — the worse it looks, the more we can tell you're going to ace the exam!

DOING THE CODE?

Good for you! Learning Morse code at the same time you study for Technician Element 2 is a great way to get started in our amateur radio service. Remember, passing the code test at the same time as passing your Element 2 examination gives you permanent operating privileges on 10 meters single-sideband voice, plus CW privileges on 10-, 15-, 40-, and 80-meters. It also gives you 365-day exam credit so that you will only have to take the Element 3 written exam to upgrade to General Class.

You'll get a kick out of the author's 6-tape code course, or other combinations of his code courses that can be found at most RadioShack stores and at those ham radio stores where you may have purchased this book. The code course is available on CDs, also.

There also is Morse code learning software for your computer. Software has the advantage of generating unique code text and random characters that cannot be memorized easily. Software from the W5YI Group has code learning and proficiency games that make telegraphy fun! Set the code program for the 5 to 7-wpm *word* rate, the 16 to 17-wpm *character* rate, and a tone of around 777 Hz. This is called the "Farnsworth method" of learning the code, and this is how the code will sound when your Volunteer Examiners give you the code test.

Another great way in learning the code to pass the Element 1, 5-wpm test is to get together with a local ham radio club and let fellow hams help teach you the code. Classroom code practice is fun! You also can get a pair of code-sending oscillators and send back and forth to a friend who is also learning the code.

What the heck — why not buy one of those brand new, $700, worldwide, high-frequency transceivers, and listen to live code over the airwaves? Keep in mind that once you pass the 5-wpm code test, you can actually begin sending Morse code as a Technician Class operator on 4 different worldwide bands, plus use the mike on the 10-meter band. And without any further code test, you'll have 365 days to upgrade to General Class, and then you get access to a portion of *all* of the ham bands on that new worldwide set. Upgrading will be easy using your author's *General Class* book to study for the Element 3 written exam.

So do the code. Do it during your Technician Class, or soon thereafter, or even before. Learning the code so you can easily upgrade to General, and even Extra, will really make your ham radio operation *fun!*

HOME STUDY

You're just a couple of pages away from the Element 2 question pool. Here are some suggestions to make your learning easier:

1. Begin with sub-element 1, Rules and Regulations, and work from the front of the question pool to the back. Don't start out in the middle, and forget about doing it backwards. TRUST ME!

2. I know many of you are planning on getting your General license, now that the code test is only 5-wpm. But don't start out with the General Class book now, because you first need to pass the Element 2 exam. You can't jump over an examination element.

3. Read over each multiple-choice answer carefully. Some answers start out looking good, but turn bad during the last 2 or 3 words. If you speed read the answers, you could very easily go for a wrong answer because you didn't read them all the way through. Also, don't count on the multiple-choice answers always appearing in the exact same A-B-C-D order on your actual computer-generated test. While they won't change any words in the answers, they will sometimes scramble the A-B-C-D order.

4. Keep in mind that there is only one question on your test that will come from each group, and track how many groups in each sub-element.

5. Give this book to a friend, and ask them to read you the correct answer. You now give them the question wording.

6. Mark the heck out of your book! When the pages begin to fall out, you're probably ready for the exam!

7. Take this book along with you everywhere you go. Avoid reading it while driving the car or riding a bicycle. Remember audio cassette tapes on the theory are available, too, so if you want the questions and answers spoken to you by your author, he can do this.

THE QUESTSION POOL, PLEASE

Okay, this is the big moment — your Technician Class, Element 2, question pool. Don't freak out and get overwhelmed with the prospect of learning 384 Q & A's. You will find that the topic content is repeated many times, so you're really going to breeze through this test without any problems!

QUESTION POOL SYLLABUS

The syllabus used for the development of the question pool is included here as an aid in studying the subelements and topic groups. Review the syllabus before you start to study to gain an understanding of how the question pool is used to develop the Element 2 written examination. Remember, one question will be taken from each topic group within each subelement to create your exam.

Element 2 (Technician Class) Syllabus

T1 – Commission's Rules (9 exam questions – 9 groups)
T1A Basis and purpose of amateur service and definitions; Station /Operator license; classes of US amateur licenses, including basic differences; privileges of the various license classes; term of licenses; grace periods; modifications of licenses; current mailing address on file with FCC
T1B Frequency privileges authorized to the Technician control operator (VHF/UHF and HF)
T1C Emission privileges authorized to the Technician control operator (VHF/UHF and HF)
T1D Responsibility of licensee; station control; control operator requirements; station identification; points of communication and operation; business communications
T1E Third-party communication; authorized and prohibited transmissions; permissible one-way communication
T1F Frequency selection and sharing; transmitter power; digital communications
T1G Satellite and space communications; false signals or unidentified communications; malicious interference
T1H Correct language; phonetics; beacons; radio control of model craft and vehicles
T1I Emergency communications; broadcasting; indecent and obscene language

T2 – Operating Procedures (5 exam questions – 5 groups)
T2A Preparing to transmit; choosing a frequency for tune-up; operating or emergencies; Morse code; repeater operations and autopatch
T2B Definition and proper use; courteous operation; repeater frequency coordination; Morse code
T2C Simplex operations; RST signal reporting; choice of equipment for desired communications; communications modes including amateur television (ATV), packet radio; Q signals, procedural signals and abbreviations
T2D Distress calling and emergency drills and communications – operations and equipment; Radio Amateur Civil Emergency Service (RACES)
T2E Voice communications and phonetics; SSB/CW weak signal operations; radioteleprinting; packet; special operations

T3 – Radio-Wave Propagation (3 exam questions – 3 groups)
T3A Line of sight; reflection of VHF/UHF signals
T3B Tropospheric ducting or bending; amateur satellite and EME operations
T3C Ionospheric propagation, causes and variation; maximum usable frequency; Sporadic-E propagation; ground wave, HF propagation characteristics; sunspots and the sunspot cycle

T4 – Amateur Radio Practices (4 exam questions – 4 groups)
T4A Lightning protection and station grounding; safety interlocks, antenna installation safety procedures; dummy antennas
T4B Electrical wiring, including switch location, dangerous voltages and currents; SWR meaning and measurements; SWR meters
T4C Meters and their placement in circuits, including volt, amp, multi, peak-reading and RF watt; ratings of fuses and switches

T4D RFI and its complications, resolution and responsibility

T5 – Electrical Principles (3 exam questions – 3 groups)
T5A Metric prefixes, e.g. pico, nano, micro, milli, centi, kilo, mega, giga; concepts, units and measurement of current, voltage; concept of conductor and insulator; concept of open and short circuits
T5B Concepts, units and calculation of resistance, inductance and capacitance values in series and parallel circuits
T5C Ohm's Law (any calculations will be kept to a very low level – no fractions or decimals) and the concepts of energy and power; concepts of frequency, including AC vs. DC, frequency units, and wavelength

T6 – Circuit Components (2 exam questions – 2 groups)
T6A Electrical function and/or schematic representation of resistor, switch, fuse, or battery; resistor construction types, variable and fixed, color code, power ratings, schematic symbols
T6B Electrical function and/or schematic representation of a ground, antenna, inductor, capacitor, transistor, integrated circuit; construction of variable and fixed inductors and capacitors; factors affecting inductance and capacitance

T7 – Practical Circuits (2 exam questions – 2 groups)
T7A Functional layout of station components including transmitter, transceiver, receiver, power supply, antenna, antenna switch, antenna feed line, impedance-matching device, SWR meter; station layout and accessories for radiotelephone, radioteleprinter (RTTY) or packet
T7B Transmitter and receiver block diagrams; purpose and operation of low-pass, high-pass and band-pass filters

T8 – Signals and Emissions (2 exam questions – 2 groups)
T8A RF carrier, definition and typical bandwidths; harmonics and unwanted signals; chirp; superimposed hum; equipment and adjustments to help reduce interference to others
T8B Concepts and types of modulation: CW, phone, RTTY and data emission types; FM deviation

T9 – Antennas and Feed Lines (2 exam questions – 2 groups)
T9A Wavelength vs. antenna length; 1/2 wavelength dipole and 1/4 wavelength vertical antennas; multiband antennas
T9B Parasitic beam directional antennas; polarization, impedance matching and SWR, feed lines, balanced vs. unbalanced (including baluns)

T0 – RF Safety (3 exam questions – 3 groups)
T0A RF safety fundamentals, terms and definitions
T0B RF safety rules and guidelines
T0C Routine station evaluation (Practical applications for VHF/UHF and above operations)

NOTE: Official illustrations (schematics and block diagrams) numbered N-x and T-x that appear as part of questions in subelements T6 and T7 will be provided to you when you take your written examination.

Subelement T1 — Commission's Rules [9 Exam Questions — 9 Groups]

Note: A § Part 97 reference is enclosed in brackets, i.e. [97], after each correct answer explanation in this subelement.

T1A Basis and purpose of amateur service and definitions; Station /Operator license; classes of U.S. amateur licenses, including basic differences; privileges of the various license classes; term of licenses; grace periods; modifications of licenses; current mailing address on file with FCC

T1A01 Who makes and enforces the rules and regulations of the amateur service in the U.S.?
  A. The Congress of the United States
  B. The Federal Communications Commission (FCC)
  C. The Volunteer Examiner Coordinators (VECs)
  D. The Federal Bureau of Investigation (FBI)
ANSWER B: The Federal Communications Commission (FCC) makes and enforces all Amateur Radio rules in the United States. [97]

T1A02 What are two of the five purposes for the amateur service?
  A. To protect historical radio data, and help the public understand radio history
  B. To help foreign countries improve communication and technical skills, and encourage visits from foreign hams
  C. To modernize radio schematic drawings, and increase the pool of electrical drafting people
  D. To increase the number of trained radio operators and electronics experts, and improve international goodwill
ANSWER D: The Federal Communications Commission rules, found in Part 97, describe the amateur service as "a radio communications service for the purpose of self-training, intercommunication and technical investigation, carried out by amateurs, that is, duly authorized persons interested in radio technique solely with a personal aim and without pecuniary interest." Hams are well-known for their emergency communications capabilities; and when we are not handling disaster radio traffic, we can be found on the airwaves finding new ways to send signals from here to there as a hobby and service. [97.1]

T1A03 What is the definition of an amateur station?
  A. A station in a public radio service used for radiocommunications
  B. A station using radiocommunications for a commercial purpose
  C. A station using equipment for training new broadcast operators and technicians
  D. A station in the Amateur Radio service used for radiocommunications
ANSWER D: Your ham station will consist of a radio device, at a particular location, that will be used for amateur communications. This station can go anywhere that you go, and might be mobile, a base, or a handheld set. You also are allowed to choose any authorized frequency in any authorized band. You can change radio equipment type at anytime. [97.3a5]

T1A04 What is the definition of a control operator of an amateur station?
  A. Anyone who operates the controls of the station
  B. Anyone who is responsible for the station's equipment

C. Any licensed amateur operator who is responsible for the station's transmissions

D. The amateur operator with the highest class of license who is near the controls of the station

ANSWER C: This is a fancy name for you, the person who holds an amateur operator/primary station license. You, or any other ham you designate, are in control of all transmissions, and are responsible for the proper operation of the station. [97.3a12]

T1A05 Which of the following is required before you can operate an amateur station in the U.S.?

A. You must hold an FCC operator's training permit for a licensed radio station

B. You must submit an FCC Form 605 together with a license examination fee

C. The FCC must grant you an amateur operator/primary station license

D. The FCC must issue you a Certificate of Successful Completion of Amateur Training

ANSWER C: When you pass your examination, your accredited Volunteer Examination Team may electronically file the test results, and many times your call letters will be granted by the FCC in less than a week! As soon as you find out your new call letters, you can go on the air. It will take approximately 30 days for your actual paper license to arrive in the mail. Ask your Volunteer Examination Team what phone number to call, or what computer address to access, to find out what your new call letters are. You will not need to wait for that paper license — you can go on the air immediately with your new call sign. [97.5a]

UNITED STATES OF AMERICA
FEDERAL COMMUNICATIONS COMMISSION

 ## AMATEUR RADIO LICENSE

KB9SMG

DETER E TROTTER

Ham License

T1A06 What must happen before you are allowed to operate an amateur station?

A. The FCC database must show that you have been granted an amateur license

B. You must have written authorization from the FCC

C. You must have written authorization from a Volunteer Examiner Coordinator

D. You must have a copy of the FCC Rules, Part 97, at your station location

ANSWER A: When your name, address and call sign show up on the FCC database, this is considered a "grant" and you are on the air with the privileges you have earned. You may begin operating immediately, and are no longer required to wait for your new license to arrive in the mail from Gettysburg. [97.9a]

T1A07 What are the U.S. amateur operator licenses that a new amateur might earn?

A. Novice, Technician, General, Advanced
B. Technician, Technician Plus, General, Advanced
C. Novice, Technician, General, Advanced
D. Technician, Technician with Morse code, General, Amateur Extra

ANSWER D: Beginning April 15, 2000, there are now 3 amateur radio classes — Technician with or without Morse code, General class, and amateur Extra class. Any answer with "Novice" or "Advanced" in it would be wrong because the question reads, "A new amateur might earn." Even though there are grandfathered Novice and Advanced class operators out there in radio land, the question really wants you to know the answer as new Technician class, plus Technician class with Morse Code, General class, and amateur Extra class. [97.9a]

T1A08 How soon after you pass the elements required for your first Amateur Radio license may you transmit?

A. Immediately
B. 30 days after the test date
C. As soon as the FCC grants you a license
D. As soon as you receive your license from the FCC

ANSWER C: Good news! You will not need to wait very long to begin operating with your first Amateur Radio license. As soon as you see your FCC license grant on the Internet, or make a phone call to someone who can read you your new call sign from the FCC database, YOU ARE ON THE AIR! The paper copy of your license will come in about three to four weeks. If your Volunteer Examination Team and Coordinator file electronically, you should see a grant within 48 hours of electronic submission. [97.5a]

T1A09 How soon before the expiration date of your license should you send the FCC a completed Form 605 or file with the Universal Licensing System on the World Wide Web for a renewal?

A. No more than 90 days
B. No more than 30 days
C. Within 6 to 9 months
D. Within 6 months to a year

ANSWER A: Don't try to renew your license too early! Whether you renew on the computer or use Form 605, don't try to renew until your license is within 90 days of expiration. Licenses are good for 10 years, so keep it in a safe place where you're going to remember what you did with it 10 years from now! [97.21a3i]

T1A10 What is the normal term for which a new amateur station license is granted?

A. 5 years
B. 7 years
C. 10 years
D. For the lifetime of the licensee

ANSWER C: Amateur station licenses are granted for a term of ten years. You will need to renew your license at that time, and renewing will probably be as simple as e-mail to the FCC. There won't be any reminder notices sent out, so every now and then check the expiration date of your license and don't forget to renew! [97.25a]

T1A11 What is the "grace period" during which the FCC will renew an expired 10-year license?
- A. 2 years
- B. 5 years
- C. 10 years
- D. There is no grace period

ANSWER A: You are not allowed to operate during a grace period; however, you can keep your privileges for 2 years. After that, they are lost for good. So is your call sign. Don't forget to renew! [97.21b]

T1A12 What is one way you may notify the FCC if your mailing address changes?
- A. Fill out an FCC Form 605 using your new address, attach a copy of your license, and mail it to your local FCC Field Office
- B. Fill out an FCC Form 605 using your new address, attach a copy of your license, and mail it to the FCC office in Gettysburg, PA
- C. Call your local FCC Field Office and give them your new address over the phone or e-mail this information to the local Field Office
- D. Call the FCC office in Gettysburg, PA, and give them your new address over the phone or e-mail this information the FCC

ANSWER B: It is very important you notify the Federal Communications Commission if you change your mailing address. You will fill out FCC Form 605 and show your new address, plus attach a copy of your present license that shows your OLD address. This form is mailed to the Federal Communications Commission licensing office in Gettysburg, Pennsylvania. [97.23b]

FCC Form 605

T1B Frequency privileges authorized to the Technician control operator (VHF/UHF and HF)

T1B01 What are the frequency limits of the 6-meter band in ITU Region 2?
A. 52.0 - 54.5 MHz
B. 50.0 - 54.0 MHz
C. 50.1 - 52.1 MHz
D. 50.0 - 56.0 MHz

ANSWER B: First of all, "ITU Region 2" is here in the United States, up to Alaska and Greenland, and all the way down to South America. Region 1 is Europe and Africa, and Region 3 is the South Seas and the Far East. Here in Region 2, our 6-meter band extends from 50 to 54 MHz. [97.301a]

50 MHz   54 MHz

6-Meter Wavelength Band Privileges

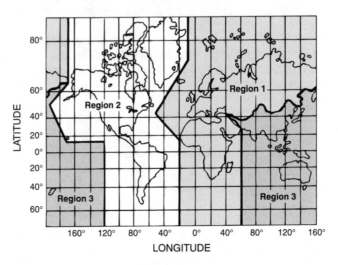

ITU Regions

T1B02 What are the frequency limits of the 2-meter band in ITU Region 2?
A. 145.0 - 150.5 MHz
B. 144.0 - 148.0 MHz
C. 144.1 - 146.5 MHz
D. 144.0 - 146.0 MHz

ANSWER B: Here in the USA, our 2-meter band extends from 144 MHz to 148 MHz. [97.301a]

144 MHz   148 MHz

2-Meter Wavelength Band Privileges

T1B03 What are the frequency limits of the 1.25-meter band in ITU Region 2?
    A. 225.0 - 230.5 MHz
    B. 222.0 - 225.0 MHz
    C. 224.1 - 225.1 MHz
    D. 220.0 - 226.0 MHz
ANSWER B: The 1.25 meter band is the popular "222" band, extending from 222 MHz to 225 MHz. We originally had a couple more MHz of this band, but the Federal Communications Commission took it away because it was underutilized by ham operators. We should use all of our frequencies, or stand the chance of losing them. [97.301f]

25 WATTS

222 MHz   225 MHz

1.25-Meter Wavelength Band Privileges

T1B04 What are the frequency limits of the 70-centimeter band in ITU Region 2?
    A. 430.0 - 440.0 MHz
    B. 430.0 - 450.0 MHz
    C. 420.0 - 450.0 MHz
    D. 432.0 - 435.0 MHz
ANSWER C: The 70 cm band is also known as the "440" band. Our privileges extend all the way down to 420 MHz, and all the way up to 450 MHz. When you buy a new dual-band radio, one band is usually 2 meters, and the other band is this band, the 440 MHz band. [97.301a]

420 MHz   450 MHz

70-CM Wavelength Band Privileges

T1B05 What are the frequency limits of the 33-centimeter band in ITU Region 2?
    A. 903 - 927 MHz
    B. 905 - 925 MHz
    C. 900 - 930 MHz
    D. 902 - 928 MHz
ANSWER D: The 33 cm band extends from 902 MHz to 928 MHz, and we compete with a lot of low-power, unlicensed equipment that may share these same frequencies. There is very little commercial ready-made equipment for this band, so we must continue to develop our own equipment for these frequencies and use all portions of the band, or stand the chance of losing this band to the low-power, unlicensed, cordless phones and garage door openers on these frequencies. [97.301a]

902 MHz   928 MHz

33-CM Wavelength Band Privileges

T1B06 What are the frequency limits of the 23-centimeter band?
 A. 1260 - 1270 MHz
 B. 1240 - 1300 MHz
 C. 1270 - 1295 MHz
 D. 1240 - 1246 MHz
ANSWER B: The 23 cm band extends from 1240 MHz to 1300 MHz, and is a good one for amateur television, repeater operation, and point-to-point simplex where there is plenty of ready-made equipment for this band. If you buy a "tri-band" transceiver, chances are it will have 2 meters, 440 MHz, and full capabilities for the 23 cm band from 1240 MHz to 1300 MHz. [97.301a]

0.23 m
1240 MHz   1300 MHz

0.23-Meter (23-Centimeters) Wavelength Band Privileges

T1B07 What are the frequency limits of the 13-centimeter band in ITU Region 2?
 A. 2300 - 2310 MHz and 2390 - 2450 MHz
 B. 2300 - 2350 MHz and 2400 - 2450 MHz
 C. 2350 - 2380 MHz and 2390 - 2450 MHz
 D. 2300 - 2350 MHz and 2380 - 2450 MHz
ANSWER A: We are just beginning to explore the 13 cm band with "home brew" equipment. Another way to operate on these frequencies is with a transverter that adds microwave capabilities to your existing VHF/UHF base or mobile unit. Now the big question is, "How are you going to remember which of these frequencies is correct on the test?" A simple way is to look at the correct answer for the lower portion of the band, 2300 to 2310 MHz, and recall that you have been sitting for the exam for about 10 minutes — and this is the only correct answer that has 10 MHz for the lower portion of the correct band. Keep in mind that some computer-generated exams will scramble the A, B, C, D answer order. 10 MHz, 10 minutes. Got it? [97.301a]

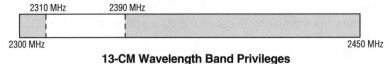

2310 MHz   2390 MHz

2300 MHz   2450 MHz

13-CM Wavelength Band Privileges

T1B08 What are the frequency limits of the 80-meter band for Technician class licensees who have passed a Morse code exam?
 A. 3500 - 4000 kHz
 B. 3675 - 3725 kHz
 C. 7100 - 7150 kHz
 D. 7000 - 7300 kHz
ANSWER B: Pass that simple 5 wpm code test when you take your first Element 2 written exam. Passing the code test gives you exciting CW privileges on the 80-meter band from 3675 kHz to 3725 kHz. [97.301e]

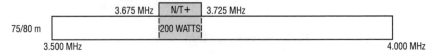

3.675 MHz   N/T+   3.725 MHz

75/80 m   200 WATTS

3.500 MHz   4.000 MHz

75/80-Meter Wavelength Band Privileges

T1B09 What are the frequency limits of the 40-meter band in ITU Region 2 for Technician class licensees who have passed a Morse code exam?
A. 3500 - 4000 kHz
B. 3700 - 3750 kHz
C. 7100 - 7150 kHz
D. 7000 - 7300 kHz

ANSWER C: Passing the 5 wpm code test with your Element 2 Technician class ticket allows you some great worldwide contacts, at night, on 40 meters from 7100 kHz to 7150 kHz. [97.301e]

40-Meter Wavelength Band Privileges

T1B10 What are the frequency limits of the 15-meter band for Technician class licensees who have passed a Morse code exam?
A. 21.100 - 21.200 MHz
B. 21.000 - 21.450 MHz
C. 28.000 - 29.700 MHz
D. 28.100 - 28.200 MHz

ANSWER A: Passing the 5 wpm code test in addition to Technician Element 2 will give you exciting daytime around-the-world Morse Code capabilities from 21.100 MHz to 21.200 MHz. [97.301e]

15-Meter Wavelength Band Privileges

T1B11 What are the frequency limits of the 10-meter band for Technician class licensees who have passed a Morse code exam?
A. 28.000 - 28.500 MHz
B. 28.100 - 29.500 MHz
C. 28.100 - 28.500 MHz
D. 29.100 - 29.500 MHz

ANSWER C: Ten meters is an exciting band for Technician class operators who also pass the Element 1 Morse Code test. Your privileges will extend from 28.100 MHz to 28.500 MHz, and the region between 28.300 MHz to 28.500 MHz is for single-sideband voice, too! Get that code test out of the way at the same time you take your Element 2 Technician written exam. Trust me, you will be glad you learned the code. [97.301e]

10-Meter Wavelength Band Privileges

T1B12 If you are a Technician licensee who has passed a Morse code exam, what is one document you can use to prove that you are authorized to use certain amateur frequencies below 30 MHz?

A. A certificate from the FCC showing that you have notified them that you will be using the HF bands

B. A certificate showing that you have attended a class in HF communications

C. A Certificate of Successful Completion of Examination showing that you have passed a Morse code exam

D. No special proof is required

ANSWER C: When you successfully pass your Morse code examination, you will be issued a Certificate of Successful Completion of Examination that is valid for 365 days as credit when you next go for Element 3, the worldwide General class license. But that CSCE is permanent proof that you have passed the 5 wpm code test; and if you want to wait a few years before finally going to General class, you may continue to operate on those 4 worldwide bands even though your certificate is more than 365 days old. But what the heck — once you get the code out of the way, the General class license is just one more simple written exam of just 35 questions found in my SECOND test preparation book. [97.9b]

Don't Lose Your CSCE

T1C Emission privileges authorized to the Technician control operator (VHF/UHF and HF)

T1C01 On what HF band may a Technician licensee use FM phone emission?

A. 10 meters

B. 15 meters

C. 75 meters

D. None

ANSWER D: If you are taking the code test and pass becoming a Technician with code credit, you gain access to four worldwide bands: 10 meters, 15 meters, 40 meters and 80 meters. Single sideband, using upper sideband, will give you the best range on 10 meters, and on 10 meters you can use voice, too! Although there are portions at the top end of the 10-meter band for FM, you are not permitted 10 meters FM because it is outside of your Technician frequency privileges, and there is no FM activity below 29.5 MHz because it would exceed the bandwidth limits. [97.305c]

T1C02 On what frequencies within the 6-meter band may phone emissions be transmitted?
- A. 50.0 - 54.0 MHz only
- B. 50.1 - 54.0 MHz only
- C. 51.0 - 54.0 MHz only
- D. 52.0 - 54.0 MHz only

ANSWER B: The term "phone" means voice, and as a new Technician class operator, you are allowed voice on the 6-meter band from 50.1 to 54 MHz. The area below 50.1 MHz to 50 MHz is reserved for CW only. [97.305c] Always follow the band plan (see *Table 2-2,* page 17).

50.1 MHz

50.0 MHz   54.0 MHz

6-Meter Phone Privileges

T1C03 On what frequencies within the 2-meter band may image emissions be transmitted?
- A. 144.1 - 148.0 MHz only
- B. 146.0 - 148.0 MHz only
- C. 144.0 - 148.0 MHz only
- D. 146.0 - 147.0 MHz only

ANSWER A: The term "image emissions" could relate to the portable, slow-scan, video transponders that send color, still images in about 30 seconds over worldwide and VHF/UHF frequencies. This slow-scan television does not occupy any more bandwidth than voice, and is permitted throughout the entire 2-meter band except below 144.1 MHz, which is reserved for CW only. The slow-scan signals are many times heard over repeaters and on FM simplex frequencies. Also please keep in mind that the lower portion of the 2-meter band below 144.300 MHz is restricted to weak signal emissions only, and no FM below 144.300. [97.305c]

T1C04 What frequencies within the 2-meter band are reserved exclusively for CW operations?
- A. 146 - 147 MHz
- B. 146.0 - 146.1 MHz
- C. 145 - 148 MHz
- D. 144.0 - 144.1 MHz

ANSWER D: Most new Technician Class operators begin operating FM voice on the 2-meter band. Most will purchase dual-band equipment for both 2 meters and 440 MHz. But not all of the 2-meter band may be used for FM voice. The 144.0 to 144.3 portion of the band is reserved for weak signal work and no FM. 144.0 to 144.1, MHz is reserved exclusively for CW operations. Absolutely no FM down here! [97.305c]

2-Meter CW-only — No Voice

T1C05 What emission types are Technician control operators who have passed a Morse code exam allowed to use in the 80-meter band?
- A. CW only
- B. Data only
- C. RTTY only
- D. Phone only

ANSWER A: As a Technician class operator who has passed the 5-wpm Element 1 Morse code test, you are allowed Morse code CW only on the 80-meter band. Remember the exact frequencies? 3675-3725 kHz. [97.305/.307f9]

Emission Definitions

CW — International Morse code telegraphy emissions.
Data — Telemetry, telecommand and computer communications emissions.
RTTY (Radioteletype) — Narrow-band, direct-printing telegraphy emissions.
Phone — Speech and other sound emissions.

T1C06 What emission types are Technician control operators who have passed a Morse code exam allowed to use from 7100 to 7150 kHz in ITU Region 2?
- A. CW and data
- B. Phone
- C. Data only
- D. CW only

ANSWER D: As a Technician class operator having passed the 5-wpm Element 1 Morse code test, you are allowed CW ONLY from 7100 to 7150 kHz, the 40-meter band. [97.305/.307f9]

T1C07 What emission types are Technician control operators who have passed a Morse code exam allowed to use on frequencies from 28.1 to 28.3 MHz?
- A. All authorized amateur emission privileges
- B. Data or phone
- C. CW, RTTY and data
- D. CW and phone

ANSWER C: As a Technician class operator who has successfully passed the 5-wpm Element 1 Morse code test, you get a little bit more on the lower portion of the 10-meter band from 28.1 MHz to 28.3 MHz—you also may transmit CW, RTTY radioteleprinter, and data packet or PSK (phased shift keying) emissions. [97.305]

T1C08 What emission types are Technician control operators who have passed a Morse code exam allowed to use on frequencies from 28.3 to 28.5 MHz?
A. All authorized amateur emission privileges
B. CW and data
C. CW and single-sideband phone
D. Data and phone

ANSWER C: Pass the Morse code Element 1 exam with your Technician written Element 2, because the 10-meter band from 28.3 MHz to 28.5 MHz allows you not only Morse code, but also exciting SINGLE-SIDEBAND PHONE transmissions, too. [97.305/ 307f10]

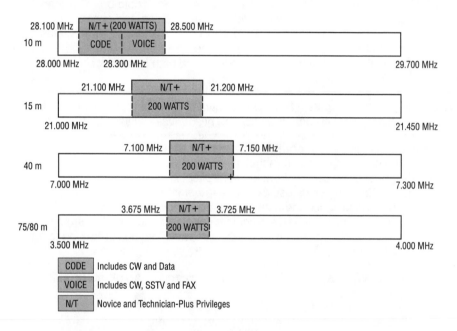

Additional Technician Class Privileges on HF Bands with CW Credit

T1C09 What emission types are Technician control operators allowed to use on the amateur 1.25-meter band in ITU Region 2?
A. Only CW and phone
B. Only CW and data
C. Only data and phone
D. All amateur emission privileges authorized for use on the band

ANSWER D: When you pass your upcoming Element 2, 35-question Tech exam, you will have all amateur emission privileges from 6 meters and shorter wavelength bands including all amateur emission privileges on the 1.25-meter band. How many MHz is 1.25 meters? That's right — 222 MHz to 225 MHz. [97.305]

T1C10 What emission types are Technician control operators allowed to use on the amateur 23-centimeter band?
A. Only data and phone
B. Only CW and data

C. Only CW and phone
D. All amateur emission privileges authorized for use on the band

ANSWER D: You may operate any emission — including television and all forms and speeds of packet. [97.305]

T1C11 On what frequencies within the 70-centimeter band in ITU Region 2 may image emissions be transmitted?
A. 420.0 - 420.1 MHz only
B. 430.0 - 440.0 MHz only
C. 420.0 - 450.0 MHz only
D. 440.0 - 450.0 MHz only

ANSWER C: Up on the "440 MHz" band, image emissions could be slow-scan television up and back from the international space station and space shuttles, plus fast-scan television on specific 440 MHz frequencies authorized for this wide-band image emission. So on 70 cm, have fun over the entire band with image emissions, but pay careful attention to the recommended band plan for fast-scan or slow-scan imaging. [97.305c]

T1D Responsibility of licensee; station control; control operator requirements; station identification; points of communication and operation; business communications

T1D01 What is the control point of an amateur station?
A. The on/off switch of the transmitter
B. The input/output port of a packet controller
C. The variable frequency oscillator of a transmitter
D. The location at which the control operator function is performed

ANSWER D: This is where you have complete capabilities to turn the equipment on, or shut it off in case of a malfunction. Every ham radio station is required to have a control point. [97.3a13]

T1D02 Who is responsible for the proper operation of an amateur station?
A. Only the control operator
B. Only the station licensee
C. Both the control operator and the station licensee
D. The person who owns the station equipment

ANSWER C: If you are visiting another ham's station and you operate the equipment with you acting as a control operator, both you and the other ham are jointly responsible for the proper operation of the station. [97.103a]

T1D03 What is your responsibility as a station licensee?
A. You must allow another amateur to operate your station upon request
B. You must be present whenever the station is operated
C. You must notify the FCC if another amateur acts as the control operator
D. You are responsible for the proper operation of the station in accordance with the FCC rules

ANSWER D: When a fellow ham is using your equipment and station call sign, remember your responsibility of making sure everything is legal. [97.103a]

T1D04 Who may be the control operator of an amateur station?
A. Any person over 21 years of age
B. Any person over 21 years of age with a General class license or higher

C. Any licensed amateur chosen by the station licensee

D. Any licensed amateur with a Technician class license or higher

ANSWER C: When you pass your upcoming Technician class exam with some friends, you may pick or choose who might be the control operator of a Technician class station on Technician class authorized frequencies. Just keep in mind that when you choose someone to be in control of your station, they must have the correct grade of license for the particular frequencies the equipment is operating on. [97.103b]

T1D05 If you are the control operator at the station of another amateur who has a higher class license than yours, what operating privileges are you allowed?

A. Any privileges allowed by the higher license

B. Only the privileges allowed by your license

C. All the emission privileges of the higher license, but only the frequency privileges of your license

D. All the frequency privileges of the higher license, but only the emission privileges of your license

ANSWER B: If you operate another amateur's equipment, you may operate only with the privileges allowed by your license, even though the equipment is owned by another ham with more privileges. [97.105b]

T1D06 When an amateur station is transmitting, where must its control operator be?

A. At the station's control point

B. Anywhere in the same building as the transmitter

C. At the station's entrance, to control entry to the room

D. Anywhere within 50 km of the station location

ANSWER A: If you let another ham use your station, your control operator responsibilities require you to stay in the room, right at the radio equipment, supervising the communications. [97.109b]

The control operator must be present in the ham shack whenever his station is transmitting.

T1D07 How often must an amateur station be identified?

A. At the beginning of a contact and at least every ten minutes after that

B. At least once during each transmission

C. At least every ten minutes during and at the end of a contact

D. At the beginning and end of each transmission

ANSWER C: Give your call letters regularly. Remember, even though the law doesn't require that you give them at the beginning of the transmission, it makes good sense to start out with your call letters. [97.119a]

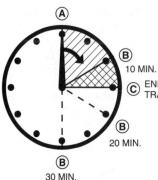

(A) START OF TRANSMISSION—EVEN THOUGH IT IS NOT REQUIRED, MOST HAMS IDENTIFY THEIR STATION AT THE START OF A TRANSMISSION.

TRANSMISSIONS LONGER THAN 10 MINUTES:
(B) AN AMATEUR STATION MUST IDENTIFY ITSELF EVERY 10 MINUTES OF TRANSMISSION, AND (C) AT THE END OF A TRANSMISSION.

(C) END OF TRANSMISSION

TRANSMISSIONS LESS THAN 10 MINUTES:
(C) FOR TRANSMISSIONS LESS THAN 10 MINUTES, THE AMATEUR STATION MUST IDENTIFY ITSELF AT THE END OF THE TRANSMISSION.

10 MIN.

20 MIN.

30 MIN.

Identifying Amateur Transmissions

T1D08 What identification, if any, is required when two amateur stations begin communications?
A. No identification is required
B. One of the stations must give both stations' call signs
C. Each station must transmit its own call sign
D. Both stations must transmit both call signs

ANSWER A: Isn't that strange! By FCC law, you can actually communicate for nearly 10 minutes without identifying. You must identify at the 10 minute point — or at the end of the communication, whichever comes first. Most hams identify when signing on a specific frequency so the other person will know who they are talking to. It is a good idea. [97.119a]

T1D09 What identification, if any, is required when two amateur stations end communications?
A. No identification is required
B. One of the stations must transmit both stations' call signs
C. Each station must transmit its own call sign
D. Both stations must transmit both call signs

ANSWER C: Use your own call sign — not someone else's call sign — when operating from your own station. [97.119a]

T1D10 What is the longest period of time an amateur station can operate without transmitting its call sign?
A. 5 minutes
B. 10 minutes
C. 15 minutes
D. 30 minutes

ANSWER B: Some hams use a 10-minute timer to remind them to give their call signs. §Part 97 stipulates: "Each amateur shall give its call sign at the end of each communication, and every ten minutes or less during a communication." [97.119a]

T1D11 What emission type may always be used for station identification, regardless of the transmitting frequency?
A. CW
B. RTTY

C. MCW

D. Phone

ANSWER A: CW stands for continuous wave. We use an interrupted continuous wave to transmit the dots and dashes of telegraphy. Telegraphy may be used for all station identification. [97.305a]

T1D12 If you are a Technician licensee with a Certificate of Successful Completion of Examination (CSCE) for a Morse code exam, how should you identify your station when transmitting on the 10 meter band?

A. You must give your call sign followed by the words "plus plus"

B. You must give your call sign followed by the words "temporary plus"

C. No special form of identification is needed

D. You must give your call sign and the location of the VE examination where you obtained the CSCE

ANSWER C: Pass your upcoming Element 1 Morse code 5-wpm exam! When you are operating on the 10-meter band, just give your regular Technician class call sign without the need to add any other words after it indicating you have indeed passed the 5 wpm requirements to operate on 10 meters. Remember, if you don't pass the code test, Technician privileges would NOT convey 10-meter voice and CW and data, 15-meter CW, 40-meter CW, and 80-meter CW sub-band privileges. Pass that code test! Listen to my voice getting you through the test on cassettes and CDs. [97.119e]

T1E Third-party communication; authorized and prohibited transmissions; permissible one-way communication

---

T1E01 What kind of payment is allowed for third-party messages sent by an amateur station?

A. Any amount agreed upon in advance

B. Donation of repairs to amateur equipment

C. Donation of amateur equipment

D. No payment of any kind is allowed

ANSWER D: You may not receive payment for handling any type of third-party traffic. This includes payment for long-distance charges incurred during the third-party traffic. [97.11a2]

T1E02 What is the definition of third-party communications?

A. A message sent between two amateur stations for someone else

B. Public service communications for a political party

C. Any messages sent by amateur stations

D. A three-minute transmission to another amateur

ANSWER A: Did you know you can let other people talk over your ham set who might not be ham radio operators? That's right, but you must stay right at the microphone to act as a "control operator" and make sure that they abide by the rules. When you link your ham radio into the telephone service, the people you can call would be considered "third-party." [97.3a44]

T1E03 What is a "third party" in amateur communications?

A. An amateur station that breaks in to talk

B. A person who is sent a message by amateur communications other than a control operator who handles the message

C. A shortwave listener who monitors amateur communications

D. An unlicensed control operator

ANSWER B: When third-party traffic is taking place, never leave the room. You must supervise the conversation at all times to ensure that the rules concerning illegal messages are being obeyed. Messages involving "business interest" and material compensation are prohibited, as well as messages to individuals of certain countries that do not permit Amateur Radio message traffic on behalf of others. [97.3a44]

T1E04 When are third-party messages allowed to be sent to a foreign country?

A. When sent by agreement of both control operators

B. When the third party speaks to a relative

C. They are not allowed under any circumstances

D. When the U.S. has a third-party agreement with the foreign country or the third party is qualified to be a control operator

ANSWER D: Your ham radio station is not a substitute for the regular international telephone service. If a third party wishes to use your ham station to talk with another ham in a foreign country (with which there is a third-party agreement), the third party's communications must be of a personal nature and relatively unimportant. [97.115a2]

List of Countries Permitting Third-Party Traffic

Country	Call Sign Prefix	Country	Call Sign Prefix	Country	Call Sign Prefix
Antigua and Barbuda	V2	El Salvador	YS	Paraguay	ZP
Argentina	LU	The Gambia	C5	Peru	OA
Australia	VK	Ghana	9G	Philippines	DU
Austria, Vienna	4U1VIC	Grenada	J3	St. Christopher & Nevis	V4
Belize	V3	Guatemala	TG	St. Lucia	J6
Bolivia	CP	Guyana	8R	St. Vincent & Grenadines	J8
Bosnia-Herzegovina	T9	Haiti	HH	Sierra Leone	9L
Brazil	PY	Honduras	HR	South Africa	ZS
Canada	VE, VO, VY	Israel	4X	Swaziland	3D6
Chile	CE	Jamaica	6Y	Trinidad and Tobago	9Y
Colombia	HK	Jordan	JY	Turkey	TA
Comoros	D6	Liberia	EL	United Kingdom	GB*
Costa Rica	TI	Marshall Is.	V6	Uruguay	CX
Cuba	CO	Mexico	XE	Venezuela	YV
Dominica	J7	Micronesia	V6	ITU-Geneva	4U1ITU
Dominican Republic	HI	Nicaragua	YN	VIC-Vienna	4U1VIC
Ecuador	HC	Panama	HP		

T1E05 If you let an unlicensed third party use your amateur station, what must you do at your station's control point?

A. You must continuously monitor and supervise the third-party's participation

B. You must monitor and supervise the communication only if contacts are made in countries that have no third-party communications agreement with the U.S.

C. You must monitor and supervise the communication only if contacts are made on frequencies below 30 MHz

D. You must key the transmitter and make the station identification

ANSWER A: Don't even leave the room when a third party is using your ham set. Your license is at stake, so stay right there with the third party to insure compliance with all FCC rules. See list at T1E04. [97.115b1]

T1E06 Besides normal identification, what else must a U.S. station do when sending third-party communications internationally?
    A. The U.S. station must transmit its own call sign at the beginning of each communication, and at least every ten minutes after that
    B. The U.S. station must transmit both call signs at the end of each communication
    C. The U.S. station must transmit its own call sign at the beginning of each communication, and at least every five minutes after that
    D. Each station must transmit its own call sign at the end of each transmission, and at least every five minutes after that
ANSWER B: It's common for U.S. amateur operators to handle third-party communications with those countries with whom we have a third-party agreement. The U.S. station must transmit both their call sign and the call sign of the foreign operator at the end of each communication. [97.115c]

T1E07 When is an amateur allowed to broadcast information to the general public?
    A. Never
    B. Only when the operator is being paid
    C. Only when broadcasts last less than 1 hour
    D. Only when broadcasts last longer than 15 minutes
ANSWER A: News bulletins broadcast over the ham radio airwaves must relate solely to Amateur Radio matters or be of interest to [97.305] amateur operators who tune in, not to the general public. [97.113b]

T1E08 When is an amateur station permitted to transmit music?
    A. Never, except incidental music during authorized rebroadcasts of space shuttle communications
    B. Only if the transmitted music produces no spurious emissions
    C. Only if it is used to jam an illegal transmission
    D. Only if it is above 1280 MHz, and the music is a live performance
ANSWER A: Music is generally not allowed on the ham bands. No playing the violin or piano, and no singing happy birthday. However, a little known rule COULD permit you to blow your trumpet for revelry when sending up an authorized signal to the space shuttle or international space station. Answer A calls this "incidental music during authorized space shuttle communications." You DO play the trumpet, right? [97.113a4/.113e]

T1E09 When is the use of codes or ciphers allowed to hide the meaning of an amateur message?
    A. Only during contests
    B. Only during nationally declared emergencies
    C. Never, except when special requirements are met
    D. Only on frequencies above 1280 MHz
ANSWER C: Secret codes are not allowed. It's even considered poor practice to use police-type "ten codes" on the air. [97.113a4]

T1E10 Which of the following one-way communications may not be transmitted in the amateur service?
    A. Telecommands to model craft
    B. Broadcasts intended for the general public

C. Brief transmissions to make adjustments to the station

D. Morse code practice

ANSWER B: This is one of those questions where you are to look for the "not" answer. No, you may not broadcast information intended for the general public. Only commercial broadcast stations may do that. [97.3a10, 97.113b]

T1E11 If you are allowing a non-amateur friend to use your station to talk to someone in the U.S., and a foreign station breaks in to talk to your friend, what should you do?

A. Have your friend wait until you find out if the U.S. has a third-party agreement with the foreign station's government

B. Stop all discussions and quickly sign off

C. Since you can talk to any foreign amateurs, your friend may keep talking as long as you are the control operator

D. Report the incident to the foreign amateur's government

ANSWER A: The U.S. must have a third-party agreement to allow your friend to talk to a foreign Amateur Radio operator. [97.115a2]

T1E12 When are you allowed to transmit a message to a station in a foreign country for a third party?

A. Anytime

B. Never

C. Anytime, unless there is a third-party agreement between the U.S. and the foreign government

D. If there is a third-party agreement with the U.S. government, or if the third party is eligible to be the control operator

ANSWER D: The following list is an example of countries with whom we have a third-party agreement. As you will see, most of our third-party agreements are with South American countries, with a few countries to our west, but almost no countries in Europe. [97.115a2]

T1F Frequency selection and sharing; transmitter power; digital communications

T1F01 If the FCC rules say that the amateur service is a secondary user of a frequency band, and another service is a primary user, what does this mean?

A. Nothing special; all users of a frequency band have equal rights to operate

B. Amateurs are only allowed to use the frequency band during emergencies

C. Amateurs are allowed to use the frequency band only if they do not cause harmful interference to primary users

D. Amateurs must increase transmitter power to overcome any interference caused by primary users

ANSWER C: We share the 900-MHz band with the vehicle locator service, which is primary user of the frequencies. Same thing with 70 cm—we share it with military radio location services. They have first rights to these frequencies. [97.303]

T1F02 What rule applies if two amateur stations want to use the same frequency?

A. The station operator with a lesser class of license must yield the frequency to a higher-class licensee

B. The station operator with a lower power output must yield the frequency to the station with a higher power output

C. Both station operators have an equal right to operate on the frequency

D. Station operators in ITU Regions 1 and 3 must yield the frequency to stations in ITU Region 2

ANSWER C: Hams must share the amateur frequencies. No ham owns a specific spot on the dial! All hams have an equal right to operate on any frequency that their class of license authorizes. [97.101b]

T1F03 If a repeater is causing harmful interference to another repeater and a frequency coordinator has recommended the operation of one repeater only, who is responsible for resolving the interference?

A. The licensee of the unrecommended repeater

B. Both repeater licensees

C. The licensee of the recommended repeater

D. The frequency coordinator

ANSWER A: It's important to remember that all amateur repeaters must receive coordination. If you operate an amateur repeater that is uncoordinated, you are responsible for resolving interference to a coordinated repeater. [97.205c]

T1F04 If a repeater is causing harmful interference to another amateur repeater and a frequency coordinator has recommended the operation of both repeaters, who is responsible for resolving the interference?

A. The licensee of the repeater that has been recommended for the longest period of time

B. The licensee of the repeater that has been recommended the most recently

C. The frequency coordinator

D. Both repeater licensees

ANSWER D: If both repeater stations are coordinated, both repeater licensees must mutually work out the interference problem. [97.205c]

T1F05 What is the term for the average power supplied to an antenna transmission line during one RF cycle at the crest of the modulation envelope?

A. Peak transmitter power

B. Peak output power

C. Average radio-frequency power

D. Peak envelope power

ANSWER D: If we measure to the crest of the modulation envelope, this is at its peak, and is called peak envelope power (PEP). [97.3b6]

T1F06 What is the maximum transmitting power permitted an amateur station on 146.52 MHz?

A. 200 watts PEP output

B. 500 watts ERP

C. 1000 watts DC input

D. 1500 watts PEP output

ANSWER D: You could transmit 1500 watts peak envelope power output on 146.52 MHz, 2 meters FM simplex, but 50 watts would be more appropriate unless you're doing some deep space work. On the 2-meter band, 1500 watts peak envelope power output is usually reserved for moon bounce or single-sideband, weak-signal work. [97.313b]

A Professional Wattmeter

T1F07 On which band(s) may a Technician licensee who has passed a Morse code exam use up to 200 watts PEP output power?
A. 80, 40, 15, and 10 meters
B. 80, 40, 20, and 10 meters
C. 1.25 meters
D. 23 centimeters

ANSWER A: If you pass your Element 1 Morse code 5-wpm exam when you also take and pass your Element 2 Technician written exam, you will be allow CW and a little bit of 10-meter voice on 80 meters, 40 meters, 15 meters, and 10 meters, sharing the sub-bands with grandfathered Novice operators. On these Novice CW and 10-meter voice sub-bands, a Technician class licensee holding code credit would be limited to no more than 200 watts of peak envelope power output. But hey, gang, 200 watts is plenty to easily work the world. That's about all your author runs at his station in Southern California. [97.313c]

T1F08 What amount of transmitter power must amateur stations use at all times?
A. 25 watts PEP output
B. 250 watts PEP output
C. 1500 watts PEP output
D. The minimum legal power necessary to communicate

ANSWER D: Be careful of this one — the answer is not a numerical one, but rather a philosophical one. Always run the minimum amount of power to make contact with another station. [97.313a]

T1F09 What name does the FCC use for telemetry, telecommand or computer communications emissions?
A. CW
B. Image
C. Data
D. RTTY

ANSWER C: The FCC name "data" may be used for indicating telemetry communications, telecommand communications, or sending radio signals from your laptop or home computer. [97.3c2]

T1F10 What name does the FCC use for narrow-band direct-printing telegraphy emissions?
A. CW
B. Image
C. MCW
D. RTTY

ANSWER D: Radio teleprinting is a form of narrow-band, direct-printing telegraphy. It is abbreviated "RTTY", and there are still some hams who enjoy sending RTTY narrow-band, direct-printing signals over the air waves as their way of preserving one of the earliest forms of sending signals that can be read as plain text on paper. [97.3c7]

T1F11 What is the maximum symbol rate permitted for packet transmissions on the 2-meter band?
A. 300 bauds
B. 1200 bauds

C. 19.6 kilobauds
D. 56 kilobauds

ANSWER C: The higher we go in frequency, the faster we may send our data transmissions. On 2 meters, we may step up to 19.6 kilobauds. [97.307f5]

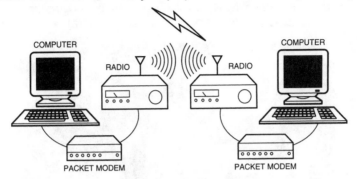

A Packet Radio System

T1F12 What is the maximum symbol rate permitted for RTTY or data transmissions on the 6- and 2-meter bands?
   A. 56 kilobauds
   B. 19.6 kilobauds
   C. 1200 bauds
   D. 300 bauds

ANSWER B: 19.6 kilobauds (kilo means 1000). 19,600 bauds is real quick! [97.307f5]

Amateur Band (meters)	Maximum Symbol Rate (bauds)
160 to 12 m	300 bauds
10 m	1200 bauds
6 and 2 m	19,600 bauds
1.25 and 0.70 m	56,000 bauds
33 cm and higher	Not Specified

T1G Satellite and space communications; false signals or unidentified communications; malicious interference

T1G01 What is an amateur space station?
   A. An amateur station operated on an unused frequency
   B. An amateur station awaiting its new call letters from the FCC
   C. An amateur station located more than 50 kilometers above the Earth's surface
   D. An amateur station that communicates with the International Space Station

ANSWER C: Special rules pertain to amateur operation in a space station. A space station is considered any amateur station located more than 50 kilometers above the earth's surface. Remote control of a model aircraft at 1000 feet is not considered a space station. [97.3a38]

T1G02 Who may be the licensee of an amateur space station?
   A. An amateur holding an Amateur Extra class operator license
   B. Any licensed amateur operator

C. Anyone designated by the commander of the spacecraft

D. No one unless specifically authorized by the government

ANSWER B: It doesn't take any special grade of amateur operator license to be the licensee of an amateur space station. Years ago, only Extra Class amateur operators could go into space. Now, any licensed amateur operator may receive space station authorization. Shall we beam you up? [97.207a]

Author's Space Shuttle QSL Card Contacts

T1G03 Which band may NOT be used by Earth stations for satellite communications?

A. 6 meters

B. 2 meters

C. 70 centimeters

D. 23 centimeters

ANSWER A: There are no uplink frequencies on the 6-meter band for satellite communications. [97.209b2]

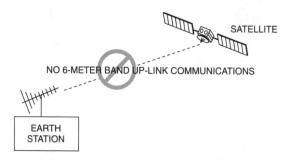

Earth-Station-to-Satellite Communications Restriction

T1G04 When may false or deceptive amateur signals or communications be transmitted?

A. Never

B. When operating a beacon transmitter in a "fox hunt" exercise

C. When playing a harmless "practical joke"

D. When you need to hide the meaning of a message for secrecy

ANSWER A: Going on the air using someone else's call sign, or reporting a false emergency, is strictly forbidden! [97.113a4]

T1G05 If an amateur pretends there is an emergency and transmits the word "MAYDAY," what is this called?

A. A traditional greeting in May

B. An emergency test transmission

C. False or deceptive signals

D. Nothing special; "MAYDAY" has no meaning in an emergency

ANSWER C: It's wise not to even utter the word "MAYDAY" in the course of your conversation. Reserve this word for the highest of emergencies over the worldwide bands. On local VHF and UHF repeaters, the equivalent of the worldwide word "MAYDAY" is the phrase "Break, break, break." A triple break signifies a local emergency. [97.113a4]

T1G06 When may an amateur transmit unidentified communications?

A. Only for brief tests not meant as messages

B. Only if it does not interfere with others

C. Never, except transmissions from a space station or to control a model craft

D. Only for two-way or third-party communications

ANSWER C: Normally we would NEVER transmit communications without giving our FCC call sign. However, transmissions from a space station or transmitting up to a 6-meter model aircraft may take place without station I.D. So look for the answer that begins with "never," and then double check that it says "space station" and "model aircraft." [97.119a]

T1G07 What is an amateur communication called that does not have the required station identification?

A. Unidentified communications or signals

B. Reluctance modulation

C. Test emission

D. Tactical communication

ANSWER A: Although not required, it's common practice to use your call sign at the beginning of a transmission. The law does allow you to begin communicating without your call sign for up to 10 minutes. While it's not required at the beginning of a transmission, it's required when you sign off. [97.119a]

T1G08 If an amateur transmits to test access to a repeater without giving any station identification, what type of communication is this called?

A. A test emission; no identification is required

B. An illegal unmodulated transmission

C. An illegal unidentified transmission

D. A non-communication; no voice is transmitted

ANSWER C: Every now and then you may hear a repeater being "keyed up" by another station, but the other station that is accessing the repeater as a test never gives their official FCC call sign. This is sometimes called "kerchunking" a repeater, and without call letters, this is absolutely illegal and is considered an unidentified transmission. [97.119a]

T1G09 When may you deliberately interfere with another station's communications?
    A. Only if the station is operating illegally
    B. Only if the station begins transmitting on a frequency you are using
    C. Never
    D. You may expect, and cause, deliberate interference because it can't be
        helped during crowded band conditions
ANSWER C: Ham radio operators pride themselves on being polite. Deliberate interference is rare, and will not be tolerated. The FCC will respond to jamming complaints from the amateur community. You could lose your amateur operator/primary station license permanently if found guilty of intentional interference. [97.101d]

T1G10 If an amateur repeatedly transmits on a frequency already occupied by a group of amateurs in a net operation, what type of interference is this called?
    A. Break-in interference
    B. Harmful or malicious interference
    C. Incidental interference
    D. Intermittent interference
ANSWER B: Regularly amateur operators will conduct organized round-table gatherings on a specific frequency. This is called a "net", and "nets" are a fun way to meet new friends and get started on ham radio. If another amateur operator repeatedly transmits on a frequency that is already in use by members of the net, and if that operator does not stop transmitting when requested by the net control, this would be considered harmful or malicious interference and is absolutely illegal. Luckily, occurrences like this bad behavior are relatively rare on the ham bands. And the very best procedure to discourage harmful interference is simply to ignore the interfering station and make absolutely no reference that someone is out there trying to break up the net. Without recognition, they will probably go away. [97.3a22]

T1G11 What is a transmission called that disturbs other communications?
    A. Interrupted CW
    B. Harmful interference
    C. Transponder signals
    D. Unidentified transmissions
ANSWER B: Intentionally transmitting over another station already on the air is not courteous, not legal, and out of the spirit of good ham radio operating. [97.3a22]

T1H Correct language; phonetics; beacons; radio control of model craft and vehicles

T1H01 If you are using a language besides English to make a contact, what language must you use when identifying your station?
    A. The language being used for the contact
    B. The language being used for the contact, provided the U.S. has a third-party
        communications agreement with that country
    C. English
    D. Any language of a country that is a member of the International
        Telecommunication Union
ANSWER C: It is okay to talk with another amateur in a foreign language to practice the other language as long as you identify your station in English every 10 minutes. FCC rules require U.S. amateurs to give their call signs in English. [97.119b2]

T1H02 What do the FCC Rules suggest you use as an aid for correct station identification when using phone?

A. A speech compressor
B. Q signals
C. A phonetic alphabet
D. Unique words of your choice

ANSWER C: When talking with a new station that is unfamiliar with your call sign, use the phonetic alphabet. This is especially helpful when communicating with a foreign station that may not speak good English. Everyone uses the same phonetics, and it makes it easy to pick out someone's call sign. [97.119b2]

Table T1H02. Phonetic Alphabet
Adopted by the International Telecommunication Union

A - Alpha	F - Foxtrot	K - Kilo	P - Papa	U - Uniform	Z - Zulu
B - Bravo	G - Golf	L - Lima	Q - Quebec	V - Victor	
C - Charlie	H - Hotel	M - Mike	R - Romeo	W- Whiskey	
D - Delta	I - India	N - November	S - Sierra	X - X-Ray	
E - Echo	J - Juliette	O - Oscar	T - Tango	Y - Yankee	

T1H03 What is the advantage in using the International Telecommunication Union (ITU) phonetic alphabet when identifying your station?

A. The words are internationally recognized substitutes for letters
B. There is no advantage
C. The words have been chosen to be easily pronounced by Asian cultures
D. It preserves traditions begun in the early days of Amateur Radio

ANSWER A: When you get your new call sign, hardly anyone else on the repeater will be familiar with it, and you should use the International Phonetic Alphabet to make your individual letters recognized by substituting a word for each letter. Memorize the phonetic alphabet, and use it often. [97.119b2]

T1H04 What is one reason to avoid using "cute" phrases or word combinations to identify your station?

A. They are not easily understood by non-English-speaking amateurs
B. They might offend English-speaking amateurs
C. They do not meet FCC identification requirements
D. They might be interpreted as codes or ciphers intended to obscure the meaning of your identification

ANSWER A: When communicating through satellites or to other operators who may not speak English well, always stick with the International Phonetic Alphabet. Some amateurs say the last three letters of my call sign as "Never-Outof-Answers!" While this may be cute, November-Oscar-Alpha might be better so a foreign station would know exactly my "NOA" call sign. [97.119b2]

T1H05 What is an amateur station called that transmits communications for the purpose of observation of propagation and reception?

A. A beacon
B. A repeater
C. An auxiliary station
D. A radio control station

ANSWER A: You can tune in radio beacons on 14.100, 18.110, 21.150, 24.930, and 28.200 MHz. They use CW to send their call signs over and over again for propagation phenomena information. [97.3a9]

T1H06 What is the maximum transmitting power permitted an amateur station in beacon operation?
 A. 10 watts PEP output
 B. 100 watts PEP output
 C. 500 watts PEP output
 D. 1500 watts PEP output

ANSWER B: Radio beacons automatically transmit a distinctive call sign on a specific beacon band frequency. This allows hams to tune them in from far away to determine band conditions. If you can hear a distant beacon thousands of miles away, chances are you can communicate on that Amateur Radio band to other stations thousands of miles away in the direction of the propagational beacon. [97.203c]

Radio Beacon Stations

Slot	Country	Call	14.100	18.110	21.150	24.930	28.200	Operator
1	United Nations	4U1UN	00:00	00:10	00:20	00:30	00:40	UNRC
2	Canada	VE8AT	00:10	00:20	00:30	00:40	00:50	RAC
3	USA	W6WX	00:20	00:30	00:40	00:50	01:00	NCDXF
4	Hawaii	KH6WO	00:30	00:40	00:50	01:00	01:10	UHRO
5	New Zealand	ZL	00:40	00:50	01:00	01:10	01:20	NZART
6	Australia	VK8	00:50	01:00	01:10	01:20	01:30	W1A
7	Japan	JA21CY	01:00	01:10	01:20	01:30	01:40	JARL
8	China	BY	01:10	01:20	01:30	01:40	01:50	CRSA
9	Russia	UA	01:20	01:30	01:40	01:50	02:00	TBO
10	Sri Lanka	4S7B	01:30	01:40	01:50	02:00	02:10	RSSL
11	South Africa	ZS6DN	01:40	01:50	02:00	02:10	02:20	ZS6DN
12	Kenya	5Z4B	01:50	02:00	02:10	02:20	02:30	RSK
13	Israel	4X6TU	02:00	02:10	02:20	02:30	02:40	U of Tel Aviv
14	Finland	OH2B	02:10	02:20	02:30	02:40	02:50	U oh Helsinki
15	Madeira	CS3B	02:20	02:30	02:40	02:50	00:00	ARRM
16	Argentina	LU4AA	02:30	02:40	02:50	00:00	00:10	RCA
17	Peru	OA4B	02:40	02:50	00:00	00:10	00:20	RCP
18	Venezuela	YV5B	02:50	00:00	00:10	00:20	00:30	RCV

The 10-second, phase-3, message format is: "W6WX dah-dah-dah-dah" — each "dah" lasts a little more than one second. W6WX is transmitted at 100 watts, then each "dah" is attenuated in order, beginning at 100 watts, then 10 watts, then 1 watt, and finally 0.1 watt.
Courtesy CQ Magazine

T1H07 What minimum class of amateur license must you hold to operate a beacon or a repeater station?
 A. Technician with credit for passing a Morse code exam
 B. Technician
 C. General
 D. Amateur Extra

ANSWER B: This question asks what MINIMUM class of license may operate a repeater or propagation beacon station — and guess what, you with a Technician class, even without passing the code test, may operate VHF and UHF propagational beacons and repeaters. [97.205a]

T1H08 What minimum information must be on a label affixed to a transmitter used for telecommand (control) of model craft?
 A. Station call sign
 B. Station call sign and the station licensee's name

C. Station call sign and the station licensee's name and address
D. Station call sign and the station licensee's class of license

ANSWER C: With your Technician Class license, you get to fly the coveted black flag. The black flag indicates 6-meter ham operation. Just make sure you have all of your license information on the side of your transmitter. [97.215a]

T1H09 What is the maximum transmitter power an amateur station is allowed when used for telecommand (control) of model craft?
A. One milliwatt
B. One watt
C. 25 watts
D. 100 watts

ANSWER B: If you ran more than one watt of power, every model in the country might take its command from your transmitter! One watt is a good power level to keep your model going within eyesight. [97.215c]

Radio Control Channels

Old Channels			New Channels	
Freq. (MHz)	Channel I.D.		Freq. (MHz)	Channel I.D.
53.1	Black	Brown	50.80	00
53.2	Black	Red	50.82	01
53.3	Black	Orange	50.84	02
53.4	Black	Yellow	50.86	03
53.5	Black	Green	50.88	04
53.6	Black	Blue	50.90	05
53.7	Black	Violet	50.92	06
53.8	Black	Grey	50.94	07
53.9	Black	White	50.96	08
			50.98	09

T1I Emergency communications; broadcasting; indecent and obscene language

T1I01 If you hear a voice distress signal on a frequency outside of your license privileges, what are you allowed to do to help the station in distress?
A. You are NOT allowed to help because the frequency of the signal is outside your privileges
B. You are allowed to help only if you keep your signals within the nearest frequency band of your privileges
C. You are allowed to help on a frequency outside your privileges only if you use international Morse code
D. You are allowed to help on a frequency outside your privileges in any way possible

ANSWER D: In an emergency, anything goes! If you hear someone calling "MAYDAY" on a frequency outside of your normal operating privileges, it's perfectly okay to transmit on any frequency to save someone's life. [97.405a]

T1I02 When may you use your amateur station to transmit an "SOS" or "MAYDAY"?
A. Never
B. Only at specific times (at 15 and 30 minutes after the hour)
C. In a life- or property-threatening emergency
D. When the National Weather Service has announced a severe weather watch

ANSWER C: As mentioned previously, don't even utter the word "MAYDAY" in the course of your conversation. Only in the highest of emergencies would you "MAYDAY" over the worldwide bands. The same applies, of course, for "SOS" when transmitting with CW. [97.403]

T1I03 When may you send a distress signal on any frequency?
- A. Never
- B. In a life- or property-threatening emergency
- C. Only at specific times (at 15 and 30 minutes after the hour)
- D. When the National Weather Service has announced a severe weather watch

ANSWER B: In a life and death situation, you may send out a distress signal on any frequency and any band, regardless of the license you may hold. [97.405a]

T1I04 If a disaster disrupts normal communication systems in an area where the amateur service is regulated by the FCC, what kinds of transmissions may stations make?
- A. Those that are necessary to meet essential communication needs and facilitate relief actions
- B. Those that allow a commercial business to continue to operate in the affected area
- C. Those for which material compensation has been paid to the amateur operator for delivery into the affected area
- D. Those that are to be used for program production or news gathering for broadcasting purposes

ANSWER A: If you do take part in emergency communications, keep your transmissions as short as possible. Listen to airline pilots communications over the airwaves — you should adopt their brief style when taking part in emergency communications. [97.401a]

T1I05 What information is included in an FCC declaration of a temporary state of communication emergency?
- A. A list of organizations authorized to use radio communications in the affected area
- B. A list of amateur frequency bands to be used in the affected area
- C. Any special conditions and special rules to be observed during the emergency
- D. An operating schedule for authorized amateur emergency stations

ANSWER C: If you are asked to stop transmitting on a certain frequency because it is reserved only for emergency communications, then by all means comply! Do listen in to see if there is anything that you might do to help — but avoid transmitting on the frequency unless directed to do so by the emergency net controller. If they are not asking for outside help, then don't transmit an offer for assistance. [97.401c]

In a Blizzard, Ham Emergency Calls Have High Priority

T1I06 What is meant by the term broadcasting?
  A. Transmissions intended for reception by the general public, either direct or relayed
  B. Retransmission by automatic means of programs or signals from non-amateur stations
  C. One-way radio communications, regardless of purpose or content
  D. One-way or two-way radio communications between two or more stations
ANSWER A: You may not operate your station like an AM, FM, or shortwave broadcast station. You cannot transmit to the public directly. [97.3a10]

T1I07 When may you send obscene words from your amateur station?
  A. Only when they do not cause interference to other communications
  B. Never; obscene words are not allowed in amateur transmissions
  C. Only when they are not retransmitted through a repeater
  D. Any time, but there is an unwritten rule among amateurs that they should not be used on the air
ANSWER B: Using indecent or obscene language is not permitted on the ham bands. Watch your tongue, and communicate like a professional. [97.113a4]

T1I08 When may you send indecent words from your amateur station?
  A. Only when they do not cause interference to other communications
  B. Only when they are not retransmitted through a repeater
  C. Any time, but there is an unwritten rule among amateurs that they should not be used on the air
  D. Never; indecent words are not allowed in amateur transmissions
ANSWER D: Any type of questionable language is frowned upon by other hams. Remember, ham radio is a family hobby, and there may be young kids out there listening. [97.113a4]

T1I09 Why is indecent and obscene language prohibited in the Amateur Service?
  A. Because it is offensive to some individuals
  B. Because young children may intercept amateur communications with readily available receiving equipment
  C. Because such language is specifically prohibited by FCC Rules
  D. All of these choices are correct
ANSWER D: Bad language is OUT on amateur radio frequencies. If ever I encounter a ham using bad language, I politely and abruptly sign off, and hopefully they will get the message. No bad language on ham frequencies! [97.113a4]

T1I10 Where can the official list of prohibited obscene and indecent words be found?
  A. There is no public list of prohibited obscene and indecent words; if you believe a word is questionable, don't use it in your communications
  B. The list is maintained by the Department of Commerce
  C. The list is International, and is maintained by Industry Canada
  D. The list is in the "public domain," and can be found in all amateur study guides
ANSWER A: No, there is not a list of the 10 worst words to not ever be found on ham frequencies. We don't need a list to know what's proper or improper. If you find yourself in contact with someone going over the line, just abruptly sign off, and hopefully they will get the message loud and clear. [97.113a4]

T1I11 Under what conditions may a Technician class operator use his or her station to broadcast information intended for reception by the general public?
- A. Never, broadcasting is a privilege reserved for Extra and General class operators only
- B. Only when operating in the FM Broadcast band (88.1 to 107.9 MHz)
- C. Only when operating in the AM Broadcast band (530 to 1700 kHz)
- D. Never, broadcasts intended for reception by the general public are not permitted in the Amateur Service

ANSWER D: Sometimes you will hear a repeater station transmitting a professional-sounding amateur radio news service for hams. This is perfectly legal. But what is NOT legal would be a news broadcast talking about non-ham subjects that was intended to be received by non-ham public listeners on scanners. This is not allowed. All ham news bulletins are broadcast specifically for other hams, not the general public. [97.113b]

Subelement T2 — Operating Procedures   [5 Exam Questions — 5 Groups]

T2A Preparing to transmit; choosing a frequency for tune-up; operating or emergencies; Morse code; repeater operations and autopatch

T2A01 What should you do before you transmit on any frequency?
- A. Listen to make sure others are not using the frequency
- B. Listen to make sure that someone will be able to hear you
- C. Check your antenna for resonance at the selected frequency
- D. Make sure the SWR on your antenna feed line is high enough

ANSWER A: Always listen for a few seconds before initiating a transmitted call. On worldwide, ask, "Is the frequency in use?" Always choose a frequency within your privileges, within the American Radio Relay League (ARRL) suggested band plan, and clear of an ongoing conversation.

T2A02 If you are in contact with another station and you hear an emergency call for help on your frequency, what should you do?
- A. Tell the calling station that the frequency is in use
- B. Direct the calling station to the nearest emergency net frequency
- C. Call your local Civil Preparedness Office and inform them of the emergency
- D. Stop your QSO immediately and take the emergency call

ANSWER D: An emergency call always has the highest priority. Do what you can to take down the message accurately, and then call the proper authorities.

T2A03 Why should local amateur communications use VHF and UHF frequencies instead of HF frequencies?
- A. To minimize interference on HF bands capable of long-distance communication
- B. Because greater output power is permitted on VHF and UHF
- C. Because HF transmissions are not propagated locally
- D. Because signals are louder on VHF and UHF frequencies

ANSWER A: We use VHF and UHF frequencies for operating on the 6-meter, 2-meter, 222-MHz, 450-MHz, and 1270-MHz FM ham bands. These bands are so high in frequency that they are line-of-sight to repeaters. We would use worldwide frequencies below 30 MHz for longer sky-wave range. If we wish to talk locally, we go to local VHF and UHF band frequencies.

T2A04 How can on-the-air interference be minimized during a lengthy transmitter testing or loading-up procedure?

A. Choose an unoccupied frequency
B. Use a dummy load
C. Use a non-resonant antenna
D. Use a resonant antenna that requires no loading-up procedure

ANSWER B: If you work on your transmitter a lot, you may wish to test it without actually putting a signal out on the airwaves. A dummy antenna might be a 50-ohm noninductive resistance. The energy doesn't go very far. It's a great way to test your set before adding the antenna to it. It lets you run your rig at full output, but without actually going on the air.

A Dummy Load

T2A05 At what speed should a Morse code CQ call be transmitted?

A. Only speeds below five WPM
B. The highest speed your keyer will operate
C. Any speed at which you can reliably receive
D. The highest speed at which you can control the keyer

ANSWER C: We use CQ for a general call to communicate with anyone, about anything, on worldwide frequencies. When using telegraphy, a fast CW CQ call will result in a very fast reply since it will be assumed that you can receive Morse code as fast as you can send it. Don't transmit CW faster than you can receive it.

T2A06 What is an autopatch?

A. An automatic digital connection between a U.S. and a foreign amateur
B. A digital connection used to transfer data between a hand-held radio and a computer
C. A device that allows radio users to access the public telephone system
D. A video interface allowing images to be patched into a digital data stream

ANSWER C: One benefit of becoming an amateur operator is using an autopatch to access the public telephone system. There are autopatches on the 2-meter band, and on the 70-cm (440-MHz) band. Most autopatches are offered through club and organization participation. If you are operating on an open repeater, and hear someone making a phone call over it, ask that person how to join the club for the additional benefit of autopatch. Most clubs include local dialing autopatch privileges as part of their $15 to $30 yearly dues. If the autopatch has long-distance capabilities, you would pay for the long-distance calls just like you do when dialing from home. You may not use your autopatch to stay in touch with your own business. However, new rules may now allow you to use autopatch to order a pizza, make dinner reservations, or to call an auto parts store to see whether or not they have that specific auto part in stock. Autopatch is a fringe benefit to ham radio operating, and under no circumstances should you rely on an autopatch solely to beat long-distance charges or substitute for your cellular phone.

T2A07 How do you call another station on a repeater if you know the station's call sign?
   A. Say "break, break 79," then say the station's call sign
   B. Say the station's call sign, then identify your own station
   C. Say "CQ" three times, then say the station's call sign
   D. Wait for the station to call "CQ," then answer it
ANSWER B: Before transmitting on any frequency, be sure to listen for a few seconds to insure the channel is clear. Then depress the microphone push-to-talk button and say the call sign of the station you are wishing to hook up with, followed by your call sign, and the optional word "over." If you are placing a repeater call to ANY station, state your call sign a couple of times phonetically, and just say the fact that you are on the air looking for a contact with anyone else monitoring. You will find plenty of friends responding to your call.

T2A08 What is a courtesy tone (used in repeater operations)?
   A. A sound used to identify the repeater
   B. A sound used to indicate when a transmission is complete
   C. A sound used to indicate that a message is waiting for someone
   D. A sound used to activate a receiver in case of severe weather
ANSWER B: Most repeaters have a beep tone that lets you know when the other person has stopped transmitting. Wait at least a second before continuing the conversation.

T2A09 What is the meaning of the procedural signal "DE"?
   A. "From" or "this is," as in "W0AIH DE KA9FOX"
   B. "Directional Emissions" from your antenna
   C. "Received all correctly"
   D. "Calling any station"
ANSWER A: When working CW, it's much easier to send abbreviations than the whole word or phrase. Abbreviations are very important for you to know for both your written and code examinations.

T2A10 During commuting rush hours, which type of repeater operation should be discouraged?
   A. Mobile stations
   B. Low-power stations
   C. Highway traffic information nets
   D. Third-party communications nets
ANSWER D: It's not a good idea to let a friend talk over your microphone as a third party during heavy repeater use time. During rush hours, most repeaters are used for traffic advisories and traffic accident reports.

T2A11 What is the proper way to break into a conversation on a repeater?
   A. Wait for the end of a transmission and start calling the desired party
   B. Shout, "break, break!" to show that you're eager to join the conversation
   C. Turn on an amplifier and override whoever is talking
   D. Say your call sign during a break between transmissions

ANSWER D: If you tune into a repeater transmission between 2 hams, and they are talking about something YOU really know about and want to share with them, quickly drop your call sign in between the time one station releases their push-to-talk button and the few seconds before the other station begins to return onto the airwaves. Usually stations leave about a 2-second gap for this type of call sign drop-in. They will usually immediately recognize you, and welcome you to the conversation. Never enter a conversation with the word "break" unless it is a priority or emergency call. Stay away from the word "break" at all times on ham frequencies except for very important matters that just can't wait.

T2B Definition and proper use; courteous operation; repeater frequency coordination; Morse code

T2B01 When using a repeater to communicate, which of the following do you need to know about the repeater?
A. Its input frequency and offset
B. Its call sign
C. Its power level
D. Whether or not it has an autopatch

ANSWER A: When you first get started on the VHF and UHF airwaves with your new Technician class license, operating through repeaters will be a great way to extend your local communications range. All repeaters transmit on one frequency, and listen on another simultaneously. This means you need to know ahead of time what the repeater input is and the offset to hear the repeater output. Some amateur mobile and handheld VHF/UHF transceivers have an automatic repeater offset feature. This is good. But what is BETTER is to ask the sales personnel at the location where you buy your equipment to please clone your new radio to local frequencies in your area so you can begin tuning in all of the radio excitement without having to search for local repeaters and local simplex traffic in your area. Preprogrammed equipment is a terrific way to start out operating on repeater channels with everything preset and cloned for your local area of repeater operation. You should also buy local repeater directories at the same time that you purchase your new equipment so you know what repeaters are where in your area, or where you plan to travel.

T2B02 What is an autopatch?
A. Something that automatically selects the strongest signal to be repeated
B. A device that connects a mobile station to the next repeater if it moves out of range of the first
C. A device that allows repeater users to make telephone calls from their stations
D. A device that locks other stations out of a repeater when there is an important conversation in progress

ANSWER C: Now you have a car phone — and a pocket phone! Many ham repeaters are tied into automatic telephone system interconnections. Once you join a repeater group, you may be given the specific access code for making local phone calls. Remember, it's not legal to call the office or make business phone calls from an Amateur Radio set. Don't confuse your new pleasure telephone patch capabilities with the utility of a regular cellular telephone. For business, you should use cellular telephone or CB. For strictly personal phone calls, use your ham autopatch, and be aware that the whole world is listening! Phone patches are anything but private.

T2B03 What is the purpose of a repeater time-out timer?

A. It lets a repeater have a rest period after heavy use
B. It logs repeater transmit time to predict when a repeater will fail
C. It tells how long someone has been using a repeater
D. It limits the amount of time someone can transmit on a repeater

ANSWER D: Time-out timers keep repeater operators from getting long-winded. The repeater cycles off the air if it doesn't get a few seconds break during one long transmission. Some timers are as short as 30 seconds. It's always good practice to keep your transmissions shorter than a one-half minute period. If you need to talk longer, announce, "Reset," release the mike button, and let the repeater reestablish its time-out timer.

T2B04 What is a CTCSS (or PL) tone?

A. A special signal used for telecommand control of model craft
B. A sub-audible tone, added to a carrier, which may cause a receiver to accept a signal
C. A tone used by repeaters to mark the end of a transmission
D. A special signal used for telemetry between amateur space stations and Earth stations

ANSWER B: CTCSS stands for Continuous Tone Coded Squelch System. This is a sub-audible tone that rides along with your FM carrier to access other stations using the same CTCSS tone.

Table T2B04. EIA Standard Subaudible CTCSS (PL) Tone Frequencies

Freq.	Tone No.	Tone Code	Freq.	Tone No.	Tone Code	Freq.	Tone No.	Tone Code
67.0	01	XZ	110.9	15	2Z	179.9	29	6B
71.9	02	XA	114.8	16	2A	186.2	30	7Z
74.4	03	WA	118.8	17	2B	192.8	31	7A
77.0	04	XB	123.0	18	3Z	203.5	32	M1
79.7	05	SP	127.3	19	3A	206.5		8Z
82.5	06	YZ	131.8	20	3B	210.7	33	M2
85.4	07	YA	136.5	21	4Z	218.8	34	M3
88.5	08	YB	141.3	22	4A	225.7	35	M4
91.5	09	ZZ	146.2	23	4B	229.2		9Z
94.8	10	ZA	151.4	24	5Z	233.6	36	
97.4	11	ZB	156.7	25	5A	241.8		M5
100.0	12	1Z	162.2	26	5B	250.3		M6
103.5	13	1A	167.9	27	6Z	256.3		M7
107.2	14	1B	173.8	28	6A			

T2B05 What is the usual input/output frequency separation for repeaters in the 2-meter band?

A. 600 kHz
B. 1.0 MHz
C. 1.6 MHz
D. 5.0 MHz

ANSWER A: You will have this question, or one of the next three questions, on your exam, for sure. These are important to remember. Although some sets already come with the repeater splits memorized, some sets require initializing. On the 2-meter wavelength band, repeater inputs and outputs are usually separated by 600 kHz.

T2B06 What is the usual input/output frequency separation for repeaters in the 1.25-meter band?
A. 600 kHz
B. 1.0 MHz
C. 1.6 MHz
D. 5.0 MHz
ANSWER C: The 1.25-meter wavelength band is 222 MHz, and repeater separation is 1.6 MHz.

T2B07 What is the usual input/output frequency separation for repeaters in the 70-centimeter band?
A. 600 kHz
B. 1.0 MHz
C. 1.6 MHz
D. 5.0 MHz
ANSWER D: 70 centimeters (0.70 meters) is the 450-MHz band, and input and output repeater separation is 5 MHz.

T2B08 What is the purpose of repeater operation?
A. To cut your power bill by using someone else's higher power system
B. To help mobile and low-power stations extend their usable range
C. To transmit signals for observing propagation and reception
D. To communicate with stations in services other than amateur
ANSWER B: Repeaters are sponsored by ham radio clubs and individual hams for everyone to use. They are usually placed high atop a mountain or a very tall building. Mobile and portable sets operate through repeaters with dramatically extended range. Even base stations are permitted to use repeaters for added communications distance. There is usually no charge for joining a repeater group. Some repeaters have autopatch, and those repeaters may require special access codes and financial support.

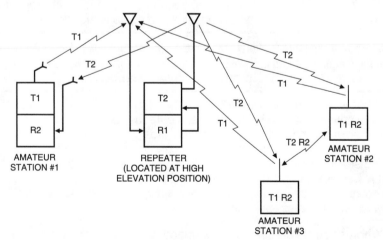

Repeater

Source: *Mobile 2-Way Radio Communications,* G. West, © 1993, Master Publishing, Inc.

T2B09 What is a repeater called that is available for anyone to use?
  A. An open repeater
  B. A closed repeater
  C. An autopatch repeater
  D. A private repeater
ANSWER A: If you buy your first new VHF/UHF transceiver without getting it cloned or preprogrammed, you won't really know what repeaters are available for you to use in your local area. Repeater atlases and repeater directories are available at the same place you buy your equipment, so get one that will illustrate all of the many open repeaters where you live or where you plan to travel. An open repeater is one that anyone may use without needing to join an organization.

T2B10 Why should you pause briefly between transmissions when using a repeater?
  A. To check the SWR of the repeater
  B. To reach for pencil and paper for third-party communications
  C. To listen for anyone wanting to break in
  D. To dial up the repeater's autopatch
ANSWER C: A repeater is like a party line — there may be others who may wish to use the system. In an emergency, stations may break in saying "Break, Break, Break". Give up the channel immediately. Always leave enough time between picking up the conversation for other stations to break in. It's a pause that may refresh someone else's day in an emergency.

T2B11 Why should you keep transmissions short when using a repeater?
  A. A long transmission may prevent someone with an emergency from using the repeater
  B. To see if the receiving station operator is still awake
  C. To give any listening non-hams a chance to respond
  D. To keep long-distance charges down
ANSWER A: During peak traffic hours, keep your transmissions short. Repeaters are a great way to find out traffic reports and for reporting traffic accidents.

T2C Simplex operations; RST signal reporting; choice of equipment for desired communications; communications modes including amateur television (ATV), packet radio; Q signals, procedural signals and abbreviations

T2C01 What is simplex operation?
  A. Transmitting and receiving on the same frequency
  B. Transmitting and receiving over a wide area
  C. Transmitting on one frequency and receiving on another
  D. Transmitting one-way communications
ANSWER A: Simplex means same frequency. Operate simplex on VHF or UHF when the other station is within a few miles of your station. The opposite of simplex is duplex, a type of repeater operation.

T2C02 When should you use simplex operation instead of a repeater?
  A. When the most reliable communications are needed
  B. When a contact is possible without using a repeater
  C. When an emergency telephone call is needed
  D. When you are traveling and need some local information

ANSWER B: If you are communicating with a station that is located within 10 miles of you, go "simplex" (or direct) rather than through a repeater. This localizes your transmissions and frees the repeater for more distant contacts.

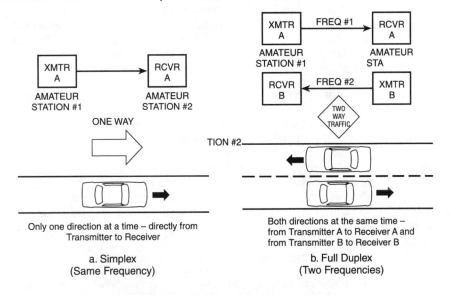

Only one direction at a time – directly from Transmitter to Receiver

a. Simplex
(Same Frequency)

Both directions at the same time – from Transmitter A to Receiver A and from Transmitter B to Receiver B

b. Full Duplex
(Two Frequencies)

Simplex and Duplex Communications

T2C03 Why should simplex be used where possible, instead of using a repeater?

A. Signal range will be increased
B. Long distance toll charges will be avoided
C. The repeater will not be tied up unnecessarily
D. Your antenna's effectiveness will be better tested

ANSWER C: If you are close to the station you are communicating with, switch over to a direct channel. This is called simplex. Every band has several simplex channels specifically designed to relieve repeater congestion. You might be surprised how far simplex will go.

T2C04 If you are talking to a station using a repeater, how would you find out if you could communicate using simplex instead?

A. See if you can clearly receive the station on the repeater's input frequency
B. See if you can clearly receive the station on a lower frequency band
C. See if you can clearly receive a more distant repeater
D. See if a third station can clearly receive both of you

ANSWER A: Almost all portable, mobile, and base VHF/UHF FM equipment have a small button marked "REV." Momentarily push the button, and it causes your receiver to quickly shift to the input frequency of the repeater. This allows you to see whether or not you can pick up the other station direct. If so, suggest that you switch over to simplex for the remainder of the communications.

T2C05 What does RST mean in a signal report?

A. Recovery, signal strength, tempo
B. Recovery, signal speed, tone

C. Readability, signal speed, tempo

D. Readability, signal strength, tone

ANSWER D: We use the RST signal reporting system on the worldwide bands regularly. Sometimes we use the RST system when operating weak signal equipment on VHF and UHF frequencies. Readability is how well you can audibly make out the signal with your ears, and signal strength is usually indicated on an LCD bar graph scale or a needle movement signal strength meter. Tone is something that you judge with your own ears and brain when receiving a CW signal.

T2C06 What is the meaning of: "Your signal report is five nine plus 20 dB..."?

A. Your signal strength has increased by a factor of 100

B. Repeat your transmission on a frequency 20 kHz higher

C. The bandwidth of your signal is 20 decibels above linearity

D. A relative signal-strength meter reading is 20 decibels greater than strength 9

ANSWER D: Any signal over S9 is an excellent one. Most worldwide sets have well-calibrated S-meters that register 10, 20, 40, and 60 dB over S9. Your signal is plenty strong! Although the question and answer is worded technically correct, most hams would simply state that "your signal is 20 over 9". Same thing, but less formal on the air. See Table.

Table T2C06. RST Signal Reporting System

The RST System is a way of reporting on the quality of a received signal by using a three digit number. The first digit indicates *Readability* (R), the second digit indicates received *Signal Strength* (S) and the third digit indicates *Tone* (T).

READABILITY (R) Voice and CW

1 – Unreadable

2 – Barely readable, occasional words distinguishable

3 – Readable with considerable difficulty

4 – Readable with practically no difficulty

5 – Perfectly readable

SIGNAL STRENGTH (S) Voice and CW

1 – Faint and barely perceptible signals

2 – Very weak signals

3 – Weak signals

4 – Fair signals

5 – Fairly good signals

6 – Good signals

7 – Moderately strong signals

8 – Strong signals

9 – Extremely strong signals

*TONE (T) Use on CW only

1 – Very rough, broad signals, 60 cycle AC may be present

2 – Very rough AC tone, harsh, broad

3 – Rough, low pitched AC tone, no filtering

4 – Rather rough AC tone, some trace of filtering

5 – Filtered rectified AC note, musical, ripple modulated

6 – Slight trace of filtered tone but with ripple modulation

7 – Near DC tone but trace of ripple modulation

8 – Good DC tone, may have slight trace of modulation

9 – Purest, perfect DC tone with no trace of ripple or modulation.

* The TONE report refers only to the purity of the signal, and has no connection with its stability or freedom from clicks or chirps. If the signal has the characteristic steadiness of crystal control, add X to the report (e.g., RST 469X). If it has a chirp or "tail" (either on "make" or "break") add C (e.g., RST 469C). If it has clicks or other noticeable keying transients, add K (e.g., RST 469K). If a signal has both chirps and clicks, add both C and K (e.g., RST 469CK).

T2C07 What is the meaning of the procedural signal "CQ"?
A. "Call on the quarter hour"
B. "New antenna is being tested" (no station should answer)
C. "Only the called station should transmit"
D. "Calling any station"

ANSWER D: The 2 letters "CQ" mean calling any station, and we use this on all worldwide bands and weak signal calls over VHF and UHF frequencies. But the CQ is NOT EVER USED when operating on FM repeater and simplex frequencies because the presence of your FM carrier is strong enough to let everyone else know you are on the air. Instead of calling "CQ" over a repeater, you would simply announce your call letters, and indicate you are monitoring for a call. And if you're on the air for the very first time, tell them you are a Gordo grad, and that may be all that is necessary to bring back plenty of responses from the ham community welcoming you to the exciting airwaves.

T2C08 What is a QSL card in the amateur service?
A. A letter or postcard from an amateur pen pal
B. A Notice of Violation from the FCC
C. A written acknowledgment of communications between two amateurs
D. A postcard reminding you when your license will expire

ANSWER C: Hams exchange colorful postcard QSLs to confirm contacts. Always take a look at another ham's QSL card collection. You will find it fascinating! Here is your author's QSL card.

T2C09 What is the correct way to call CQ when using voice?
A. Say "CQ" once, followed by "this is," followed by your call sign spoken three times
B. Say "CQ" at least five times, followed by "this is," followed by your call sign spoken once
C. Say "CQ" three times, followed by "this is," followed by your call sign spoken three times
D. Say "CQ" at least ten times, followed by "this is," followed by your call sign spoken once

ANSWER C: We use "CQ" as a general call only on the worldwide bands. On the FM, VHF and UHF bands, we are less formal, and simply announce ourselves as being on the air by just giving our call sign.

T2C10 How should you answer a voice CQ call?

A. Say the other station's call sign at least ten times, followed by "this is," then your call sign at least twice

B. Say the other station's call sign at least five times phonetically, followed by "this is," then your call sign at least once

C. Say the other station's call sign at least three times, followed by "this is," then your call sign at least five times phonetically

D. Say the other station's call sign once, followed by "this is," then your call sign given phonetically

ANSWER D: If you hear a lively CQ call, then go ahead and respond to that station and enjoy a great conversation. If the station is coming in clear, you would only need to call it once, followed by "This is," and then give your call sign, slowly, and phonetically. Your author also likes to give his location.

T2C11 What is the meaning of: "Your signal is full quieting..."?

A. Your signal is strong enough to overcome all receiver noise

B. Your signal has no spurious sounds

C. Your signal is not strong enough to be received

D. Your signal is being received, but no audio is being heard

ANSWER A: When transmitting on VHF or UHF FM equipment, the S meter is simply a row of LCD bars that may illustrate relative signal strength. It's much easier to relate signal strength to how well the signal is quieting the background white noise.

T2D Distress calling and emergency drills and communications — operations and equipment; Radio Amateur Civil Emergency Service (RACES)

T2D01 What is the proper distress call to use when operating phone?

A. Say "MAYDAY" several times

B. Say "HELP" several times

C. Say "EMERGENCY" several times

D. Say "SOS" several times

ANSWER A: The word "Mayday" deserves the highest priority. Always stand by and prepare to copy a "Mayday" message.

T2D02 What is the proper distress call to use when operating CW?

A. MAYDAY

B. QRRR

C. QRZ

D. SOS

ANSWER D: In Morse code (CW), send "SOS" to indicate a grave emergency.

T2D03 What is the proper way to interrupt a repeater conversation to signal a distress call?

A. Say "BREAK" twice, then your call sign

B. Say "HELP" as many times as it takes to get someone to answer

C. Say "SOS," then your call sign

D. Say "EMERGENCY" three times

ANSWER A: On repeater frequencies, the word "break" is spoken several times to indicate a priority or emergency distress call. Keep this in mind when operating routinely on a repeater — don't say the word "break" unless it's an emergency or something very, very important.

T2D04 What is one reason for using tactical call signs such as "command post" or "weather center" during an emergency?
    A. They keep the general public informed about what is going on
    B. They are more efficient and help coordinate public-service communications
    C. They are required by the FCC
    D. They increase goodwill between amateurs

ANSWER B: It's perfectly legal to use such tactical words as "command post," "triage team," or "disaster communicator" during an emergency. This promotes efficiency in the ham radio communications being provided. BREAK means "important," and the words BREAK BREAK means "emergency." The words BREAK BREAK BREAk indicate a life-or-death emergency call.

**Hams Operating from an
Emergency Communications Trailer**

T2D05 What type of messages concerning a person's well-being are sent into or out of a disaster area?
    A. Routine traffic
    B. Tactical traffic
    C. Formal message traffic
    D. Health and Welfare traffic
ANSWER D: This type of traffic deserves priority because we are talking about the welfare of human lives.

T2D06 What are messages called that are sent into or out of a disaster area concerning the immediate safety of human life?
    A. Tactical traffic
    B. Emergency traffic
    C. Formal message traffic
    D. Health and Welfare traffic
ANSWER B: Any communications relating to the safety of human life or the immediate protection of property are considered emergency calls. They deserve the highest priority.

T2D07 Why is it a good idea to have a way to operate your amateur station without using commercial AC power lines?
    A. So you may use your station while mobile
    B. So you may provide communications in an emergency
    C. So you may operate in contests where AC power is not allowed
    D. So you will comply with the FCC rules
ANSWER B: Your author's station operates on solar panel power. The battery is safely outside, and the solar panels keep the battery charged even though his ham station is used often.

T2D08 What is the most important accessory to have for a hand-held radio in an emergency?

A. An extra antenna
B. A portable amplifier
C. Several sets of charged batteries
D. A microphone headset for hands-free operation

ANSWER C: Rechargeable nickel cadmium batteries self-discharge up to 10 percent per week. This means a nickel-cadmium battery will need frequent charging. Alkaline batteries have long shelf life, but cannot be recharged.

T2D09 Which type of antenna would be a good choice as part of a portable HF amateur station that could be set up in case of an emergency?

A. A three-element quad
B. A three-element Yagi
C. A dipole
D. A parabolic dish

ANSWER C: A simple antenna for high-frequency worldwide emergency communications would be the dipole. The dipole can be easily deployed up a tree with each side of the dipole's one-quarter wavelength wire extending out and tied off with nonconducting line. The dipole is one-half wavelength long, and you can easily coil it up to fit inside a padded brown envelope. All good worldwide emergency communicators carry a dipole for each band of operation.

T2D10 What is the maximum number of hours allowed per week for RACES drills?

A. One
B. Seven, but not more than one hour per day
C. Eight
D. As many hours as you want

ANSWER A: The term "RACES" stands for Radio Amateur Civil Emergency Service, a descendant of the original Civil Defense Service years ago. Many ham radio operators are members of local RACES units, and they will send and receive mock emergency drills no more than 1 hour per week for these test messages. If you are interested in emergency communications, contact your local city's communications department, and ask whether or not they have an amateur radio RACES unit. If they don't, have them refer you to your local county communications coordinator.

RACES Logo

T2D11 How must you identify messages sent during a RACES drill?
A. As emergency messages
B. As amateur traffic
C. As official government messages
D. As drill or test messages

ANSWER D: To eliminate any misunderstanding of a drill message versus the real thing, always announce messages for practice as drill or test messages. You never know how many scanner monitor listeners are out there tuning in the ham bands!

T2E Voice communications and phonetics; SSB/CW weak signal operations; radioteleprinting; packet; special operations

T2E01 To make your call sign better understood when using voice transmissions, what should you do?
A. Use Standard International Phonetics for each letter of your call
B. Use any words that start with the same letters as your call sign for each letter of your call
C. Talk louder
D. Turn up your microphone gain

ANSWER A: When you voice your call sign, a "P" might sound like a "B", and that sounds like a "C", or maybe it was "D". To end the confusion, use the phonetic alphabet the first time you make contact with a new station. The standard phonetic alphabet adopted by the International Telecommunication Union is shown in Table T2E01.

Table T2E01. Phonetic Alphabet
Adopted by the International Telecommunication Union

A - Alpha	F - Foxtrot	K - Kilo	P - Papa	U - Uniform	Z - Zulu
B - Bravo	G - Golf	L - Lima	Q - Quebec	V - Victor	
C - Charlie	H - Hotel	M - Mike	R - Romeo	W- Whiskey	
D - Delta	I - India	N - November	S - Sierra	X - X-Ray	
E - Echo	J - Juliette	O - Oscar	T - Tango	Y - Yankee	

T2E02 What does the abbreviation "RTTY" stand for?
A. "Returning to you", meaning "your turn to transmit"
B. Radioteletype
C. A general call to all digital stations
D. Morse code practice over the air

ANSWER B: Although radioteletype, abbreviated RTTY, is a relatively outmoded type of communication on worldwide frequencies, there is still some RTTY traffic that you might want to tune into and decode. At night, tune in RTTY on 80 meters near 3600 kHz. During the day, try 15 meters around 21,080 kHz.

T2E03 What does "connected" mean in a packet-radio link?
A. A telephone link is working between two stations
B. A message has reached an amateur station for local delivery
C. A transmitting station is sending data to only one receiving station; it replies that the data is being received correctly
D. A transmitting and receiving station are using a digipeater, so no other contacts can take place until they are finished

ANSWER C: Your packet radio system gives you many winking lights that indicate your station is interacting with another station.

T2E04 What does "monitoring" mean on a packet-radio frequency?
A. The FCC is copying all messages
B. A member of the Amateur Auxiliary to the FCC's Compliance and Information Bureau is copying all messages
C. A receiving station is displaying all messages sent to it, and replying that the messages are being received correctly
D. A receiving station is displaying all messages on the frequency, and is not replying to any messages

ANSWER D: Eavesdropping is a favorite practice on packet radio — and no one will know that you are there.

T2E05 What is a digipeater?
A. A packet-radio station that retransmits only data that is marked to be retransmitted
B. A packet-radio station that retransmits any data that it receives
C. A repeater that changes audio signals to digital data
D. A repeater built using only digital electronics parts

ANSWER A: Longtime ham radio operators have established excellent repeater stations and packet repeater setups for everyone to use. We strongly support those hams that give of their time to help you extend your communications range, and we hope that you will support their stations by joining their membership organizations.

T2E06 What does "network" mean in packet radio?
A. A way of connecting terminal-node controllers by telephone so data can be sent over long distances
B. A way of connecting packet-radio stations so data can be sent over long distances
C. The wiring connections on a terminal-node controller board
D. The programming in a terminal-node controller that rejects other callers if a station is already connected

ANSWER B: If you're into computers and ham radio, chances are you are really going to get some excitement on the 2-meter band where packet and automatic position/packet reporting system (APRS) could allow you to send messages over a network from coast to coast and even get into regular e-mail through a packet I-Gate. Modern ham radio handhelds and VHF/UHF mobile radios may have a terminal node controller already built in for exciting data connections where packet-radio signals can be sent over long distances by means of the "network."

T2E07 When should digital transmissions be used on 2-meter simplex voice frequencies?
A. In between voice syllables
B. Digital operations should be avoided on simplex voice frequencies
C. Only in the evening
D. At any time, so as to encourage the best use of the band

ANSWER B: Do you own a computer? You can easily tie your computer into your handheld for digital communications. You can transmit digital communications on specific 2-meter frequencies reserved for digital traffic: 145.01, 145.03, 145.05, 145.07, and 145.09 MHz unattended packet operations. Avoid operating digital transmissions on voice simplex frequencies.

T2E08 Which of the following modes of communication are NOT available to a Technician class operator?
    A. CW and SSB on HF bands
    B. Amateur television (ATV)
    C. EME (Moon bounce)
    D. VHF packet, CW and SSB
ANSWER A: Until you pass the 5-wpm Element 1 code test as a Technician class operator or higher, you will get everything BUT Morse code and single sideband on the worldwide high-frequency bands. But a Technician class operator with the code certificate may then include Answer A as part of their fun operating areas.

T2E09 What speed should you use when answering a CQ call using RTTY?
    A. Half the speed of the received signal
    B. The same speed as the received signal
    C. Twice the speed of the received signal
    D. Any speed, since RTTY systems adjust to any signal speed
ANSWER B: Operating an RTTY station with your home computer is fun. It's also challenging. Not only do you need to tune in the station correctly, but you also need to match the speed of your equipment with the sending rate of the station on the air. The sending rate of 45 baud is common on worldwide bands.

T2E10 When may you operate your amateur station aboard a commercial aircraft?
    A. At any time
    B. Only while the aircraft is not in flight
    C. Only with the pilot's specific permission and not while the aircraft is operating under Instrument Flight Rules
    D. Only if you have written permission from the commercial airline company and not during takeoff and landing
ANSWER C: In rare circumstances a commercial aircraft pilot may give you specific permission to operate your handheld transceiver. You will never be able to operate your equipment when the aircraft is operating under instrument flight rules (IFR). With everyone very concerned about air safety, the likelihood of a pilot giving you permission is next to zip. But if you get stuck down on the ground, away from the gate, and you are going to be holding for a long period of time on the deck (as I was once in a snow storm), you may ask the pilot if you can make a handheld call when you are waiting out the storm.

T2E11 When may you operate your amateur station somewhere in the U.S. besides the address listed on your license?
    A. Only during times of emergency
    B. Only after giving proper notice to the FCC
    C. During an emergency or an FCC-approved emergency practice
    D. Whenever you want to
ANSWER D: Just because your license has a permanent station location on it, don't think for a second that this is the only place you may operate your ham set. You can operate it anywhere in the U.S. and its territories and possessions without notifying the FCC. However, using your portable ham set on a commercial airplane is taboo. Using your ham set on cruise ships requires the permission of the captain.

Once you are a licensed amateur operator, your amateur station can operate from anywhere within the U.S., its territories and possessions — even remote mountain lakes and wilderness areas — without notifying the FCC.

Subelement T3 — Radio-Wave Propagation   [3 Exam Questions — 3 Groups]

T3A Line of sight; reflection of VHF/UHF signals

T3A01 How are VHF signals propagated within the range of the visible horizon?
- A. By sky wave
- B. By line of sight
- C. By plane wave
- D. By geometric refraction

ANSWER B: If you can see it, you can work it on VHF and UHF via direct wave.

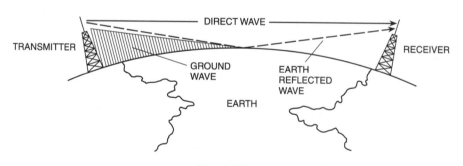

Direct Wave
Source: *Antennas — Selection and Installation,* © 1986, Master Publishing, Inc., Lincolnwood, Illinois

T3A02 When a signal travels in a straight line from one antenna to another, what is this called?
- A. Line-of-sight propagation
- B. Straight line propagation
- C. Knife-edge diffraction
- D. Tunnel ducting

ANSWER A: As a new Technician class operator, you will enjoy line-of-sight propagation on all of the VHF and UHF bands from 2 meters and higher. But keep in mind that the international space station and overhead space shuttles are also line-of-sight, so many times line-of-sight transmissions can take place over hundreds and even thousands of miles!

T3A03 How do VHF and UHF radio waves usually travel from a transmitting antenna to a receiving antenna?
A. They bend through the ionosphere
B. They go in a straight line
C. They wander in any direction
D. They move in a circle going either east or west from the transmitter
ANSWER B: VHF and UHF radio signals travel line of sight. They do not bend through the ionosphere.

T3A04 What type of propagation usually occurs from one hand-held VHF transceiver to another nearby?
A. Tunnel propagation
B. Sky-wave propagation
C. Line-of-sight propagation
D. Auroral propagation
ANSWER C: You can compute your line-of-sight range to the horizon by multiplying 1.2 times the square root of the height of your antenna. (Here is an example for an antenna that is 36 feet high:

$$1.2 \times \sqrt{36} = 7.2 \text{ miles}$$

T3A05 What causes the ionosphere to form?
A. Solar radiation ionizing the outer atmosphere
B. Temperature changes ionizing the outer atmosphere
C. Lightning ionizing the outer atmosphere
D. Release of fluorocarbons into the atmosphere
ANSWER A: The ionosphere surrounds us 24 hours a day. It is constantly "recharged" by the sun's solar radiation. When it gets "overcharged," you may see the effects as the Northern Lights.

The ionosphere is the electrified atmosphere from 40 miles to 400 miles above the earth. You can sometimes see it as "northern lights." It is charged up daily by the sun, and does some miraculous things to radio waves that strike it. Some radio waves are absorbed during daylight hours by the ionosphere's D layer. Others are bounced back to earth. Yet others penetrate the ionosphere and never come back again. The wavelength of the radio waves determines whether the waves will be absorbed, refracted, or will penetrate. Here's a quick way to memorize what the different layers do during day and nighttime hours:

The D layer is about 40 miles up. The D layer is a Daylight layer; it almost disappears at night. D for Daylight. The D layer absorbs radio waves between 1 MHz to 7 MHz. These are long wavelengths. All others pass through.

The E layer is also a daylight layer, and it is very Eccentric. E for Eccentric. Patches of E layer ionization may cause some surprising reflections of signals on both high frequency as well as very-high frequency. The E layer height is usually 70 miles.

The F1 layer is one of the layers furthest away. The F layer gives us those Far away signals. F for Far away. The F1 layer is present during daylight hours, and is up around 150 miles. The F2 layer is also present during daylight hours, and it gives us the Furthest range. The F2 layer is 250 miles high, and it's the best for the Furthest range on medium and short waves. At nighttime, the F1 and F2 layers combine to become just the F layer at 180 miles. This F layer at nighttime will usually bend radio waves between 1 MHz and 15 MHz back to earth. At night, the D and E layers disappear.

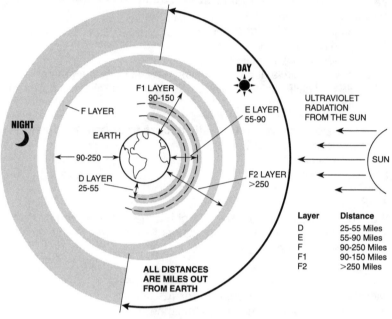

Layer	Distance
D	25-55 Miles
E	55-90 Miles
F	90-250 Miles
F1	90-150 Miles
F2	>250 Miles

Ionosphere Layers

Source: *Antennas — Selection and Installation,* © 1986, Master Publishing, Inc., Lincolnwood, Illinois

---

T3A06 What type of solar radiation is most responsible for ionization in the outer atmosphere?
- A. Thermal
- B. Non-ionized particle
- C. Ultraviolet
- D. Microwave

ANSWER C: It's the ultraviolet component of the sun's radiation that creates our ionosphere. More ultraviolet radiation on any one day will lead us to either improved or disturbed radio conditions.

T3A07 Which two daytime ionospheric regions combine into one region at night?
- A. E and F1
- B. D and E
- C. F1 and F2
- D. E1 and E2

ANSWER C: As you prepare for your Element 2 written exam, why not learn the Morse code at a simple 5 wpm rate, and qualify for worldwide operation as well? At nighttime, the F-1 and F-2 layers combine, and you can get some exciting 75-meter and 40-meter CW contacts all over the world.

T3A08 Which ionospheric region becomes one region at night, but separates into two separate regions during the day?
A. D
B. E
C. F
D. All of these choices
ANSWER C: So you're going to do it, huh? Okay, glad you are going to learn the code at a simple 5 wpm that will carry you all the way to Extra class. During the day, high-frequency signals on 15 meters and many times 10 meters will bounce around within the 2 F-layers, and give you worldwide contacts.

T3A09 Ultraviolet solar radiation is most responsible for ionization in what part of the atmosphere?
A. Inner
B. Outer
C. All of these choices
D. None of these choices
ANSWER B: Have you seen the Northern Lights? These auroras are what effect ham frequencies, and ultraviolet solar radiation that can actually glow takes part in our OUTER atmosphere.

T3A10 What part of our atmosphere is formed by solar radiation ionizing the outer atmosphere?
A. Ionosphere
B. Troposphere
C. Ecosphere
D. Stratosphere
ANSWER A: The ionization of the outer atmosphere takes place specifically in the IONOSPHERE.

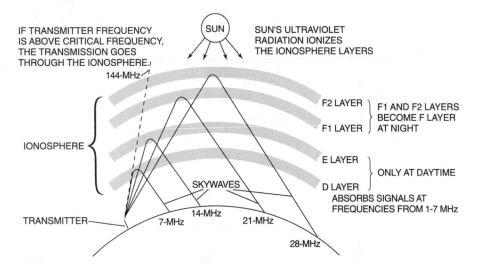

Ionosphere and Its Layers

T3A11 What can happen to VHF or UHF signals going towards a metal-framed building?
A. They will go around the building
B. They can be bent by the ionosphere
C. They can be easily reflected by the building
D. They are sometimes scattered in the ecosphere

ANSWER C: Okay, so you're going to wait on the code until a later date. No rush — there is plenty of excitement on the VHF and UHF frequency bands. Up on these frequencies, you would be surprised how signals behave when they strike a metal-framed building or aircraft — they are easily reflected by the buildings, and this is what gives us some exciting 2-meter and 440 MHz operation with a handheld actually INSIDE a building where our signals somehow bounce around and reflect OUTSIDE.

T3B Tropospheric ducting or bending; amateur satellite and EME operations

T3B01 Ducting occurs in which region of the atmosphere?
A. F2
B. Ecosphere
C. Troposphere
D. Stratosphere

ANSWER C: The key word in this question is "ducting." In your home you use ducts to shuffle that warm or cool air around the house. Out in radio land, natural atmospheric ducts form that shuffle VHF and UHF radio waves well beyond line-of-sight range. Tropospheric ducting occurs most often during the summer months, and sometimes occurs in the presence of large storm systems. Your author is one of the record holders in tropospheric ducting on VHF line-of-sight frequencies between his home near Los Angeles all the way over to Hawaii. This is not a skip wave off the ionosphere, but rather tropospheric ducting several hundred feet above the water traveling thousands of miles away!

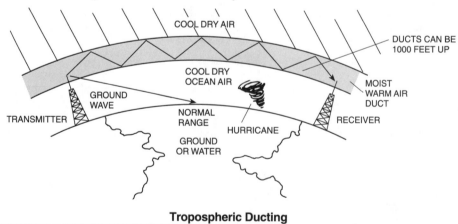

Tropospheric Ducting

T3B02 What effect does tropospheric bending have on 2-meter radio waves?
A. It lets you contact stations farther away
B. It causes them to travel shorter distances
C. It garbles the signal
D. It reverses the sideband of the signal

ANSWER A: Tropospheric bending and ducting gives us some extraordinary range that we normally don't get under average weather conditions.

T3B03 What causes tropospheric ducting of radio waves?
A. A very low pressure area
B. An aurora to the north
C. Lightning between the transmitting and receiving stations
D. A temperature inversion

ANSWER D: Have you ever seen a mirage? Out on the desert, it looks like blue water instead of sand ahead. Actually, that's the blue sky you are looking at. Light waves that normally travel in straight lines bounce off the super-heated, windless sand and pavement and are reflected back to your eyes. Same concept during a tropospheric duct — but just backwards. Typically straight-line VHF and UHF signals begin to travel up and away, but are bent back by a sharp boundary layer of warm, moist air overlying cool, dry air below and above. In the city, this is what traps the smog and gives us one of those unbearable days. Get on the radio — it will be unbelievable.

T3B04 What causes VHF radio waves to be propagated several hundred miles over oceans?
A. A polar air mass
B. A widespread temperature inversion
C. An overcast of cirriform clouds
D. A high-pressure zone

ANSWER B: Some of these tropospheric ducts may extend out to 1000 miles. The record is between Gordon West's (your author) home in California and Hawaii. Any hams in the area are invited to stop by and see his record-breaking tropo station.

T3B05 In which of the following frequency ranges does tropospheric ducting most often occur?
A. UHF
B. MF
C. HF
D. VLF

ANSWER A: When you obtain your new Technician class license, why not look into equipment that operates multi-mode on 2 meters and 440 MHz? Using single sideband on 2 meters and 440 MHz allows you to take advantage of a summertime condition called tropospheric ducting. Here is where your signal will travel hundreds and sometimes thousands of miles over oceans. And if you're in the middle of the country, land, too. "Tropo" is most pronounced on frequencies between 300 MHz and 3000 MHz, ultra high frequency (UHF). While it also occurs on 2 meters, too, for the test go with Answer A, UHF.

T3B06 What weather condition may cause tropospheric ducting?
A. A stable high-pressure system
B. An unstable low-pressure system
C. A series of low-pressure waves
D. Periods of heavy rainfall

ANSWER A: You can watch your local weather maps for signs of temperature inversions. If they predict bad air quality, you can predict good band qualities on VHF and UHF.

T3B07 How does the signal loss for a given path through the troposphere vary with frequency?
  A. There is no relationship
  B. The path loss decreases as the frequency increases
  C. The path loss increases as the frequency increases
  D. There is no path loss at all

ANSWER C: Bouncing signals within tropospheric layers of warm and cool air is a popular sport among no-code Technician Class operators. Remember, your no-code license allows unlimited privileges within the VHF and UHF Amateur Radio bands — microwave too. But the higher you go in frequency, the greater the path loss. Half loss (a decrease in signal levels to one-half of that at the antenna) increases as the frequency increases. If you are talking 500 miles away, simplex, with a station on 2 meters, up on the 70-cm (440-MHz) band, your signals will be much weaker.

T3B08 Why are high-gain antennas normally used for EME (moon bounce) communications?
  A. To reduce the scattering of the reflected signal as it returns to Earth
  B. To overcome the extreme path losses of this mode
  C. To reduce the effects of polarization changes in the received signal
  D. To overcome the high levels of solar noise at the receiver

ANSWER B: If you have understanding neighbors and multi-mode VHF/UHF equipment, you may wish to try your hand at bouncing the signal off of the moon. But you're going to need a pair of very-high-gain antennas to overcome the extreme path loses all the way out to the moon and back again.

T3B09 Which of the following antenna systems would be the best choice for an EME (moon bounce) station?
  A. A single dipole antenna
  B. An isotropic antenna
  C. A ground-plane antenna
  D. A high-gain array of Yagi antennas

ANSWER D: Very long boom high-gain Yagi antennas are required for moon bounce. You can get by with just one big long "boomer", but two or four in an array would be better. Let's hope you have understanding neighbors!

T3B10 When is it necessary to use a higher transmitter power level when conducting satellite communications?
  A. When the satellite is at its perigee
  B. When the satellite is low to the horizon
  C. When the satellite is fully illuminated by the sun
  D. When the satellite is near directly overhead

ANSWER B: Try NOT to run more power than necessary to operate through orbiting satellites. If you run too much power through a satellite, it pulls down all of the other signals from the translator circuits. About the only time you need to increase your power level is when the satellite is low to the horizon, either coming up or going down.

T3B11 Which of the following conditions must be met before two stations can conduct real-time communications through a satellite?
A. Both stations must use circularly polarized antennas
B. The satellite must be illuminated by the sun during the communications
C. The satellite must be in view of both stations simultaneously
D. Both stations must use high-gain antenna systems

ANSWER C: If you're going to communicate "real-time" through a satellite, you and the other station must be in view of that satellite at the same time. There are some great computer programs that will graphically show you your communications opportunity to different places of the world through a mutually viewed satellite. For digital communications, the satellite may hold the data, and retransmit it at a later time when it's on the other side of the Earth. But for voice, CW, and live keyboard-to-keyboard communications, the satellite must be in view by both stations for real-time communications to take place.

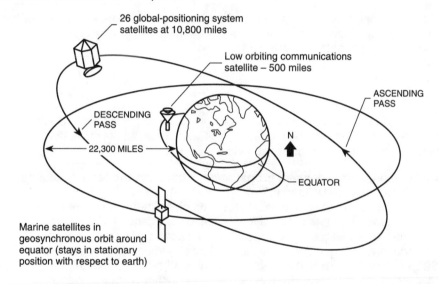

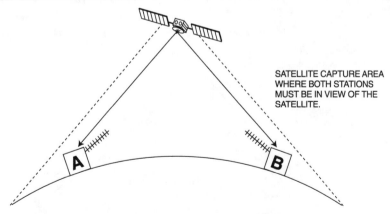

Successful Earth-to-Satellite Communications

T3C Ionospheric propagation, causes and variation; maximum usable frequency; Sporadic-E propagation; ground wave, HF propagation characteristics; sunspots and the sunspot cycle

T3C01 Which region of the ionosphere is mainly responsible for absorbing MF/HF radio signals during the daytime?
A. The F2 region
B. The F1 region
C. The E region
D. The D region

ANSWER D: The key word in this question is "absorption." Only one layer absorbs radio signals like a sponge, and that's the D layer during daylight hours. It absorbs medium- and low-frequency signals only. Higher frequencies pass through the D layer, and bounce off of other layers.See illustration at T3A10, page 83.

T3C02 If you are receiving a weak and distorted signal from a distant station on a frequency close to the maximum usable frequency, what type of propagation is probably occurring?
A. Ducting
B. Line-of-sight
C. Scatter
D. Ground-wave

ANSWER C: It's unbelievable, but sometimes you can talk to stations in South America with your antenna pointed west, and with better results in the evening hours. The unusual propagation is due to scattering.

T3C03 In relation to sky-wave propagation, what does the term "maximum usable frequency" (MUF) mean?
A. The highest frequency signal that will reach its intended destination
B. The lowest frequency signal that will reach its intended destination
C. The highest frequency signal that is most absorbed by the ionosphere
D. The lowest frequency signal that is most absorbed by the ionosphere

ANSWER A: Maximum usable frequency is abbreviated "MUF." Monthly magazines predict the maximum usable frequency from here to there, anywhere in the world, at any time.

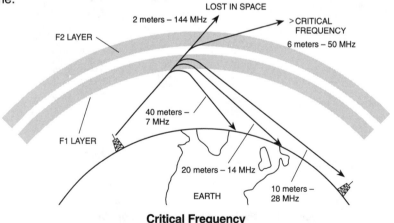

Critical Frequency
Source: *Antennas — Selection and Installation,* © 1986, Master Publishing, Inc.

T3C04 When a signal travels along the surface of the Earth, what is this called?
A. Sky-wave propagation
B. Knife-edge diffraction
C. E-region propagation
D. Ground-wave propagation

ANSWER D: All stations on all frequencies emit radio waves that hug the earth, called ground waves. They travel out from your transmitter antenna up to approximately 100 miles. The better the conductivity of the soil, the more intense your ground wave propagation.

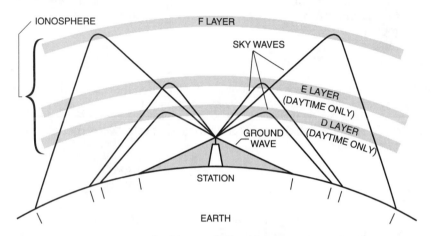

Radio Wave Propagation
Source: *Mobile 2-Way Radio Communications*, G. West, © 1993, Master Publishing, Inc.

T3C05 When a signal is returned to Earth by the ionosphere, what is this called?
A. Sky-wave propagation
B. Earth-Moon-Earth propagation
C. Ground-wave propagation
D. Tropospheric propagation

ANSWER A: What you couldn't do on CB (Citizen's Band) is a way of life on ham radio! Radio waves are bounced off of the ionospheric E or F layer and may return to earth thousands of miles away! This 10-meter propagation occurs in daylight and evening hours — seldom beyond 9:00 PM. The ionosphere becomes mirror-like due to ultraviolet radiation given off by the sun. The mirror may be so intense during daylight hours that 10-meter signals may travel halfway around the world.

T3C06 What is a skip zone?
A. An area covered by ground-wave propagation
B. An area covered by sky-wave propagation
C. An area that is too far away for ground-wave propagation, but too close for sky-wave propagation
D. An area that is too far away for ground-wave or sky-wave propagation

ANSWER C: Increasing your power won't help establish communications with a station that is being missed within your skip zone. If you switch to other bands, chances are good that lower frequencies (longer wavelength) may skip in closer.

T3C07 Which ionospheric region is closest to the Earth?
A. The A region
B. The D region
C. The E region
D. The F region

ANSWER B: Be careful on this question — they simply ask for the lowest ionospheric layer, not necessarily the lowest one that gives us skip. Since the D layer is the lowest, this is the correct answer.

T3C08 Which region of the ionosphere is mainly responsible for long-distance sky-wave radio communications?
A. D region
B. E region
C. F1 region
D. F2 region

ANSWER D: Since the F2 layer is higher than the F1 layer, it would be mainly responsible for the longest distance skywave hop back to earth.

T3C09 Which of the ionospheric regions may split into two regions only during the daytime?
A. Troposphere
B. F
C. Electrostatic
D. D

ANSWER B: During daylight hours, the sun is so powerful it actually breaks the F layer into two distinct regions — F1 and F2.

T3C10 How does the number of sunspots relate to the amount of ionization in the ionosphere?
A. The more sunspots there are, the greater the ionization
B. The more sunspots there are, the less the ionization
C. Unless there are sunspots, the ionization is zero
D. Sunspots do not affect the ionosphere

ANSWER A: The higher the solar activity, the greater the ionization. Listen to WWV, 10 or 15 MHz, at 18 minutes past every hour. They will report on the amount of solar activity, and you can many times predict whether 10 meters is going to be hot, or not, the next day.

T3C11 How long is an average sunspot cycle?
A. 2 years
B. 5 years
C. 11 years
D. 17 years

ANSWER C: Our sun exhibits periods of high solar activity, peaking every 11 years. During the peak of the sunspot cycles, you will be able to reach out with your 6-meter station over thousands of miles. Sunspot peaks will occur in 2001 and 2012. But if you learn the code at 5 wpm and get up to General class, you can operate all over the world OFF PEAK quite nicely by choosing the lower bands, too. There is always worldwide propagation on the high-frequency band as soon as you get your 5 wpm Morse code credit.

Subelement T4 — Amateur Radio Practices   [4 Exam Questions — 4 Groups]

T4A Lightning protection and station grounding; safety interlocks, antenna installation safety procedures; dummy antennas

T4A01 How can an antenna system best be protected from lightning damage?
A. Install a balun at the antenna feed point
B. Install an RF choke in the antenna feed line
C. Ground all antennas when they are not in use
D. Install a fuse in the antenna feed line
ANSWER C: Always use a good quality amateur-grade grounded antenna selector switch for lightning protection. You also can install lightning arrestors.

T4A02 How can amateur station equipment best be protected from lightning damage?
A. Use heavy insulation on the wiring
B. Never turn off the equipment
C. Disconnect the ground system from all radios
D. Disconnect all equipment from the power lines and antenna cables
ANSWER D: If you suspect a lightning storm approaching, unplug everything, and actually remove the set from other grounded equipment in your ham shack.

T4A03 For best protection from electrical shock, what should be grounded in an amateur station?
A. The power supply primary
B. All station equipment
C. The antenna feed line
D. The AC power mains
ANSWER B: When you add new gear to your ham station setup, always connect the chassis to the other gear with a good common braid or foil connection. Be certain all connections are tight! You will have less ground noise interference.

T4A04 Why would there be an interlock switch in a high-voltage power supply to turn off the power if its cabinet is opened?
A. To keep dangerous RF radiation from leaking out through an open cabinet
B. To keep dangerous RF radiation from coming in through an open cabinet
C. To turn the power supply off when it is not being used
D. To keep anyone opening the cabinet from getting shocked by dangerous high voltages
ANSWER D: Most linear amplifiers incorporate an automatic disconnect switch when you lift the cover. This usually shorts out the high voltage that may still remain in big capacitors. Never circumvent this switch — it's there for your safety.

T4A05 Why should you wear a hard hat and safety glasses if you are on the ground helping someone work on an antenna tower?
A. So you won't be hurt if the tower should accidentally fall
B. To keep RF energy away from your head during antenna testing
C. To protect your head from something dropped from the tower
D. So someone passing by will know that work is being done on the tower and will stay away

ANSWER C: Local hams may invite you to an "antenna party." As a group, you may help another ham put the antenna up atop a tower. If you are on the ground, make sure you wear a hard hat and safety glasses.

Always wear a hard hat and safety glasses when working on an antenna tower.

T4A06 What safety factors must you consider when using a bow and arrow or slingshot and weight to shoot an antenna-support line over a tree?
- A. You must ensure that the line is strong enough to withstand the shock of shooting the weight
- B. You must ensure that the arrow or weight has a safe flight path if the line breaks
- C. You must ensure that the bow and arrow or slingshot is in good working condition
- D. All of these choices are correct

ANSWER D: Amateur operators have some ingenious ways of getting antenna support lines up and over a tall tree. I like the sling shot as my best tool for this job, making sure my line is nice and strong — and if it should break, the weight out of the sling shot does not go through my next door neighbor's window. Be careful not to allow the bare antenna wire to be pulled up into the tree limbs because your neighbor is really not going to like that tree catching on fire as soon as you transmit over high frequency.

T4A07 Which of the following is the best way to install your antenna in relation to overhead electric power lines?
- A. Always be sure your antenna wire is higher than the power line, and crosses it at a 90-degree angle
- B. Always be sure your antenna and feed line are well clear of any power lines
- C. Always be sure your antenna is lower than the power line, and crosses it at a small angle
- D. Only use vertical antennas within 100 feet of a power line

ANSWER B: Be particularly careful of the two wires atop telephone poles. These are bare wires and can carry as much as 15,000 volts. Make sure your antenna and feed lines are well clear of all power lines!

T4A08 What device is used in place of an antenna during transmitter tests so that no signal is radiated?
- A. An antenna matcher
- B. A dummy antenna

C. A low-pass filter
D. A decoupling resistor

ANSWER B: Here's yet another question about that antenna that doesn't radiate — the dummy load or dummy antenna.

T4A09 Why would you use a dummy antenna?
A. For off-the-air transmitter testing
B. To reduce output power
C. To give comparative signal reports
D. To allow antenna tuning without causing interference

ANSWER A: Another question about the dummy load — just remember, it doesn't radiate, and allows you to run your transmitter full bore without causing interference.

T4A10 What minimum rating should a dummy antenna have for use with a 100 watt single-sideband phone transmitter?
A. 100 watts continuous
B. 141 watts continuous
C. 175 watts continuous
D. 200 watts continuous

ANSWER A: Your single-sideband phone transmitter will put out about 100 watts. This means you need a dummy load capable of handling that power — 100 watts continuous.

T4A11 Would a 100 watt light bulb make a good dummy load for tuning a transceiver?
A. Yes; a light bulb behaves exactly like a dummy load
B. No; the impedance of the light bulb changes as the filament gets hot
C. No; the light bulb would act like an open circuit
D. No; the light bulb would act like a short circuit

ANSWER B: Back in the good old days, a 100-watt light bulb was a pretty neat way of testing the output of a 100-watt radio. Simply tune the output for a nice bright bulb, and chances were that the transmitter was working properly. But this is a dangerous procedure because you're putting power output right into your face as you tune for maximum white! The light bulb is no longer used as a dummy load because the impedance of the light bulb changes as the filament gets hot. Your radio usually will cycle off detecting that the cold filament looks almost like a short circuit. If the radio does light the bulb, the bright bulb will then look like a mismatched circuit, and the radio may automatically protect the final transistor outputs by pulling back the power. You may think you have a bad transmitter when really the radio is simply self-protecting itself from a lousy dummy load. Don't use a light bulb.

T4B Electrical wiring, including switch location, dangerous voltages and currents; SWR meaning and measurements; SWR meters

T4B01 Where should the green wire in a three-wire AC line cord be connected in a power supply?
A. To the fuse
B. To the "hot" side of the power switch
C. To the chassis
D. To the white wire

ANSWER C: Green is ground. That's easy to remember. The chassis of our radio equipment is the metal top, bottom, and side covers that keep everything together on the inside. Most radio sets offer a ground connection at the back of the chassis. A green ground connection conductor will let you keep your colors straight.

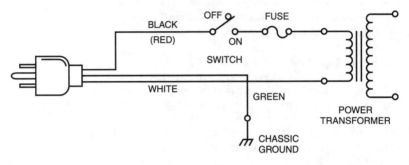

AC Line Connections

T4B02 What is the minimum voltage that is usually dangerous to humans?
    A. 30 volts
    B. 100 volts
    C. 1000 volts
    D. 2000 volts

ANSWER A: Even a couple of golf cart batteries could kill you if you aren't careful. This is why you must be especially careful not to touch any bare wires or connections when leaning across a bank of batteries because that would allow current to flow through your body accidentally.

T4B03 How much electrical current flowing through the human body will probably be fatal?
    A. As little as 1/10 of an ampere
    B. Approximately 10 amperes
    C. More than 20 amperes
    D. Current through the human body is never fatal

ANSWER A: One-tenth of a ampere (amp) is the same as 100 millamperes. One-tenth of an amp is as little as the small current drawn by a tiny dial light. It is enough to zap you for good if it travels through your body and heart in the right path. Never, never, never work without shoes on a concrete garage floor. Never let any metal electrical appliance get near a bathtub.

T4B04 Which body organ can be fatally affected by a very small amount of electrical current?
    A. The heart
    B. The brain
    C. The liver
    D. The lungs

ANSWER A: Your heart is a pump that is powered by your own electricity. If you disturb the natural flow of electricity driving the heart, it could be fatal. This is why you never work on electrical equipment in the garage with a cement floor when you are not wearing shoes. Electricity could flow through your hands, through your heart, and out of your feet to ground. Not good.

T4B05 What does an SWR reading of less than 1.5:1 mean?
A. An impedance match that is too low
B. An impedance mismatch; something may be wrong with the antenna system
C. A fairly good impedance match
D. An antenna gain of 1.5

ANSWER C: If you have a 1.5:1 SWR, not bad! But again, this reading is meaningless as a guarantee of good range. Location, height, and surroundings all contribute to the effectiveness of the antenna once you make sure you are transferring maximum power from your transmitter to the antenna by a good impedance match.

*SWR Reading	Antenna Condition
1:1	Perfectly Matched
1.5:1	Good Match
2:1	Fair Match
3:1	Poor Match
4:1	Something Definitely Wrong

*Constant Frequency

SWR Meter and Readings

T4B06 What does a very high SWR reading mean?
A. The antenna is the wrong length, or there may be an open or shorted connection somewhere in the feed line
B. The signals coming from the antenna are unusually strong, which means very good radio conditions
C. The transmitter is putting out more power than normal, showing that it is about to go bad
D. There is a large amount of solar radiation, which means very poor radio conditions

ANSWER A: Another cause of high SWR, not mentioned in the answer, is your antenna is too close to the earth. The 10-meter dipole for your voice privileges should be at least 15 feet above the ground. It won't work on the ground. Pass that code test!

T4B07 If an SWR reading at the low frequency end of an amateur band is 2.5:1, increasing to 5:1 at the high frequency end of the same band, what does this tell you about your 1/2-wavelength dipole antenna?
A. The antenna is broadbanded
B. The antenna is too long for operation on the band
C. The antenna is too short for operation on the band
D. The antenna is just right for operation on the band

ANSWER B: If you go slightly higher in frequency, and the SWR continues to climb, your antenna is too long. Cut off an inch and see what happens.

T4B08 If an SWR reading at the low frequency end of an amateur band is 5:1, decreasing to 2.5:1 at the high frequency end of the same band, what does this tell you about your 1/2-wavelength dipole antenna?
A. The antenna is broadbanded
B. The antenna is too long for operation on the band
C. The antenna is too short for operation on the band
D. The antenna is just right for operation on the band

ANSWER C: Are you working on the code? I hope so — I want to hear you on the worldwide bands. You can easily build a simple dipole to get a signal out on worldwide frequencies. Once that dipole is built, you can borrow an SWR analyzer from a friend and see how the dipole is tuned. If you find that the tuning is rotten at the bottom end of the band at 5:1 SWR, but relatively okay at the top of the band at 2.5:1, it means you need to LOWER the resonant frequency of the dipole by lengthening it by a couple of inches — right now the antenna is too short for operation on the band.

T4B09 What instrument is used to measure the relative impedance match between an antenna and its feed line?
A. An ammeter
B. An ohmmeter
C. A voltmeter
D. An SWR meter

ANSWER D: We use an SWR meter to measure the relative match between an antenna and the coaxial cable feedline. I like the battery-operated SWR analyzer because it allows me to measure the match between the antenna and the feedline without needing to go back and forth between the radio and my SWR bridge.

T4B10 If you use an SWR meter designed to operate on 3-30 MHz for VHF measurements, how accurate will its readings be?
A. They will not be accurate
B. They will be accurate enough to get by
C. If it properly calibrates to full scale in the set position, they may be accurate
D. They will be accurate providing the readings are multiplied by 4.5

ANSWER C: Most CB-type SWR bridges sometimes will work on 2-meter VHF frequencies. You should buy a special meter for these higher frequencies.

T4B11 What does an SWR reading of 1:1 mean?
A. An antenna for another frequency band is probably connected
B. The best impedance match has been attained
C. No power is going to the antenna
D. The SWR meter is broken

ANSWER B: A 1:1 SWR is a perfect match. However, it doesn't necessarily mean you're going to have a great signal on the airwaves. You can achieve a 1:1 SWR by transmitting into a non-radiating dummy load!

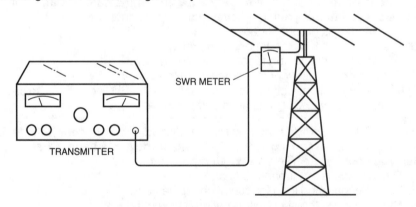

SWR METER

TRANSMITTER

Measure SWR Right at Antenna for Best Readings

T4C Meters and their placement in circuits, including volt, amp, multi, peak-reading and RF watt; ratings of fuses and switches

T4C01 How is a voltmeter usually connected to a circuit under test?
A. In series with the circuit
B. In parallel with the circuit
C. In quadrature with the circuit
D. In phase with the circuit

ANSWER B: We test for voltage by hooking our meter across the voltage source without undoing any wires — a parallel connection. Checking the voltage when operating equipment is called "checking the voltage source under load."

T4C02 How is an ammeter usually connected to a circuit under test?
A. In series with the circuit
B. In parallel with the circuit
C. In quadrature with the circuit
D. In phase with the circuit

ANSWER A: A ammeter measures current. To measure current, turn off the power, disconnect one lead of the load from its source voltage and insert a ammeter in series with that lead. If you are measuring DC current, you will need to connect the meter with the correct polarity, so the meter reads up scale when power is turned on.

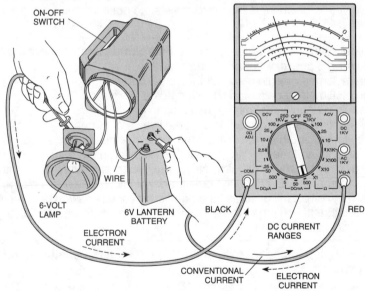

Using a Multimeter to Measure a Series Circuit
Source: *Basic Electronics* © 1994, Master Publishing, Inc., Lincolnwood, Illinois

T4C03 Where should an RF wattmeter be connected for the most accurate readings of transmitter output power?
A. At the transmitter output connector
B. At the antenna feed point
C. One-half wavelength from the transmitter output
D. One-half wavelength from the antenna feed point

ANSWER A: Right at the transmitter. It's that simple.

T4C04 For which measurements would you normally use a multimeter?
- A. SWR and power
- B. Resistance, capacitance and inductance
- C. Resistance and reactance
- D. Voltage, current and resistance

ANSWER D: Every amateur operator should own a multimeter. The multiple function meter can measure voltage, current, and resistance, and check continuity. Even an inexpensive multimeter is better than no meter when you are trying to check out a circuit in the field. You can buy an excellent multimeter for less than $25.00 at your local RadioShack store.

T4C05 What might happen if you switch a multimeter to measure resistance while you have it connected to measure voltage?
- A. The multimeter would read half the actual voltage
- B. It would probably destroy the meter circuitry
- C. The multimeter would read twice the actual voltage
- D. Nothing unusual would happen; the multimeter would measure the circuit's resistance

ANSWER B: Guess what happens to that new multimeter if you start to measure voltage on it, but you discover you left it in the ohms reading scale? Voltage will probably destroy the resistance measuring circuitry of that meter. Make sure you never leave your multimeter in the ohms resistance position when you are ready to put it away.

T4C06 If you switch a multimeter to read microamps and connect it into a circuit drawing 5 amps, what might happen?
- A. The multimeter would read half the actual current
- B. The multimeter would read twice the actual current
- C. It would probably destroy the meter circuitry
- D. The multimeter would read a very small value of current

ANSWER C: Here is another way to trash that new multimeter. If you hook it up in the microamp setting, and then try and measure straight amps through it, you will more than likely destroy the meter circuitry. Never put your meter away when it is left set to ohms or microamps. Even though old-timers will tell you leaving a big-needle in the microamp position will decrease the needle movement as you're carrying it from one job to another, if you forget to switch it out of microamps, you could very easily destroy that delicate mechanism.

T4C07 At what line impedance do most RF watt meters usually operate?
- A. 25 ohms
- B. 50 ohms
- C. 100 ohms
- D. 300 ohms

ANSWER B: Since Amateur Radio transceivers all operate at a 50-ohm impedance, our wattmeter should also be rated at 50 ohms. The impedance is kept the same for a perfect match.

T4C08 What does a directional wattmeter measure?
- A. Forward and reflected power
- B. The directional pattern of an antenna

C. The energy used by a transmitter

D. Thermal heating in a load resistor

ANSWER A: A directional wattmeter is a special wattmeter that can simultaneously measure forward and reflected power levels. Some directional wattmeters use only one needle, and a control that allows you to check for forward, and then reverse, power levels. They are a handy thing to have if you experiment with antennas.

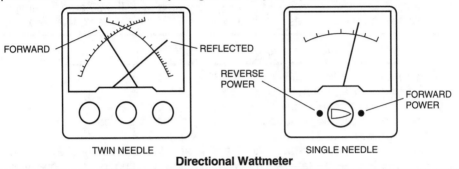

TWIN NEEDLE   SINGLE NEEDLE

Directional Wattmeter

T4C09 If a directional RF wattmeter reads 90 watts forward power and 10 watts reflected power, what is the actual transmitter output power?

A. 10 watts

B. 80 watts

C. 90 watts

D. 100 watts

ANSWER B: You can buy an inexpensive twin-needle wattmeter that allows you to simultaneously monitor forward power and reverse power in watts. Any watts reflected back to the transmitter by a poor antenna are considered lost. They go up in transmitter heat or transmission line loss.

$$\text{Forward Power} - \text{Reflected Power} = \text{Actual Power Output}$$
$$90\text{ W} \quad - \quad 10\text{ W} \quad = \quad 80\text{ W}$$

T4C10 Why might you use a peak-reading RF wattmeter at your station?

A. To make sure your transmitter's output power is not higher than that authorized by your license class

B. To make sure your transmitter is not drawing too much power from the AC line

C. To make sure all your transmitter's power is being radiated by your antenna

D. To measure transmitter input and output power at the same time

ANSWER A: An everyday wattmeter will typically show less CW or SSB power output than what is really being delivered to the antenna. The reason is the fast on-and-off duty cycle of the signal, and the lag of the needle to make it to the absolute peak of the power output. But there are more expensive peak-reading wattmeters that have internal circuits to compensate for this lag and give you a much better indication of exactly what the peak output power is. This is one good way to insure you're not putting out more power than is authorized for your license class.

T4C11 What could happen to your transceiver if you replace its blown 5 amp AC line fuse with a 30 amp fuse?

A. The 30-amp fuse would better protect your transceiver from using too much current

B. The transceiver would run cooler

C. The transceiver could use more current than 5 amps and a fire could occur

D. The transceiver would not be able to produce as much RF output

ANSWER C: A fuse is installed in both the red and black power leads of your transceivers to protect the wires from overload. Pulling too much current through the wires could cause them to heat up, and for the insulation to give off toxic smoke and eventually burst into flames. If you substitute a 30-amp fuse for a 5-amp fuse on a small radio that is malfunctioning and blowing the 5-amp fuse, the 30-amp fuse might carry the load, causing the wires to heat up and, POOF, you smoke your installation.

T4D RFI and its complications, resolution and responsibility

T4D01 What is meant by receiver overload?
 A. Too much voltage from the power supply
 B. Too much current from the power supply
 C. Interference caused by strong signals from a nearby source
 D. Interference caused by turning the volume up too high

ANSWER C: Many times a high-pass filter installed at the antenna input of a television will help reduce television interference (TVI) caused by a strong, nearby signal. It is the responsibility of the set owner — not the ham operator — to install this filter.

T4D02 What is meant by harmonic radiation?
 A. Unwanted signals at frequencies that are multiples of the fundamental (chosen) frequency
 B. Unwanted signals that are combined with a 60-Hz hum
 C. Unwanted signals caused by sympathetic vibrations from a nearby transmitter
 D. Signals that cause skip propagation to occur

ANSWER A: Every transmitted signal contains a weak second harmonic. If you operate at 7.1 MHz, your second harmonic will be 14.2 MHz, which is in another ham band. If you operate at 28.2 MHz, your second harmonic will land at 56.4 MHz, which is in the middle of television channel 2. Be aware of where your second harmonic falls to be a good operator and a good neighbor!

T4D03 What type of filter might be connected to an amateur HF transmitter to cut down on harmonic radiation?
 A. A key-click filter
 B. A low-pass filter
 C. A high-pass filter
 D. A CW filter

ANSWER B: Low-pass filters are designed for the worldwide transceivers that you will use when you pass your Technician class test plus pass the 5 wpm code exam. Never put a low-pass filter on VHF or UHF equipment. Low-pass filters are only designed for the worldwide bands.

T4D04 If your neighbor reports television interference whenever you are transmitting from your amateur station, no matter what frequency band you use, what is probably the cause of the interference?
 A. Too little transmitter harmonic suppression
 B. Receiver VR tube discharge
 C. Receiver overload
 D. Incorrect antenna length

ANSWER C: Receiver overload may be reduced by keeping your transmitting antenna as far away from other antennas as possible. Reducing power will also help. Good grounding techniques will help. Staying off the air during big ball games may also help!

T4D05 If your neighbor reports television interference on one or two channels only when you are transmitting on the 15-meter band, what is probably the cause of the interference?
- A. Too much low-pass filtering on the transmitter
- B. De-ionization of the ionosphere near your neighbor's TV antenna
- C. TV receiver front-end overload
- D. Harmonic radiation from your transmitter

ANSWER D: If your neighbor is using an outside TV antenna, they might experience multiples of your transmitted signal on the 15- and 10-meter bands. These multiples, called harmonics, are minimized by a low-pass filter on your ham set. Another cure is to encourage your neighbors to sign up for cable TV, which is less susceptible to interference.

T4D06 What type of filter should be connected to a TV receiver as the first step in trying to prevent RF overload from an amateur HF station transmission?
- A. Low-pass
- B. High-pass
- C. Band pass
- D. Notch

ANSWER B: The TV band is higher than your worldwide radio and your new voice privileges on 10 meters. Putting a high-pass filter on the TV receiver, if it's connected to an outside antenna, is a good start in cleaning up interference. Don't put a high-pass filter into a cable TV system. Cable television feeds will not work through a high-pass filter.

T4D07 What first step should be taken at a cable TV receiver when trying to prevent RF overload from an amateur HF station transmission?
- A. Install a low-pass filter in the cable system transmission line
- B. Tighten all connectors and inspect the cable system transmission line
- C. Make sure the center conductor of the cable system transmission line is well grounded
- D. Install a ceramic filter in the cable system transmission line

ANSWER B: Since most televisions are now running from cable television feedlines or from direct satellite dish systems, your first step to minimize RF overload from your nearby ham station is to ensure that all TV connections are tight and there are no breaks in the cable that leads into the house.

Make sure all coax connections are tight to help minimize interference.

T4D08 What effect might a break in a cable television transmission line have on amateur communications?
- A. Cable lines are shielded and a break cannot affect amateur communications
- B. Harmonic radiation from the TV receiver may cause the amateur transmitter to transmit off-frequency
- C. TV interference may result when the amateur station is transmitting, or interference may occur to the amateur receiver
- D. The broken cable may pick up very high voltages when the amateur station is transmitting

ANSWER C: When a cable TV coaxial cable line becomes nicked or broken, amateur signals can sometimes leak into the cable causing television interference, and TV signals will sometimes leak out of the cable causing interference on certain ham radio frequencies. You will notice this problem on the popular 2-meter band.

T4D09 If you are told that your amateur station is causing television interference, what should you do?
- A. First make sure that your station is operating properly, and that it does not cause interference to your own television
- B. Immediately turn off your transmitter and contact the nearest FCC office for assistance
- C. Connect a high-pass filter to the transmitter output and a low-pass filter to the antenna-input terminals of the television
- D. Continue operating normally, because you have no reason to worry about the interference

ANSWER A: It's unlikely that VHF and UHF signals will cause television interference to your neighbors on an outside antenna, or on the dish or on cable. However, when you pass your 5 wpm code test and go on the worldwide bands, be aware that these frequencies COULD sneak into a television set and cause problems. First, double check that your equipment is well grounded and operating properly, and double check that your TV is working okay when you are transmitting over the air. If it is, chances are your neighbors may have some loose connections on THEIR TV receivers, and this should be cured as a step to reducing the interference from your station when transmitting on high frequency.

T4D10 If harmonic radiation from your transmitter is causing interference to television receivers in your neighborhood, who is responsible for taking care of the interference?
- A. The owners of the television receivers are responsible
- B. Both you and the owners of the television receivers share the responsibility
- C. You alone are responsible, since your transmitter is causing the problem
- D. The FCC must decide if you or the owners of the television receivers are responsible

ANSWER C: A misaligned amateur transmitter may sometimes create harmonics of the fundamental frequency on the transmitter output. This usually occurs when someone gets inside the transmitter and starts adjusting things without looking at the output on a service monitor. If you are causing harmonic interference to TV receivers, you are putting out an illegal signal on the TV frequencies and you alone are responsible for solving the problem. With harmonics, it's your radio at fault.

T4D11 If signals from your transmitter are causing front-end overload in your neighbor's television receiver, who is responsible for taking care of the interference?

    A. You alone are responsible, since your transmitter is causing the problem
    B. Both you and the owner of the television receiver share the responsibility
    C. The FCC must decide if you or the owner of the television receiver are responsible
    D. The owner of the television receiver is responsible

ANSWER D: This is an idealistic answer about who is responsible for taking care of interference when your neighbor's television receiver is overloading from your nearby transmitted signal. Although the correct answer reads, "The owner of the television receiver is responsible," the GOOD Amateur Radio operator may also share some responsibility in assisting the neighbor with better shielded cable connections between the TV and VCR, as well as some bypass capacitors that might help reduce the problem. Receiver overload is a fact of life that affects anything close to your transmitter antenna, and the GOOD ham will do more than just cite Answer D as "You are the owner of the television, so you are responsible, not me." Go for this answer for the test, but in the real world of ham radio, work with your neighbors and be a good, responsible ham to resolve all forms of interference, whether it's your transmitter or their receiver.

Subelement T5 — Electrical Principles   [3 Exam Questions — 3 Groups]

T5A Metric prefixes, e.g. pico, nano, micro, milli, centi, kilo, mega, giga; concepts, units and measurement of current, voltage; concept of conductor and insulator; concept of open and short circuits

T5A01 If a dial marked in kilohertz shows a reading of 28450 kHz, what would it show if it were marked in hertz?

    A. 284,500 Hz
    B. 28,450,000 Hz
    C. 284,500,000 Hz
    D. 284,500,000,000 Hz

ANSWER B: The term kHz stands for KILO Hertz, and that means 1,000 Hz of cycles per second. If you wanted to write 28,450 kHz all the way out, it would be 28,450,000 Hz. The "k" means 1×10^3.

T5A02 If an ammeter marked in amperes is used to measure a 3000-milliampere current, what reading would it show?

    A. 0.003 amperes
    B. 0.3 amperes
    C. 3 amperes
    D. 3,000,000 amperes

ANSWER C: One milliampere equals one one-thousandth of an ampere (1×10^{-3}); therefore, one ampere equals 1000 milliamperes. Divide milliamperes by 1000 to convert to amperes. Or move the decimal point 3 places to the left. Calculator keystrokes are: CLEAR 3000 ÷ 1000 = and the answer is 3.

T5A03 How many hertz are in a kilohertz?

    A. 10
    B. 100

C. 1000

D. 1,000,000

ANSWER C: Kilo means one thousand (1 × 10³). A kilohertz is 1000 Hz.

T5A04 What is the basic unit of electric current?
A. The volt
B. The watt
C. The ampere
D. The ohm

ANSWER C: The flow of electrons in a conductor is called current. Current is measured in amperes. Amperes is often referred to as "amps."

Parameter	Basic Unit	Measuring Instrument
Voltage	Volts	Voltmeter
Current	Amperes	Ammeter
Resistance	Ohms	Ohmmeter
Power	Watts	Wattmeter

T5A05 Which instrument would you use to measure electric current?
A. An ohmmeter
B. A wavemeter
C. A voltmeter
D. An ammeter

ANSWER D: Current is measured in amperes, the unit of current. We use an ammeter to measure electrical current.

T5A06 Which instrument would you use to measure electric potential or electromotive force?
A. An ammeter
B. A voltmeter
C. A wavemeter
D. An ohmmeter

ANSWER B: Another name for electromotive force is voltage. We measure voltage with a voltmeter.

T5A07 What is the basic unit of electromotive force (EMF)?
A. The volt
B. The watt
C. The ampere
D. The ohm

ANSWER A: Voltage is an electromotive force whose basic unit is the volt.

T5A08 What are three good electrical conductors?
A. Copper, gold, mica
B. Gold, silver, wood
C. Gold, silver, aluminum
D. Copper, aluminum, paper

ANSWER C: Most wire is copper, and this is a good conductor. Some relays use gold- or silver-plated contacts, and these are also good conductors. You can use aluminum foil as a ground plane; it also is a good conductor. Always read all answers completely — mica, wood and paper are insulators!

T5A09 What are four good electrical insulators?
- A. Glass, air, plastic, porcelain
- B. Glass, wood, copper, porcelain
- C. Paper, glass, air, aluminum
- D. Plastic, rubber, wood, carbon

ANSWER A: In order for there to be current from one point to another in a circuit, current must have a good completed path of conductivity. If there is a poor or open connection, or an insulator with high resistance, there will be little or no current. An insulator has infinitely high resistance.

T5A10 Which electrical circuit can have no current?
- A. A closed circuit
- B. A short circuit
- C. An open circuit
- D. A complete circuit

ANSWER C: If you turn on your equipment and nothing happens, probably something is "open." It could be that main line power switch you hid to prevent unauthorized operation.

T5A11 Which electrical circuit draws too much current?
- A. An open circuit
- B. A dead circuit
- C. A closed circuit
- D. A short circuit

ANSWER D: Anytime you have a malfunction in a piece of equipment, and you hear a pop or smell something burning, chances are a short circuit has caused the malfunction. Some electrical connection has provided a much lower resistance path for current than is normal in the circuit.

T5B Concepts, units and calculation of resistance, inductance and capacitance values in series and parallel circuits

T5B01 What does resistance do in an electric circuit?
- A. It stores energy in a magnetic field
- B. It stores energy in an electric field
- C. It provides electrons by a chemical reaction
- D. It opposes the flow of electrons

ANSWER D: Think of resistance as stepping on a garden hose. This restricts the water flow, similar to a resistor that restricts the flow of electrons in a direct current (DC) circuit. See illustration on next page.

T5B02 What is the definition of 1 ohm?
- A. The reactance of a circuit in which a 1-microfarad capacitor is resonant at 1 MHz
- B. The resistance of a circuit in which a 1-amp current flows when 1 volt is applied
- C. The resistance of a circuit in which a 1-milliamp current flows when 1 volt is applied
- D. The reactance of a circuit in which a 1-millihenry inductor is resonant at 1 MHz

ANSWER B: A resistance of 1 ohm is calculated when there is 1 ampere of current in the circuit when 1 volt is applied to that circuit.

T5B03 What is the basic unit of resistance?
  A. The farad
  B. The watt
  C. The ohm
  D. The resistor
ANSWER C: The basic unit of resistance is the ohm. If you are taking one of my ham radio classes, we have a very special way of saying the word "ohm" so it almost sounds like a chant!

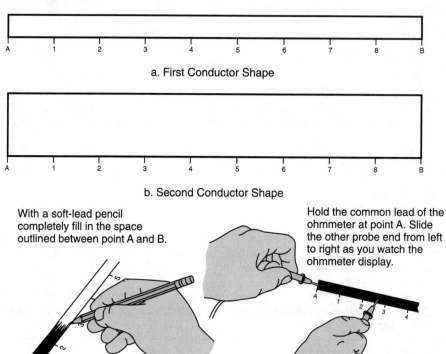

a. First Conductor Shape

b. Second Conductor Shape

With a soft-lead pencil completely fill in the space outlined between point A and B.

Hold the common lead of the ohmmeter at point A. Slide the other probe end from left to right as you watch the ohmmeter display.

Set the ohmmeter to Ω (resistance) setting.

c. Filling in Conductor with Pencil Lead   d. Measuring with Ohmmeter

Resistance of a pencil mark
Source: *Basic Electronics* © 1994, Master Publishing, Inc., Lincolnwood, Illinois

T5B04 What is one reason resistors are used in electronic circuits?
  A. To block the flow of direct current while allowing alternating current to pass
  B. To block the flow of alternating current while allowing direct current to pass
  C. To increase the voltage of the circuit
  D. To control the amount of current that flows for a particular applied voltage
ANSWER D: Resistors are found in electronic circuits to control the amount of current that flows for a particular applied voltage.

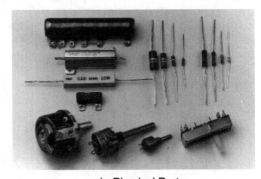

R

a. Symbol

b. Physical Part

Resistor

T5B05 What is the ability to store energy in a magnetic field called?

A. Admittance
B. Capacitance
C. Resistance
D. Inductance

ANSWER D: Place a magnetic compass near an energized inductor from DC and watch what happens! The compass needle lines up with the magnetic field, which is the basis for inductance.

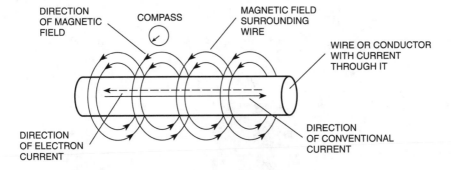

Magnetic Field Around a Conductor Carrying Current

T5B06 What is one reason inductors are used in electronic circuits?

A. To block the flow of direct current while allowing alternating current to pass
B. To reduce the flow of AC while allowing DC to pass freely
C. To change the time constant of the applied voltage
D. To change alternating current to direct current

ANSWER B: An inductor is a coil of wire. We use coils in circuits to reduce the flow of alternating current while allowing direct current to pass freely. Remember that filter you recently purchased to minimize alternator noise coming out of your new auto stereo? That filter contains an inductor (a coil) to minimize alternator AC noise from getting to your new audio system. The alternator noise is passed directly to ground with an accompanying capacitor.

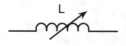

Variable Inductor

T5B07 What is the ability to store energy in an electric field called?
- A. Inductance
- B. Resistance
- C. Tolerance
- D. Capacitance

ANSWER D: Capacitors store their energy in an electric field, not a magnetic field like inductors. This is the basis for capacitance.

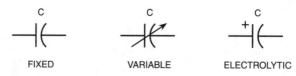

FIXED	VARIABLE	ELECTROLYTIC

a. Symbols

b. Physical Parts
Capacitors

T5B08 What is one reason capacitors are used in electronic circuits?
- A. To block the flow of direct current while allowing alternating current to pass
- B. To block the flow of alternating current while allowing direct current to pass
- C. To change the time constant of the applied voltage
- D. To change alternating current to direct current

ANSWER A: Remember that alternator filter you just bought? That filter also contains a capacitor that freely allows the alternating current to pass to ground but blocks the flow of direct current so things don't short out. That simple filter to minimize alternator noise on your new automobile radio is a coil and a capacitor, which does the job nicely because the coil blocks AC and passes DC, and the capacitor passes the AC to ground but blocks DC.

T5B09 If two resistors are connected in series, what is their total resistance?
    A. The difference between the individual resistor values
    B. Always less than the value of either resistor
    C. The product of the individual resistor values
    D. The sum of the individual resistor values
ANSWER D: Resistors in series simply add up. If you had a 5-ohm and 7-ohm resistor, in series, the total resistance would be 5 + 7 = 12 ohms. If you had a 3-ohm and 2-ohm resistor in series, your total resistance would be 5 ohms.

T5B10 If two equal-value inductors are connected in parallel, what is their total inductance?
    A. Half the value of one inductor
    B. Twice the value of one inductor
    C. The same as the value of either inductor
    D. The value of one inductor times the value of the other
ANSWER A: Inductors in parallel are treated just like resistors in parallel with respect to total value calculations. Total value is less than the value of either one.

$$\frac{L_1 \times L_2}{L_1 + L_2} = L_T$$

$$\text{When } L_1 = L_2, \quad L_T = \frac{L_2^2}{2L} = \frac{L_2}{2}$$

T5B11 If two equal-value capacitors are connected in series, what is their total capacitance?
    A. Twice the value of one capacitor
    B. The same as the value of either capacitor
    C. Half the value of either capacitor
    D. The value of one capacitor times the value of the other
ANSWER C: Capacitor values combine the opposite of resistors. The total value is less than the value of either one. The general equation for finding the equivalent capacitance of any two capacitors in series is:

$$\frac{C_1 \times C_2}{C_1 + C_2} = C_T$$

If $\qquad C_2 = C_1 \qquad$ Then $\dfrac{C_1 \times C_1}{C_1 + C_1} = C_T$

Makes Smaller Capacitor

Therefore, $\dfrac{C_1^2}{2C_1} = C_1 \qquad$ And $\dfrac{C_1}{2} = C_T$

Series Capacitance Equation

T5C *Ohm's Law (any calculations will be kept to a very low level — no fractions or decimals) and the concepts of energy and power, and; concepts of frequency, including AC vs. DC, frequency units, and wavelength*

T5C01 How is the current in a DC circuit directly calculated when the voltage and resistance are known?
    A. I = R × E [current equals resistance multiplied by voltage]
    B. I = R/E [current equals resistance divided by voltage]
    C. I = E/R [current equals voltage divided by resistance]
    D. I = E/P [current equals voltage divided by power]
ANSWER C: The relationship between voltage (E), current (I), and resistance (R) in an electronic circuit is described by Ohm's Law, which states: *the applied electromotive force, E, in volts, is equal to the circuit current, I, in amperes, times the circuit resistance, R, in ohms.* It is expressed by the equation E = I × R.

A simple way to remember how to calculate Ohm's Law is to use the magic circle. The magic circle shows E, I, and R in position so that it provides the correct equation for your problem. In this question, they ask you to solve for I (current), which is equal to E (voltage) divided by R (resistance).

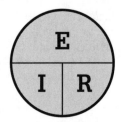

To use the magic circle, cover the letter that you are solving for with your finger. Now, plug in the other two values that they give you in the examination question. Solve the problem by performing the mathematical operation indicated by the position of the remaining letters, as shown here:

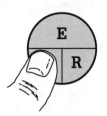

E = I × R	I = E/R	R = E/I
Finding Voltage	Finding Current	Finding Resistance

T5C02 How is the resistance in a DC circuit calculated when the voltage and current are known?
    A. R = I/E [resistance equals current divided by voltage]
    B. R = E/I [resistance equals voltage divided by current]
    C. R = I × E [resistance equals current multiplied by voltage]
    D. R = P/E [resistance equals power divided by voltage]
ANSWER B: Use the Ohm's Law magic circle in T5C01. Put your finger over the letter "R". What you have left is "E" over "I", or voltage divided by current.

T5C03 How is the voltage in a DC circuit directly calculated when the current and resistance are known?
A. E = I / R [voltage equals current divided by resistance]
B. E = R / I [voltage equals resistance divided by current]
C. E = I × R [voltage equals current multiplied by resistance]
D. E = I / P [voltage equals current divided by power]
ANSWER C: Now we are looking for voltage. Put your finger over the letter "E" in the Ohm's Law magic circle in T5C01. This leaves the letter "I" and the letter "R" on the same line. This means voltage equals current multiplied by resistance. See how simple this is.

T5C04 If a current of 2 amperes flows through a 50-ohm resistor, what is the voltage across the resistor?
A. 25 volts
B. 52 volts
C. 100 volts
D. 200 volts

ANSWER C: Since we are looking for E, the applied voltage, cover E with your finger, and you now have I (2 amps) times R (50 ohms). Multiply these two to obtain your answer of 100 volts. The calculator keystrokes are: CLEAR 2 × 50 =. And your answer is 100.

T5C05 If a 100-ohm resistor is connected to 200 volts, what is the current through the resistor?
A. 1 ampere
B. 2 amperes
C. 300 amperes
D. 20,000 amperes

ANSWER B: In this problem, you are looking for I. Using the Ohm's Law magic circle in question T5C01, cover I with your finger. You now have E over R, or 200 over 100. Do the division, and you will end up with 2 amps. See how simple this is! Calculator keystrokes are: CLEAR 200 ÷ 100 = and your answer is 2.

T5C06 If a current of 3 amperes flows through a resistor connected to 90 volts, what is the resistance?
A. 3 ohms
B. 30 ohms
C. 93 ohms
D. 270 ohms
ANSWER B: Again, use the magic circle in question T5C01. In this problem, you want to find R. Covering R with your finger leaves E over I. 90 divided by 3 gives 30 ohms. See how simple it is to use Ohm's Law. Calculator keystrokes are: CLEAR 90 ÷ 3 =. Your answer is 30.

T5C07 What term describes how fast electrical energy is used?
A. Resistance
B. Current
C. Power
D. Voltage
ANSWER C: Power indicates the rate of energy being consumed.

T5C08 What is the basic unit of electrical power?
> A. The ohm
> B. The watt
> C. The volt
> D. The ampere

ANSWER B: Power is energy, and you all have one of those energy meters on the side of your house. You know, that's the meter that keeps turning after you've turned just about everything off! Volts times amps equals watts. There is a "magic circle" for power calculation that is similar to the one for Ohm's Law.
Here it is:

$$\bigcirc \begin{array}{c} P \\ \hline I \mid E \end{array}$$

POWER CIRCLE

Power Calculation

As shown, P = power in watts, E = voltage in volts, and I = current in amperes. Use it in the same way as you use the Ohm's Law magic circle; that is, cover the unknown quantity with your finger and perform the mathematical operation represented by the remaining quantities.

T5C09 What happens to a signal's wavelength as its frequency increases?
> A. It gets shorter
> B. It gets longer
> C. It stays the same
> D. It disappears

ANSWER A: The higher we go in frequency, the more cycles per second. This means wavelength gets shorter.

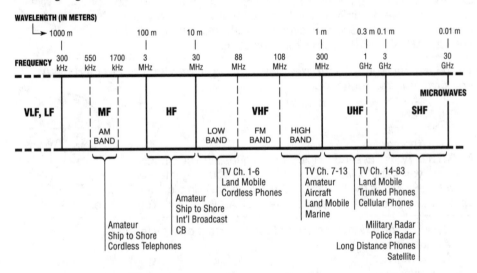

As Frequency increases, wavelength becomes shorter, as you can see from this radio frequency spectrum chart. Transmissions that require greater bandwidth, such as TV, use higher frequencies.

T5 — Electrical Principles

Category	Abbrev.	Frequency	Amateur Band Wavelength
Audio	AF	20 Hz to 20 kHz	None
Very Low Frequency	VLF	3 to 30 kHz	None
Low Frequency	LF	30 to 300 kHz	None
Medium Frequency	MF	300 to 3000 kHz	160 meters
High Frequency	HF	3 to 30 MHz	80, 40, 30, 20, 17, 15, 12, 10 meters
Very High Frequency	VHF	30 to 300 MHz	6, 2, 1.25 meters
Ultrahigh Frequency	UHF	300 to 3000 MHz	70, 33, 23, 13 centimeters
Superhigh Frequency	SHF	3 to 30 GHz	9, 5, 3, 1.2 centimeters
Extremely High Frequency	EHF	Above 30 GHz	6, 4, 2.5, 2, 1 millimeter

Frequency Spectrum

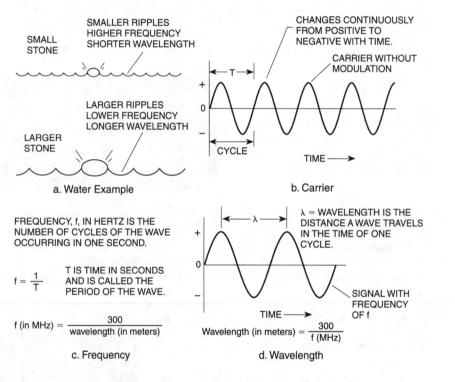

SMALL STONE

SMALLER RIPPLES
HIGHER FREQUENCY
SHORTER WAVELENGTH

LARGER RIPPLES
LOWER FREQUENCY
LONGER WAVELENGTH

LARGER STONE

a. Water Example

CHANGES CONTINUOUSLY FROM POSITIVE TO NEGATIVE WITH TIME.

CARRIER WITHOUT MODULATION

CYCLE

TIME →

b. Carrier

FREQUENCY, f, IN HERTZ IS THE NUMBER OF CYCLES OF THE WAVE OCCURRING IN ONE SECOND.

$f = \dfrac{1}{T}$ T IS TIME IN SECONDS AND IS CALLED THE PERIOD OF THE WAVE.

$f \text{ (in MHz)} = \dfrac{300}{\text{wavelength (in meters)}}$

c. Frequency

λ = WAVELENGTH IS THE DISTANCE A WAVE TRAVELS IN THE TIME OF ONE CYCLE.

TIME →

SIGNAL WITH FREQUENCY OF f

$\text{Wavelength (in meters)} = \dfrac{300}{f \text{ (MHz)}}$

d. Wavelength

Carrier, Frequency, Cycle and Wavelength

T5C10 What is the name of a current that flows back and forth, first in one direction, then in the opposite direction?

    A. An alternating current
    B. A direct current
    C. A rough current
    D. A steady state current

ANSWER A: If you have been shocked by house power, chances are you felt the "buzz." Be careful, it is very dangerous! Direct current (DC) flows in one direction; alternating current (AC) changes direction. Initially it flows in one direction, then it reverses and flows in the opposite direction.

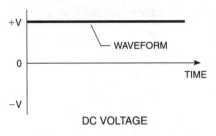

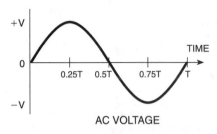

DC VOLTAGE AC VOLTAGE

DC and AC Waveforms

Direct current (dc) is a flow of charge that can change in magnitude, but not in direction (polarity). It produces a straight line when viewed on an oscilloscope. Alternating current (ac) is a flow of charge that can change both in magnitude and direction (polarity), and produces a sine wave when viewed on an oscilloscope.

T5C11 What is the name of a current that flows only in one direction?
A. An alternating current
B. A direct current
C. A normal current
D. A smooth current

ANSWER B: Batteries generate direct current. Even though a current may vary in value, if it always flows in the same direction, it is a direct current (DC).

D-Cell Batteries in Series

Subelement T6 — Circuit Components   [2 Exam Questions — 2 Groups]

T6A Electrical function and/or schematic representation of resistor, switch, fuse, or battery; resistor construction types, variable and fixed, color code, power ratings, schematic symbols

T6A01 What does a variable resistor or potentiometer do?
A. Its resistance changes when AC is applied to it
B. It transforms a variable voltage into a constant voltage
C. Its resistance changes when its slide or contact is moved
D. Its resistance changes when it is heated

ANSWER C: The volume control on your worldwide radio is a variable resistor. (Be careful: Answer D is also technically correct, but it is not the answer they want.)

Variable Resistor

T6A02 Which symbol of Figure T6-1 represents a fixed resistor?
A. Symbol 2
B. Symbol 3
C. Symbol 4
D. Symbol 5

ANSWER A: When you take your written examinations, your Volunteer Examiners will hand you the examination along with a diagram sheet that is usually stapled to the last page. Make absolutely sure the stapled diagram sheet is the correct one for your particular test. In Figure T6-1, the fixed resistor is component Symbol 2.

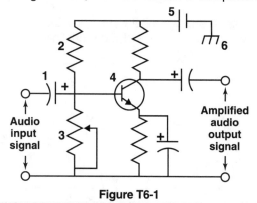

Figure T6-1

T6A03 Why would you use a double-pole, single-throw switch?
   A. To switch one input to one output
   B. To switch one input to either of two outputs
   C. To switch two inputs at the same time, one input to either of two outputs, and the other input to either of two outputs
   D. To switch two inputs at the same time, one input to one output, and the other input to the other output
ANSWER D: With this switch, you may connect two contacts to two outputs.

T6A04 In Figure N6-2, which symbol represents a single-pole, single-throw switch?
   A. Symbol 1
   B. Symbol 2
   C. Symbol 3
   D. Symbol 4
ANSWER A: Symbol 1 is an on/off switch. In one position, it opens a circuit. In the other position, it closes or completes a circuit.

Figure N6-2

T6A05 Why would you use a fuse?
   A. To create a short circuit when there is too much current in a circuit
   B. To change direct current into alternating current
   C. To change alternating current into direct current
   D. To create an open circuit when there is too much current in a circuit
ANSWER D: When a fuse passes current higher than its rating, the internal element, usually a thin wire, will heat up, melt, and then break the connection to create an open circuit.

T6A06 In Figure N6-1, which symbol represents a fuse?
  A. Symbol 1
  B. Symbol 3
  C. Symbol 5
  D. Symbol 7
ANSWER A: This is a fuse — an intentional weak link in the circuit. You want this to melt and open the circuit in case of excessive current flow.

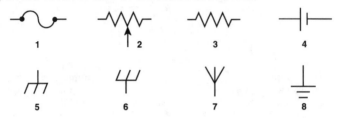

Figure N6-1

T6A07 Which of these components has a positive and a negative side?
  A. A battery
  B. A potentiometer
  C. A fuse
  D. A resistor
ANSWER A: A battery has a positive and negative terminal. We usually connect a red wire to the positive terminal and a black wire to the negative terminal.

T6A08 In Figure N6-1, which symbol represents a single-cell battery?
  A. Symbol 7
  B. Symbol 5
  C. Symbol 1
  D. Symbol 4
ANSWER D: Battery plates never touch. The symbol looks almost like a capacitor symbol. Ordinarily, the positive side (the long line) is indicated by a plus sign, and the negative side (the short line) is indicated by a minus sign.

T6A09 Why would a large size resistor be used instead of a smaller one of the same resistance value?
  A. For better response time
  B. For a higher current gain
  C. For greater power dissipation
  D. For less impedance in the circuit
ANSWER C: Besides the actual resistance and tolerance of a resistor, its power dissipation plays an important part in resistor selection. Physically larger resistors can dissipate more power than smaller resistors with the same resistance value.

T6A10 What do the first three color bands on a resistor indicate?
  A. The value of the resistor in ohms
  B. The resistance tolerance in percent
  C. The power rating in watts
  D. The resistance material

ANSWER A: You read the ohmic value of a resistor by the color of the bands. It's easy to read a resistor's color code. The first three bands indicate the resistor's resistance. The first color indicates the first number, the second color the second number, and the third color indicates the number of zeros to add after the first two numbers. For all three bands, black is zero, brown is one, red is two, orange is three, yellow is four, green is five, blue is six, violet is seven, gray is eight, and white is nine. Thus, red/black/red indicates 2-0-00 for a value of 2000 ohms. The fourth band indicates the permitted tolerance of the indicated nominal value. If the fourth band is gold, the tolerance is good at ±5 percent. Silver is an okay ±10 percent tolerance; and if there is no fourth band, the tolerance is assumed to be a ±20 percent average resistor. Thus, yellow/violet/orange/gold indicates a nominal value of 47000 ohms with a possible range from 44650 to 49350 ohms.

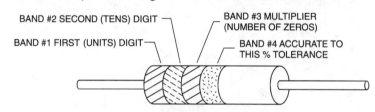

BAND #2 SECOND (TENS) DIGIT

BAND #1 FIRST (UNITS) DIGIT

BAND #3 MULTIPLIER (NUMBER OF ZEROS)

BAND #4 ACCURATE TO THIS % TOLERANCE

EXAMPLES

Band	1	2	3	4	Value
Resistor #1	Red (2)	Black (0)	Red (00)	Gold 5%	2,000 ±5%
Resistor #2	Brown (1)	Black (0)	Green (00000)	—	1,000,000 ±20%
Resistor #3	Blue (6)	White (9)	Orange (000)	Silver 10%	69,000 ±10%

Resistor Color Code (First Three Bands)

Black	0	Blue	6
Brown	1	Violet	7
Red	2	Gray	8
Orange	3	White	9
Yellow	4	Silver	0.01
Green	5	Gold	0.1

Tolerance (Fourth Band)

Gold	±5%
Silver	±10%
None	±20%

Resistor Color Code

Source: *Technology Dictionary* © 1987, Master Publishing, Inc., Lincolnwood, Illinois

T6A11 Which tolerance rating would indicate a high-precision resistor?
A. 0.1%
B. 5%
C. 10%
D. 20%

ANSWER A: In a precision circuit that you are building, you may need an very high-quality resistor, and a 0.1 percent tolerance resistor would be just fine. High-quality, high-precision resistors cost more and often are physically larger for the same power rating as a low-precision resistor.

T6B Electrical function and/or schematic representation of a ground, antenna, inductor, capacitor, transistor, integrated circuit; construction of variable and fixed inductors and capacitors; factors affecting inductance and capacitance

T6B01 Which component can amplify a small signal using low voltages?
A. A PNP transistor
B. A variable resistor
C. An electrolytic capacitor
D. A multiple-cell battery

ANSWER A: A transistor can amplify a small signal using a low-voltage power supply. (A vacuum tube amplifier requires a high-voltage power supply.)

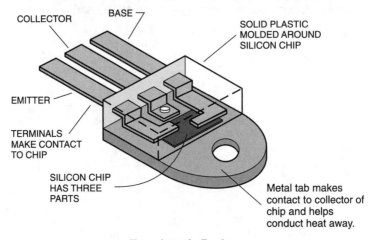

COLLECTOR
BASE
SOLID PLASTIC MOLDED AROUND SILICON CHIP
EMITTER
TERMINALS MAKE CONTACT TO CHIP
SILICON CHIP HAS THREE PARTS
Metal tab makes contact to collector of chip and helps conduct heat away.

Transistor in Package

Source: *Basic Electronics* ©1994, Master Publishing, Inc., Lincolnwood, IL

T6B02 Which component is used to radiate radio energy?
A. An antenna
B. An earth ground
C. A chassis ground
D. A potentiometer

ANSWER A: It's the job of your radio station antenna to radiate your radio energy from your station's transmitter.

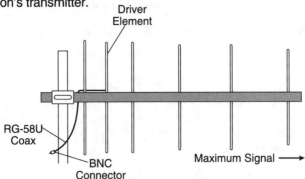

Driver Element
RG-58U Coax
BNC Connector
Maximum Signal ⟶

400-MHz Beam Antenna

T6 — Circuit Components

T6B03 In Figure N6-1, which symbol represents an earth ground?
A. Symbol 2
B. Symbol 5
C. Symbol 6
D. Symbol 8

ANSWER D: This is the classic ground symbol on worldwide radios and antenna systems. Grounding your equipment and half your antenna system is very important for safety and good range.

T6B04 In Figure N6-1, which symbol represents an antenna?
A. Symbol 2
B. Symbol 3
C. Symbol 6
D. Symbol 7

ANSWER D: Looks like an antenna, doesn't it?

Figure N6-1

T6B05 In Figure N6-3, which symbol represents an NPN transistor?
A. Symbol 1
B. Symbol 2
C. Symbol 3
D. Symbol 4

ANSWER D: An easy way to identify an NPN transistor is to first identify base (B), collector (C), and emitter (E) as shown in the schemeatics above. Then look and see which way the arrow is pointing. If the arrow is NOT POINTING IN, as in symbol 4, then it's an NPN transistor.

Figure N6-3

T6B06 Which symbol of Figure T6-2 represents a fixed-value capacitor?
A. Symbol 1
B. Symbol 2
C. Symbol 3
D. Symbol 4

ANSWER A: Symbol 1 is a fixed-value capacitor.

Figure T6-2

T6B07 In Figure T6-2, which symbol represents a variable capacitor?
A. Symbol 1
B. Symbol 2
C. Symbol 3
D. Symbol 4

ANSWER C: Symbol 2 is an adjustable coil. You want the adjustable capacitor, so symbol 3 is the correct answer.

T6B08 What does an inductor do?
A. It stores energy electrostatically and opposes a change in voltage
B. It stores energy electrochemically and opposes a change in current
C. It stores energy electromagnetically and opposes a change in current
D. It stores energy electromechanically and opposes a change in voltage

ANSWER C: Remember that coils develop a magnetic field which is indicated by a magnetic compass held near the energized coil. Energy is stored in the field.

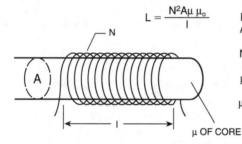

$$L = \frac{N^2 A \mu \, \mu_o}{l}$$

L = Inductance in henries
A = Cross-sectional area of coil core (m^2)
N = Number of turns on coil
l = Length of coil (m)
μ = Permeabiltiy of core material (1000 for iron)
μ_o = Permeabiltiy of air (1.26×10^{-8} henries/m)

Inductance Equation

T6B09 As an iron core is inserted in a coil, what happens to the coil's inductance?
A. It increases
B. It decreases
C. It stays the same
D. It disappears

ANSWER A: Never adjust the iron core in a coil unless you know exactly what you are doing. They are adjusted properly at the factory and wax-sealed so they seldom vibrate loose. Usually an adjustment is not necessary unless a repair has changed the circuit's characteristics.

T6B10 What does a capacitor do?
A. It stores energy electrochemically and opposes a change in current
B. It stores energy electrostatically and opposes a change in voltage
C. It stores energy electromagnetically and opposes a change in current
D. It stores energy electromechanically and opposes a change in voltage

ANSWER B: Capacitors store their energy in an electric field, not a magnetic field, as in a coil.

T6B11 What determines the capacitance of a capacitor?
A. The material between the plates, the area of one side of one plate, the number of plates and the spacing between the plates
B. The material between the plates, the number of plates and the size of the wires connected to the plates

C. The number of plates, the spacing between the plates and whether the dielectric material is N type or P type

D. The material between the plates, the area of one plate, the number of plates and the material used for the protective coating

ANSWER A: Memorize this answer for the examination. Read over the incorrect answers and see why they are wrong. Larger area of plates, larger number of plates, and closer spacing — all increase capacitance.

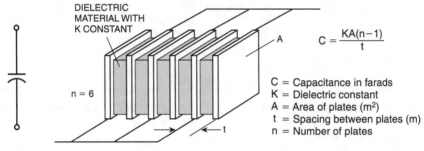

DIELECTRIC MATERIAL WITH K CONSTANT

$$C = \frac{KA(n-1)}{t}$$

C = Capacitance in farads
K = Dielectric constant
A = Area of plates (m^2)
t = Spacing between plates (m)
n = Number of plates

n = 6

a. Symbol   b. Parallel Plate Capacitor (6 Plates)

Capacitance Equation
Source: *Using You Meter*, A.J. Evans, © 1985, Master Publishing, Inc.

Subelement T7 — Practical Circuits   [2 Exam Questions — 2 Groups]

T7A *Functional layout of station components including transmitter, transceiver, receiver, power supply, antenna, antenna switch, antenna feed line, impedance-matching device, SWR meter; station layout and accessories for radiotelephone, radioteleprinter (RTTY) or packet*

T7A01 What would you connect to your transceiver if you wanted to switch it between several antennas?

A. A terminal-node switch
B. An antenna switch
C. A telegraph key switch
D. A high-pass filter

ANSWER B: We would use an antenna switch to switch between more than one type of antenna on the roof. Use a professional-quality switch like the one shown here. Stay away from inexpensive CB radio-type antenna switches — they don't work well at VHF or UHF frequencies.

T7A02 What connects your transceiver to your antenna?

A. A dummy load
B. A ground wire
C. The power cord
D. A feed line

ANSWER D: Coaxial cable is referred to as "feedline" between your transceiver and your antenna system.

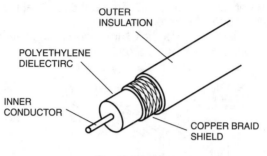

Coaxial Cable

T7A03 If your mobile transceiver works in your car but not in your home, what should you check first?
 A. The power supply
 B. The speaker
 C. The microphone
 D. The SWR meter

ANSWER A: Most ham radio sets run off of 12 volts for mobile applications. If you plan to run your equipment in your home, you will need a power supply that converts 110 VAC house power to 12 VDC.

T7A04 What does an antenna tuner do?
 A. It matches a transceiver output impedance to the antenna system impedance
 B. It helps a receiver automatically tune in stations that are far away
 C. It switches an antenna system to a transceiver when sending, and to a receiver when listening
 D. It switches a transceiver between different kinds of antennas connected to one feed line

ANSWER A: An antenna tuner will match your transceiver to an antenna system that might not be perfectly tuned to the frequency on which you wish to operate.

T7A05 In Figure N7-1, if block 1 is a transceiver and block 3 is a dummy antenna, what is block 2?
 A. A terminal-node switch
 B. An antenna switch
 C. A telegraph key switch
 D. A high-pass filter

ANSWER B: In Figure N7-1, block 2 is an antenna switch to switch between the antenna on top of block 2 or to the dummy load which is block 3.

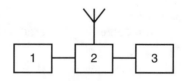

Figure N7-1

T7A06 In Figure N7-1, if block 1 is a transceiver and block 2 is an antenna switch, what is block 3?
- A. A terminal-node switch
- B. An SWR meter
- C. A telegraph key switch
- D. A dummy antenna

ANSWER D: Occasionally you may need to test your transmitter on full-power output, but you don't want to radiate a signal out on the airwaves from your antenna. You would switch the antenna selector over to the dummy antenna, and your transmitter output now goes into a noninductive resistor. The power output won't travel more than a couple hundred feet from your ham shack because it is absorbed by the dummy load.

T7A07 In Figure N7-2, if block 1 is a transceiver and block 3 is an antenna switch, what is block 2?
- A. A terminal-node switch
- B. A dipole antenna
- C. An SWR meter
- D. A high-pass filter

ANSWER C: The standing wave ratio meter, abbreviated "SWR meter," is useful in determining whether or not an antenna has been cut to perfect performance. In block diagram N7-2, block 3 is the antenna switch, so block 2 must be the SWR bridge. Block 1 is the transceiver. But if you were checking out the SWR of each antenna, it would be best to disconnect each antenna from block 3, and put it direct to the bridge. In this particular question and answer, however, block 3 is the switch, and block 2 is the SWR bridge.

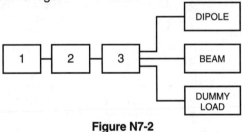

Figure N7-2

T7A08 In Figure N7-3, if block 1 is a transceiver and block 2 is an SWR meter, what is block 3?
- A. An antenna switch
- B. An antenna tuner
- C. A key-click filter
- D. A terminal-node controller

ANSWER B: There is only one antenna system in Figure N7-3, therefore, block 3 is an antenna tuner.

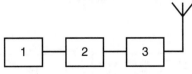

Figure N7-3

T7A09 What would you connect to a transceiver for voice operation?
  A. A splatter filter
  B. A terminal-voice controller
  C. A receiver audio filter
  D. A microphone
ANSWER D: To transmit your voice, you need a microphone.

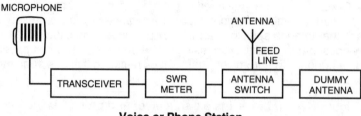

Voice or Phone Station

T7A10 What would you connect to a transceiver for RTTY operation?
  A. A modem and a teleprinter or computer system
  B. A computer, a printer and a RTTY refresh unit
  C. A data-inverter controller
  D. A modem, a monitor and a DTMF keypad
ANSWER A: "RTTY" stands for radioteleprinting, and it's a rather old way of data-sending and receiving over the airwaves. But nonetheless, it IS a data transmission, and this means you would need to hook up a modem and a printer to your transceiver to make it work — or since you already have a computer, you would hook up a computer system for RTTY operation, plus a host of other data signals that your present computer tied into a modem and printer will receive and send quite nicely. If you are into computers, you will love your new amateur radio privileges!

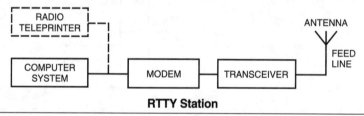

RTTY Station

T7A11 In packet-radio operation, what equipment connects to a terminal-node controller?
  A. A transceiver and a modem
  B. A transceiver and a terminal or computer system
  C. A DTMF keypad, a monitor and a transceiver
  D. A DTMF microphone, a monitor and a transceiver
ANSWER B: It's important to tell the salesperson the type of ham set and type of computer you have in order to get the right TNC and interconnecting cables.

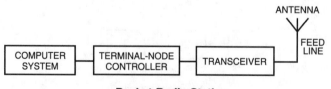

Packet-Radio Station

T7B Transmitter and receiver block diagrams; purpose and operation of low-pass, high-pass and band-pass filters

T7B01 What circuit uses a limiter and a frequency discriminator to produce an audio signal?
A. A double-conversion receiver
B. A variable-frequency oscillator
C. A superheterodyne receiver
D. An FM receiver

ANSWER D: When you see the words "frequency discriminator", you know they are talking about a stage of a frequency modulation (FM) receiver.

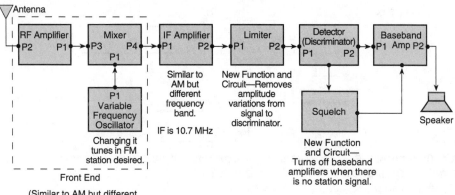

FM Receiver Block Diagram
Source: *Basic Communications Electronics*, J. Hudson & J. Luecke,
©1999, Master Publishing, Inc., Lincolnwood, IL

T7B02 What circuit is pictured in Figure T7-1 if block 1 is a variable-frequency oscillator?
A. A packet-radio transmitter
B. A crystal-controlled transmitter
C. A single-sideband transmitter
D. A VFO-controlled transmitter

ANSWER D: A variable frequency oscillator is abbreviated "VFO".

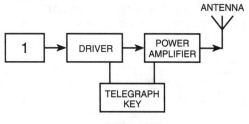

Figure T7-1

T7B03 What circuit is pictured in Figure T7-1 if block 1 is a crystal oscillator?
A. A crystal-controlled transmitter
B. A VFO-controlled transmitter
C. A single-sideband transmitter
D. A CW transceiver

ANSWER A: The question actually gives away the correct answer! If Block 1 is a crystal oscillator, it must then be a crystal controlled transmitter.

T7B04 What type of circuit does Figure T7-2 represent if block 1 is a product detector?
   A. A simple phase modulation receiver
   B. A simple FM receiver
   C. A simple CW and SSB receiver
   D. A double-conversion multiplier

ANSWER C: A product detector is necessary in a simple Morse code CW and single-sideband (SSB) receiver.

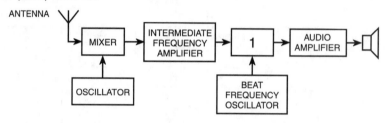

Figure T7-2

T7B05 If Figure T7-2 is a diagram of a simple single-sideband receiver, what type of circuit should be shown in block 1?
   A. A high pass filter
   B. A ratio detector
   C. A low pass filter
   D. A product detector

ANSWER D: Since Figure T7-2 is considered a simple single-sideband receiver (SSB), block 1 would be a product detector.

T7B06 What circuit is pictured in Figure T7-3, if block 1 is a frequency discriminator?
   A. A double-conversion receiver
   B. A variable-frequency oscillator
   C. A superheterodyne receiver
   D. An FM receiver

ANSWER D: Did you spot the words "frequency discriminator" in this question? This means we are looking at a frequency modulation (FM) receiver.

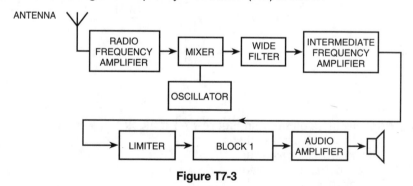

Figure T7-3

T7B07 Why do modern HF transmitters have a built-in low-pass filter in their RF output circuits?
A. To reduce RF energy below a cutoff point
B. To reduce low-frequency interference to other amateurs
C. To reduce harmonic radiation
D. To reduce fundamental radiation

ANSWER C: So how about it — are you going to learn the 5 wpm and go for the code credit with your new Technician Class license? I sure hope so! You will enjoy the worldwide bands, plus the easy upgrade to General Class. When you operate on high frequency, keep in mind that most high-frequency transmitters have a built-in, low-pass filter section that will reduce harmonic radiation.

T7B08 What circuit blocks RF energy above and below certain limits?
A. A band-pass filter
B. A high-pass filter
C. An input filter
D. A low-pass filter

ANSWER A: Read this question carefully! Since it blocks energy above and below a certain frequency, it must be a band-pass filter.

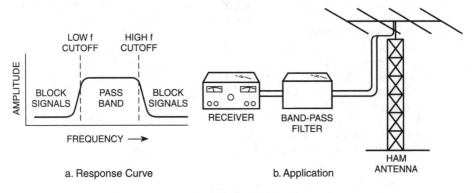

a. Response Curve   b. Application

Band-Pass Filter

T7B09 What type of filter is used in the IF section of receivers to block energy outside a certain frequency range?
A. A band-pass filter
B. A high-pass filter
C. An input filter
D. A low-pass filter

ANSWER A: Band-pass filters are used in many types of radio receivers.

T7B10 What circuit function is found in all types of receivers?
A. An audio filter
B. A beat-frequency oscillator
C. A detector
D. An RF amplifier

ANSWER C: All receivers contain a detector. Think of the detective work that a detector must do to find small signals out there on the air waves that come in from the antenna system.

T7B11 What would you use to connect a dual-band antenna to a mobile transceiver which has separate VHF and UHF outputs?
A. A dual-needle SWR meter
B. A full-duplex phone patch
C. Twin high-pass filters
D. A duplexer

ANSWER D: Mobile transceivers for dual-band operation may have two separate antenna outputs. But you only want one antenna on your vehicle. You would use a duplexer. You must also purchase a small duplexer which will combine your dual-band antenna to the double outputs on your transceiver.

Duplexer

Subelement T8 — Signals and Emissions   [2 Exam Questions — 2 Groups]

T8A RF carrier, definition and typical bandwidths; harmonics and unwanted signals; chirp; superimposed hum; equipment and adjustments to help reduce interference to others

T8A01 What is an RF carrier?
A. The part of a transmitter that carries the signal to the transmitter antenna
B. The part of a receiver that carries the signal from the antenna to the detector
C. A radio frequency signal that is modulated to produce a radiotelephone signal
D. A modulation that changes a radio frequency signal to produce a radiotelephone signal

ANSWER C: The RF carrier is a radiofrequency signal that can be modulated to produce a radio telephone signal if you use your voice. You can spot the correct answer by radiofrequency in the answer, and "RF" in the question.

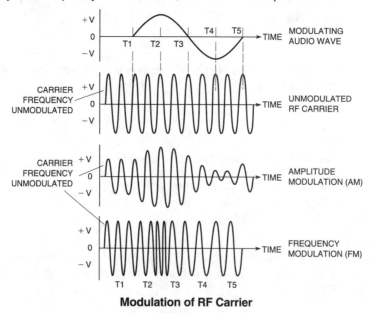

Modulation of RF Carrier

T8A02 Which list of emission types is in order from the narrowest bandwidth to the widest bandwidth?
A. RTTY, CW, SSB voice, FM voice
B. CW, FM voice, RTTY, SSB voice
C. CW, RTTY, SSB voice, FM voice
D. CW, SSB voice, RTTY, FM voice

ANSWER C: This gives you a clue why FM voice frequencies are usually found in the VHF and UHF spectrum — and the only place FM is found on worldwide frequencies is between 29.5 and 29.7 MHz. FCC rules do not permit FM repeater operation below 28.5 MHz.

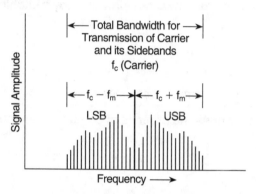

Spectral Plot of an AM Signal

T8A03 What is the usual bandwidth of a single-sideband amateur signal?
A. 1 kHz
B. 2 kHz
C. Between 3 and 6 kHz
D. Between 2 and 3 kHz

ANSWER D: A single-sideband Amateur Radio signal is typically 2 to 3 kHz wide.

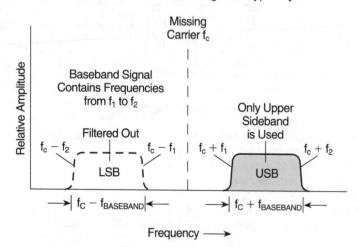

Spectral Plot of an SSB Signal

T8A04 What is the usual bandwidth of a frequency-modulated amateur signal?
A. Less than 5 kHz
B. Between 5 and 10 kHz
C. Between 10 and 20 kHz
D. Greater than 20 kHz

ANSWER C: When we transmit using frequency modulated phone (FM), our signal swings back and forth (deviates) up to ±5000 Hz. This is a total excursion of 10 kHz. Watch out for answer A — it's wrong because it does not have a "Between" (±) in front of it. Answer B is close, but answer C is the correct choice.

T8A05 What is the name for emissions produced by switching a transmitter's output on and off?
A. Phone
B. Test
C. CW
D. RTTY

ANSWER C: Morse code is a form of continuous wave, or CW.

T8A06 What term describes the process of combining an information signal with a radio signal?
A. Superposition
B. Modulation
C. Demodulation
D. Phase-inversion

ANSWER B: Combining an information signal with the carrier of a radio signal is called modulation. Think of modulation as information. An RF modulated carrier "carries" information.

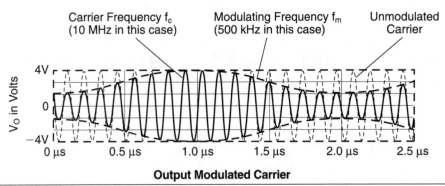

Carrier Frequency f_c (10 MHz in this case)   Modulating Frequency f_m (500 kHz in this case)   Unmodulated Carrier

V_o in Volts

4V   0   −4V

0 μs   0.5 μs   1.0 μs   1.5 μs   2.0 μs   2.5 μs

Output Modulated Carrier

T8A07 What is the result of over deviation in an FM transmitter?
A. Increased transmitter power
B. Out-of-channel emissions
C. Increased transmitter range
D. Poor carrier suppression

ANSWER B: If you overdrive the audio stage of an FM transceiver, you will create over-deviation that creates interference to adjacent channel users.

T8A08 What causes splatter interference?
A. Keying a transmitter too fast
B. Signals from a transmitter's output circuit are being sent back to its input circuit

C. Overmodulation of a transmitter

D. The transmitting antenna is the wrong length

ANSWER C: Back off the microphone if someone indicates your signal is "splattering." On some FM sets, you can turn down the modulation gain in the mike circuit. On other sets, you simply turn down the amount of deviation on the deviation pot, which is inside the transmitter.

T8A09 How does the frequency of a harmonic compare to the desired transmitting frequency?

A. It is slightly more than the desired frequency

B. It is slightly less than the desired frequency

C. It is exactly two, or three, or more times the desired frequency

D. It is much less than the desired frequency

ANSWER C: Harmonics are multiples of your fundamental frequency, and are not desirable.

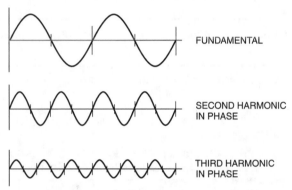

Fundamental Radio Wave and Harmonics

T8A10 What should you check if you change your transceiver's microphone from a mobile type to a base station type?

A. Check the CTCSS levels on the oscilloscope

B. Make an on-the-air radio check to ensure the quality of your signal

C. Check the amount of current the transceiver is now using

D. Check to make sure the frequency readout is now correct

ANSWER B: Many amateurs may add a headset/microphone or remote microphone to their handheld transceiver. When you do, be sure to conduct some on-the-air radio checks to ensure that the new external microphone is not over modulating (too loud) or under modulating (not enough audio). Most microphone/headsets have a microphone gain control that allows you to properly set your (transmit) audio levels.

T8A11 Why is good station grounding needed when connecting your computer to your transceiver to receive high-frequency data signals?

A. Good grounding raises the receiver's noise floor

B. Good grounding protects the computer from nearby lightning strikes

C. Good grounding will minimize stray noise on the receiver

D. FCC rules require all equipment to be grounded

ANSWER C: You will need a good earth ground system tied into your home computer chassis to minimize radiofrequency interference (RFI) to that nearby high-frequency ham set. We normally ground with copper foil to minimize the effects of "ground loops" which sometimes undo all the hard work that you have just accomplished in bringing an outside ground rod into your computer grounding circuit. Copper foil from your outside ground rod to any metal screw on the back of your home computer will usually decrease high-frequency noise.

Copper Foil Ground Strap Provides Good Surface Area Ground

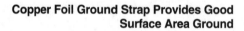

T8B Concepts and types of modulation: CW, phone, RTTY and data emission types; FM deviation

T8B01 What is the name for packet-radio emissions?
- A. CW
- B. Data
- C. Phone
- D. RTTY

ANSWER B: Sending high-speed digital packet radio emissions is called "data". CW is code, phone is voice, and RTTY is a rather slow radioteleprinter.

T8B02 What is the name of the voice emission most used on VHF/UHF repeaters?
- A. Single-sideband phone
- B. Pulse-modulated phone
- C. Slow-scan phone
- D. Frequency-modulated phone

ANSWER D: We use frequency modulation on most VHF and UHF repeaters.

T8B03 What is meant by the upper-sideband (USB)?
- A. The part of a single-sideband signal that is above the carrier frequency
- B. The part of a single-sideband signal that is below the carrier frequency
- C. Any frequency above 10 MHz
- D. The carrier frequency of a single-sideband signal

ANSWER A: USB stands for upper sideband, found on worldwide bands 10 through 20 meters. Lower sideband is found on 40 through 160 meters.

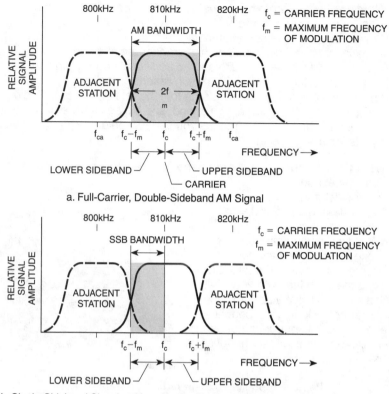

a. Full-Carrier, Double-Sideband AM Signal

b. Single-Sideband Signal — Uses No Carrier (Lower Sideband Shown)

Carrier, Sidebands and Bandwidth
Source: *Mobile 2-Way Radio Communications,*
G. West, © 1993, Master Publishing, Inc., Lincolnwood, Illinois

---

T8B04 What does the term "phone transmissions" usually mean?
A. The use of telephones to set up an amateur contact
B. A phone patch between amateur radio and the telephone system
C. AM, FM or SSB voice transmissions by radiotelephony
D. Placing the telephone handset near a transceiver's microphone and speaker to relay a telephone call

ANSWER C: Don't get "phone transmissions" mixed up with "phone patch." Phone transmissions refer to voice transmissions by telephony where you actually speak over a microphone to communicate with another operator. The term "phone patch" refers to a hook-up into your regular "Ma Bell" land-line phone system, as indicated in incorrect answers A, B and D. Go for answer C, "transmissions by radiotelephony."

T8B05 How is an HF RTTY signal usually produced?
A. By frequency-shift keying an RF signal
B. By on/off keying an RF signal
C. By digital pulse-code keying of an unmodulated carrier
D. By on/off keying an audio-frequency signal

ANSWER A: This is many times abbreviated FSK, and it's radioteletype. Here the frequency of the carrier is shifted to identify the information being transmitted.

T8B06 What are two advantages to using modern data-transmission techniques for communications?
- A. Very simple and low-cost equipment
- B. No parity-checking required and high transmission speed
- C. Easy for mobile stations to use and no additional cabling required
- D. High transmission speed and communications reliability

ANSWER D: The big advantage of using data for long lists of Amateur Radio traffic is that the traffic list may be sent at a high speed, and the accuracy of the communications will be high. This means you can rely on data communications to send long lists letter perfect.

T8B07 Which sideband is commonly used for 10-meter phone operation?
- A. Upper sideband
- B. Lower sideband
- C. Amplitude-compandored sideband
- D. Double sideband

ANSWER A: How are you doing on learning Why not take the code test at 5 wpm and g with for an easy upgrade to General Class on? Passing the code test with your Eleme Technician exam will give you 4 additional worldwide bands, including the popular 10-meter and where your upper-sideband signal will skip off of the ionosphere over thousands of miles during the day.

Popular 10-meter amateur radio SSB transceiver

T8B08 What can you do if you are told your FM hand-held or mobile transceiver is over-deviating?
- A. Talk louder into the microphone
- B. Let the transceiver cool off
- C. Change to a higher power level
- D. Talk farther away from the microphone

ANSWER D: If your set is over-deviating, it means that too much modulation is driving your signal beyond its normal bandwidth. If you talk farther away from the microphone, you will temporarily minimize over-deviation.

2-meter hand-held VHF ham transceiver

T8B09 What does chirp mean?
- A. An overload in a receiver's audio circuit whenever CW is received
- B. A high-pitched tone that is received along with a CW signal
- C. A small change in a transmitter's frequency each time it is keyed
- D. A slow change in transmitter frequency as the circuit warms up

ANSWER C: When your uncle gives you that old worldwide radio to go along with your code-passing certificate and your Tech license, chances are it may be a little unstable on the bands due to old dried-out components. If someone says you have "chirp", this is a change in your transmitter frequency each time you start sending dots and dashes. It can be fixed, but chances are you're going to need to strip down that old set and find some of the bad components.

Subelement T9 — Antennas and Feed Lines   [2 Exam Questions — 2 Groups]

T9A Wavelength vs. antenna length; 1/2 wavelength dipole and 1/4 wavelength vertical antennas; multiband antennas

T9A01 How do you calculate the length (in feet) of a half-wavelength dipole antenna?
  A. Divide 150 by the antenna's operating frequency (in MHz) [150/f(in MHz)]
  B. Divide 234 by the antenna's operating frequency (in MHz) [234/f (in MHz)]
  C. Divide 300 by the antenna's operating frequency (in MHz) [300/f (in MHz)]
  D. Divide 468 by the antenna's operating frequency (in MHz) [468/f (in MHz)]

ANSWER D: A simple antenna to build for worldwide operation is called the half-wavelength dipole. This simple antenna contains everyday wire whose length is one-half of the wavelength of the frequency being transmitted. The signal from your transmitter is applied in the exact middle of the dipole. It is best to use coaxial cable for this feed-in connection. The length of a half-wave dipole is easily calculated using the equation:

$$l = \frac{468}{f}$$

where l is the wavelength in feet and f is the frequency in MHz. To use the equation, you must convert kilohertz to megahertz. Plug this equation into your memory — you will use it often in your ham radio career.

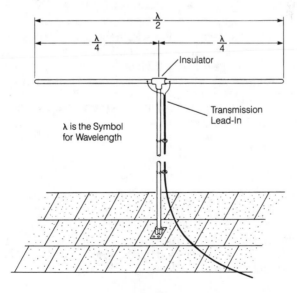

Dipole Antenna

T9A02 How do you calculate the length (in feet) of a quarter-wavelength vertical antenna?
A. Divide 150 by the antenna's operating frequency (in MHz) [150/f (in MHz)]
B. Divide 234 by the antenna's operating frequency (in MHz) [234/f (in MHz)]
C. Divide 300 by the antenna's operating frequency (in MHz) [300/f (in MHz)]
D. Divide 468 by the antenna's operating frequency (in MHz) [468/f (in MHz)]

ANSWER B: Operating ham radio in your vehicle makes good sense. Just be sure to keep your eyes on the road with a "heads up" display. Your antenna considerations may be as simple as home-brew, welding-rod elements soldered to a chassis connector that you plant smack dab in the middle of your new car's roof. Okay, I know you're not going to punch a hole in your new car roof or trunk lid, but for the next few questions, let's say you do. The quarterwave antenna is using the metal body of your vehicle as the other quarterwave counterpoise to make the whole system work. Since you have plenty of metal around the base of the antenna, your only job is to compute how long this little piece of welding rod is going to be at one quarter-wave-length of your operating frequency. So here is the formula:
Divide 234 by the antenna's operating frequency in MHz. [234/f(in MHz)]
The reason we are using 234 instead of 468 is 468 gives us a halfwave dipole, and 234 will give us the element length of a quarterwave welding rod whip. So go for Answer B — divide 234 by the antenna's operating frequency in MHz.

T9A03 How long should you make a quarter-wavelength vertical antenna for 440 MHz (measured to the nearest inch)?
A. 12 inches
B. 9 inches
C. 6 inches
D. 3 inches

ANSWER C: Oh-oh, time to find your kid's calculator. I know your math may be a little bit rusty, but a calculator can easily get you through this problem. And YES, you may bring the calculator to the test, too. First hit the CLEAR button on the calculator, and then press 2-3-4, the division sign, 4-4-0 = for an antenna quarterwave length that is .5318181 feet long. But wouldn't you know it — they want it in inches. No problem. Without removing those numbers from the screen, press the X (multiply) key and numbers 1-2, and then hit the equal button — and presto, you multiplied your fraction of a foot by 12 (remember 12 inches to the foot) and came up with 6.3818172 inches. Answer C is the closest at 6 inches. Easy, huh?

T9A04 How long should you make a quarter-wavelength vertical antenna for 28.450 MHz (measured to the nearest foot)?
A. 8 ft
B. 12 ft
C. 16 ft
D. 24 ft

ANSWER A: Now we are looking at building our own vertical ground plane antenna on the top of your car on 28.450 MHz, the 10-meter band. Using welding rod might be a little too small, so let's see what we need to do to a big long CB whip to make it work as a quarterwave length on 10 meters. Hit the CLEAR key on the calculator, and then go for keystrokes 2-3-4, divided by, 28.450 = and there it is, 8.224956 feet, with Answer A at 8 feet your best choice.

T9A05 How long should you make a quarter-wavelength vertical antenna for 146 MHz (measured to the nearest inch)?
  A. 112 inches
  B. 50 inches
  C. 19 inches
  D. 12 inches

ANSWER C: Now let's go back and see what it takes to get a good signal out with a little piece of welding rod on the top of your car roof on the 2-meter band. This time we are going for 146 MHz, and we are looking for the answer in inches. Hit the CLEAR several times and the let's go: 2-3-4, divided by, 1-4-6 = 1.6 feet as an answer. But they want it in inches, so multiple (X) 1.6 by 12 and you end up with a whip that is 19.232876 inches long, with the correct answer of Answer C, 19 inches. Now isn't that easy? Tell the kids to say goodbye to their calculator until after your exam.

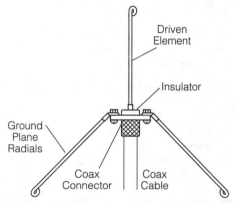

Vertical 1/4 λ Ground-Plane Antenna

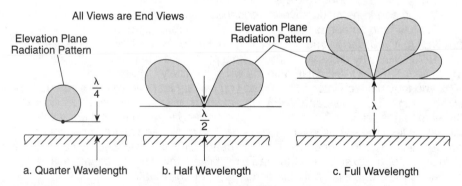

All Views are End Views

a. Quarter Wavelength   b. Half Wavelength   c. Full Wavelength

The Radiation Pattern of an Antenna Changes as Height Above Ground is Varied
Source: *Antennas*, A.J. Evans, K.E. Britain, ©1998, Master Publishing, Lincolnwood, Illinois

T9A06 If an antenna is made longer, what happens to its resonant frequency?
  A. It decreases
  B. It increases
  C. It stays the same
  D. It disappears

ANSWER A: Remember the rule: "lower-longer." If an antenna is cut a little bit too long, it works better at a lower frequency.

T9A07 If an antenna is made shorter, what happens to its resonant frequency?
A. It decreases
B. It increases
C. It stays the same
D. It disappears

ANSWER B: If you trim the tip of a vertical antenna to make it shorter, its resonant frequency will increase. If "lower is longer," "higher is shorter."

T9A08 How could you decrease the resonant frequency of a dipole antenna?
A. Lengthen the antenna
B. Shorten the antenna
C. Use less feed line
D. Use a smaller size feed line

ANSWER A: To lower the resonant frequency of an antenna, you will need to add wire to the antenna to make it longer.

T9A09 How could you increase the resonant frequency of a dipole antenna?
A. Lengthen the antenna
B. Shorten the antenna
C. Use more feed line
D. Use a larger size feed line

ANSWER B: To raise the resonant frequency of a dipole antenna, slightly shorten each end.

T9A10 What is one advantage to using a multiband antenna?
A. You can operate on several bands with a single feed line
B. Multiband antennas always have high gain
C. You can transmit on several frequencies simultaneously
D. Multiband antennas offer poor harmonic suppression

ANSWER A: If you plan to operate on 2 or 3 VHF/UHF bands like 2 meters, 440 MHz, and 1270 MHz, why dress your car up like a porcupine when one commercially made MULTI-BAND VHF/UHF antenna will work nicely? These antennas run about $75, and they have an internal spring so you can lay them down when you go to pull in the garage. The multi-band VHF/UHF antennas are manufactured specifically for the ham bands listed on the outside of the tube, and they work great for mobile use as well as fiberglass versions for home use. The multi-band antenna requires only one feedline to go to your dual-band or tri-band VHF/UHF transceiver. You may need a duplexer or triplexer down at the radio to split out this single antenna multi-band system to the 2 or 3 input antenna ports on your equipment.

T9A11 What is one disadvantage to using a multiband antenna?
A. It must always be used with a balun
B. It will always have low gain
C. It cannot handle high power
D. It can radiate unwanted harmonics

ANSWER D: They also make 5-band, 6-band, and 7-band multi-band antennas for the worldwide frequencies, too. They have little bitty ones for mobile use, and they have big tall ones for home use, and there are even directional multi-band beam antennas for home use, too. About the only precaution you must consider to use only new, high-quality, high-frequency equipment with these multi-band antennas because the antennas themselves may not minimize the transfer of harmonics generated by that old set your uncle gave you years ago. But if you use good, new equipment with harmonic filters built in, the harmonic problems with the high-frequency, multi-band antenna will be minimal.

T9B Parasitic beam directional antennas; polarization, impedance matching and SWR, feed lines, balanced vs. unbalanced (including baluns)

T9B01 What is a directional antenna?
    A. An antenna that sends and receives radio energy equally well in all directions
    B. An antenna that cannot send and receive radio energy by skywave or skip propagation
    C. An antenna that sends and receives radio energy mainly in one direction
    D. An antenna that uses a directional coupler to measure power transmitted
ANSWER C: Good examples of directional antennas are quads, rhombics, and the Yagi.

T9B02 How is a Yagi antenna constructed?
    A. Two or more straight, parallel elements are fixed in line with each other
    B. Two or more square or circular loops are fixed in line with each other
    C. Two or more square or circular loops are stacked inside each other
    D. A straight element is fixed in the center of three or more elements that angle toward the ground
ANSWER A: The Yagi antenna is really a series of dipoles, all lined up to increase the signal gain in one direction. A dipole is usually a half-wavelength long. However, on the Yagi beam, some are longer and some are shorter than the driven dipole. The ones called reflectors are slightly longer than the driven element, and the ones called directors are slightly shorter. The combination makes the Yagi antenna very directional.

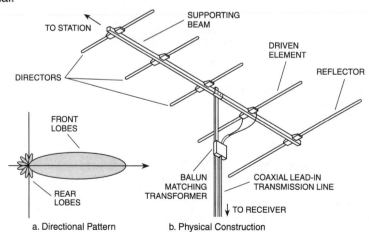

a. Directional Pattern   b. Physical Construction

A Beam Antenna — The Yagi Antenna

Source: *Antennas – Selection and Installation,* ©1986, Master Publishing, Inc., Lincolnwood, Illinois

T9B03 How many directly driven elements do most parasitic beam antennas have?
- A. None
- B. One
- C. Two
- D. Three

ANSWER B: For the examination, consider only one element as a driven element. However, in the real world of Amateur Radio, there are several manufacturers that drive more than one element on their beam antennas.

T9B04 What is a parasitic beam antenna?
- A. An antenna in which some elements obtain their radio energy by induction or radiation from a driven element
- B. An antenna in which wave traps are used to magnetically couple the elements
- C. An antenna in which all elements are driven by direct connection to the feed line
- D. An antenna in which the driven element obtains its radio energy by induction or radiation from director elements

ANSWER A: A beam antenna is an inexpensive investment for excellent power output and extraordinarily good receiving capabilities. It's much better to buy a beam antenna than a power amplifier.

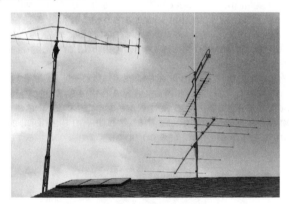

Beam Antennas

T9B05 What are the parasitic elements of a Yagi antenna?
- A. The driven element and any reflectors
- B. The director and the driven element
- C. Only the reflectors (if any)
- D. Any directors or any reflectors

ANSWER D: A parasitic element on a Yagi does not have any coaxial cable attached to it. This is why directors and reflectors are parasitic elements.

T9B06 What is a cubical quad antenna?
- A. Four straight, parallel elements in line with each other, each approximately 1/2-electrical wavelength long
- B. Two or more parallel four-sided wire loops, each approximately one-electrical wavelength long

C. A vertical conductor 1/4-electrical wavelength high, fed at the bottom

D. A center-fed wire 1/2-electrical wavelength long

ANSWER B: You can add reflectors and directors to your quad antenna system to give it some real punch in just one direction. Just like the Yagi, the reflector element is slightly larger, and the director loop is slightly smaller.

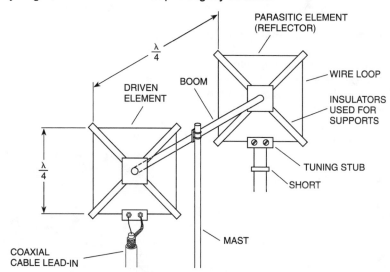

A Two-Element Cubical Quad Antenna — Horizontally Polarized

Source: *Antennas – Selection and Installation,* © 1986, Master Publishing, Inc., Lincolnwood, Illinois

---

T9B07 What type of non-directional antenna is easy to make at home and works well outdoors?

A. A Yagi

B. A delta loop

C. A cubical quad

D. A ground plane

ANSWER D: A ground plane antenna is an easy antenna to build. It is an omni-directional antenna that radiates in all directions. For 2 meters, the elements are only 18 inches long. You can even make one out of a coat hanger.

T9B08 What electromagnetic-wave polarization does most man-made electrical noise have in the HF and VHF spectrum?

A. Horizontal

B. Left-hand circular

C. Right-hand circular

D. Vertical

ANSWER D: Think of this answer as just backwards to what you might think when looking at your local horizontal power lines. Those horizontal power lines emit vertical electromagnetic waves. Most electrical interference on HF is loudest with vertically polarized antennas.

T9B09 What does standing-wave ratio mean?

A. The ratio of maximum to minimum inductances on a feed line

B. The ratio of maximum to minimum capacitances on a feed line

---

C. The ratio of maximum to minimum impedances on a feed line

D. The ratio of maximum to minimum voltages on a feed line

ANSWER D: Standing wave ratio (SWR) is the ratio of maximum voltage to minimum voltage along a transmission line. It also is a ratio of the maximum current to minimum current along a transmission line. It also is the ratio of the power fed forward along a transmission line to the power accepted by the load.

T9B10 Where would you install a balun to feed a dipole antenna with 50-ohm coaxial cable?

A. Between the coaxial cable and the antenna

B. Between the transmitter and the coaxial cable

C. Between the antenna and the ground

D. Between the coaxial cable and the ground

ANSWER A: This is a more common scenario—coaxial cable feeding a balanced dipole. In this case, the balun is installed on the antenna at the antenna feedpoint.

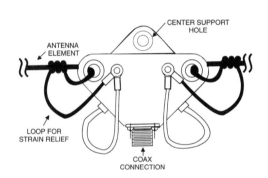

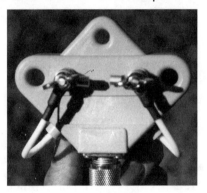

a. Balun Transformer   b. Photo

Using Balun to Feed Dipole

T9B11 Why does coaxial cable make a good antenna feed line?

A. You can make it at home, and its impedance matches most amateur antennas

B. It is weatherproof, and it can be used near metal objects

C. It is weatherproof, and its impedance is higher than that of most amateur antennas

D. It can be used near metal objects, and its impedance is higher than that of most amateur antennas

ANSWER B: You can even bury non-contaminating quality coaxial cable. Your author's station uses coaxial cable exclusively, and external runs are underground in PVC tubes so the gophers can't get to the cable.

Subelement TO — RF Safety [3 Exam Questions — 3 Groups]

TOA RF safety fundamentals, terms and definitions

Author's Note: In 1997, the FCC mandated the addition of questions on Radiofrequency (RF) Safety to the Technician and General class question pools. The addition of these questions reflects the FCC's efforts to make amateurs more aware of the potential danger to themselves and their neighbors from RF radiated energy. Remember, your antenna only emits RF radiation when you are transmitting, not when you are receiving.

The FCC's *OET Bulletin 65* and *Supplement B* contain useful equations and calculation methods for predicting the strength of RF fields when you are transmitting. You can download a copy of this information by visiting the FCC's website: www.fcc.gov. **The W5YI RF Safety Tables** appear on page 176 in the Appendix of this book. These tables also will help you determine the safe distance(s) from your antenna(s) for controlled and uncontrolled environments based on transmitting frequency and transmitter power.

Here are some terms and definitions that you need to know for the exam, and as an amateur operator in order to make sure your run your station in a safe manner in compliance with FCC RF safety regulations:

Near Field — the electromagnetic field located in the immediate vicinity of the antenna. The extent (size) of the near field depends on the size of the antenna, its wavelength, and transmission power.

Far Field — the electromagnetic field located at a great distance from a transmitting antenna. The far field begins at a distance that depends on many factors, including the wavelength and size of the antenna.

Transition Region — the area between the near and far field where power density decreases inversely with distance from the antenna.

Controlled Environment — involves people who are aware of and who can exercise control over RF exposure. Controlled exposure limits apply to both occupational workers and Amateur Radio operators and their immediate households.

Uncontrolled Environment — a location where individuals, such as your neighbors, may have no knowledge of (and therefore no control over) their exposure to RF radiation while you are operating your transmitter.

Maximum Permissible Exposure (MPE) — the maximum amount of electric and magnetic RF energy to which a person may be safely exposed.

Specific Absorption Rate (SAR) — the time rate at which RF energy is absorbed into the human body.

Thermal Effects — as applies to RF radiation, biological tissue damage resulting from the body's inability to cope with or dissipate excessive heat.

Duty Cycle — the percentage of time that a transmitter is "on" versus "off" in a 6- or 30-minute time period.

T0A01 Why is it a good idea to adhere to the FCC's Rules for using the minimum power needed when you are transmitting with your hand-held radio?
   A. Large fines are always imposed on operators violating this rule
   B. To reduce the level of RF radiation exposure to the operator's head
   C. To reduce calcification of the NiCd battery pack
   D. To eliminate self oscillation in the receiver RF amplifier

ANSWER B: The FCC adopted new rules and regulations about radiofrequency safety on August 1, 1996. These Part 97 rules send a clear signal that all amateur operators should be aware of the hazards associated with RF emissions. Always reduce power to the minimum level needed when transmitting with a handheld radio through a repeater or to another nearby ham on simplex.

T0A02 Over what frequency range are the FCC Regulations most stringent for RF radiation exposure?
   A. Frequencies below 300 kHz
   B. Frequencies between 300 kHz and 3 MHz
   C. Frequencies between 3 MHz and 30 MHz
   D. Frequencies between 30 MHz and 300 MHz

ANSWER D: The new RF exposure regulations specifically target Technician Class bands from 30 MHz to 300 MHz because these frequencies have rather short wavelengths, and the shorter the wavelength, the more susceptible our body is to RF exposure problems. Microwave ovens cook at frequencies near our popular VHF and UHF radio bands. Watch out for high power levels from 30-MHz to 300-MHz, and keep that handheld antenna away from your head and eyes!

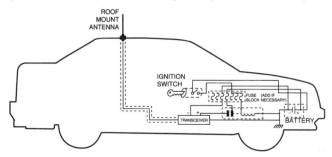

The safest place to mount the mobile antenna for minimum RF exposure is on the metal roof, as indicated

---

T0A03 What is one biological effect to the eye that can result from RF exposure?
   A. The strong magnetic fields can cause blurred vision
   B. The strong magnetic fields can cause polarization lens
   C. It can cause heating, which can result in the formation of cataracts
   D. It can cause heating, which can result in astigmatism

ANSWER C: Intense exposure to microwaves cause heating of our ocular fluids, which could result in the formation of cataracts. Don't be overly concerned that a small handheld radio or mobile VHF is going to cause you to go blind. What we are saying is don't stand in front of a 1500-watt, 5-wavelength, long moon bounce Yagi on 1296-MHz and stare down the length of the boom when the station is transmitting. As long as you take reasonable safety precautions to get out of the way of 1500-watt super-station antennas, you're going to be just fine.

T0A04 In the far field, as the distance from the source increases, how does power density vary?

A. The power density is proportional to the square of the distance
B. The power density is proportional to the square root of the distance
C. The power density is proportional to the inverse square of the distance
D. The power density is proportional to the inverse cube of the distance

ANSWER C: During our ham radio weekend class, we use a fluorescent tube to illustrate the power density around a mobile 1/4-wavelength, 10-meter antenna at 100 watts output. We use a nonconducting extension pole to hold the tube next to an antenna. When I speak in the mike, the fluorescent tube glows. But as soon as that tube is more than a foot or so away from the antenna, it no longer glows. This is a graphic example of how the power density off an antenna is proportional to the inverse square of the distance away from the antenna.

For the far-field region, the equation for power density, S, is:

$$S = \frac{PG}{4\pi R^2}$$

Where: Power desnsity, S, is in **mW/cm²**
Power input to antenna, P, is in **watts**
G is gain of antenna relative to an isotropic raditator **(a ratio)**
R is distance to center of radiation in **cm.**

We see that the far-field power density varies with the inverse square of the distance, R, from the antenna.

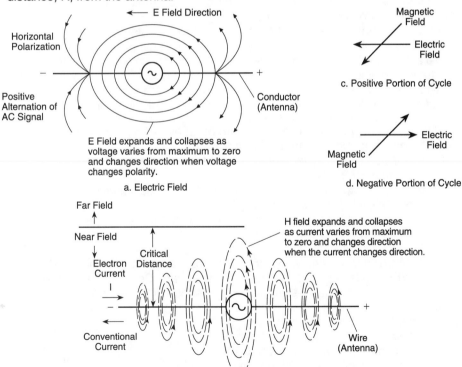

Electromagnetic Antenna Fields

Source: *Antennas*, A.J. Evans, K.E. Britain, ©1998, Master Publishing, Lincolnwood, Illinois

T0A05 In the near field, how does the field strength vary with distance from the source?
A. It always increases with the cube of the distance
B. It always decreases with the cube of the distance
C. It varies as a sine wave with distance
D. It depends on the type of antenna being used

ANSWER D: Every antenna has its own radiation pattern. On Yagi antennas, the greatest radiation is from the front director. On a dipole, there may be minimum amounts of radiation off each end, but maximum when standing broadside to the dipole. Remember that the near field strength of the signal will depend on the type of antenna that is radiating the power from the transceiver on transmit.

An antenna energized by a radio set on transmit produces strong near-field energy where power density is at a maximum. RF radiation decreases with distance. The extent of the near field can be described by the equation:

$$R_{nf} = \frac{D^2}{4\lambda}$$

where: R_{nf} = extent of near field
D = antenna diameter in **meters**
I = wavelength in **meters**

The "near field" is so close to the antenna that a person could easily touch it, or within a few steps, walk over and touch it. Because there is so much power density in close proximity to the antenna when the radio is transmitting, and there are so many other variables to consider, it is most difficult to accurately evaluate the effects of RF radiation exposure in the near field.

When you step many feet away from the antenna, you enter into the TRANSITION REGION where power density decreases inversely with distance from the antenna. When you are a safe distance from the antenna during transmit, you enter the far-field region where power density decreases inversely with the SQUARE of the distance. It is much easier to approximate far field values than it is to calculate near-field power densities and the effects of RF radiation exposure.

T0A06 Why should you never look into the open end of a microwave feed horn antenna while the transmitter is operating?
A. You may be exposing your eyes to more than the maximum permissible exposure of RF radiation
B. You may be exposing your eyes to more than the maximum permissible exposure level of infrared radiation
C. You may be exposing your eyes to more than the maximum permissible exposure level of ultraviolet radiation
D. All of these choices are correct

ANSWER A: Microwave systems may use feed horns, parabolic reflectors, or slotted wave guides to radiate the signal in a concentrated beam. Consider any microwave antenna as dangerous, regardless of the low power output that the operator may be transmitting. Never assume that a microwave system is simply receiving signals and is harmless. Always assume that the microwave antenna is transmitting a signal, and always walk behind a microwave transmitting antenna, never in front of it. Exposing your eyes to more that the maximum permissible exposure of RF radiation is very dangerous.

NEVER STAND IN FRONT OF OR TOUCH AN AMATEUR ANTENNA. IT IS EXREMELY DANGEROUS.

RF Radiation Exposure

T0A07 Why are Amateur Radio operators required to meet the FCC RF radiation exposure limits?

    A. The standards are applied equally to all radio services
    B. To ensure that RF radiation occurs only in a desired direction
    C. Because amateur station operations are more easily adjusted than those of commercial radio services
    D. To ensure a safe operating environment for amateurs, their families and neighbors

ANSWER D: By observing the new FCC RF radiation exposure limit rules you will ensure a safe operating environment for you to enjoy Amateur Radio, and your families and neighbors to live safely near you when you are on the air.

T0A08 Why are the maximum permissible exposure (MPE) levels not uniform throughout the radio spectrum?

    A. The human body absorbs energy differently at various frequencies
    B. Some frequency ranges have a cooling effect while others have a heating effect on the body
    C. Some frequency ranges have no effect on the body
    D. Radiation at some frequencies can have a catalytic effect on the body

ANSWER A: The limits are most stringent between 30-MHz to 300-MHz, covering our 6-meter band, our most popular 2-meter band, and the 220-MHz band, while still observing caution up on your new 440-MHz band. These higher frequencies are more easily absorbed by our body than lower frequencies.

T0A09 What does the term "specific absorption rate" or SAR mean?

    A. The degree of RF energy consumed by the ionosphere
    B. The rate at which transmitter energy is lost because of a poor feed line
    C. The rate at which RF energy is absorbed into the human body
    D. The amount of signal weakening caused by atmospheric phenomena

ANSWER C: Now let's examine some of the RF terminology that will help keep us safe when working with ham radio antenna systems. Remember, the dangerous radiation comes off of the antenna, not necessarily from the radio you are sitting in front of. The term "specific absorption rate" deals with how much RF energy our body absorbs when standing near an antenna while somebody is transmitting.

T0A10 On what value are the maximum permissible exposure (MPE) limits based?

    A. The square of the mass of the exposed body
    B. The square root of the mass of the exposed body
    C. The whole-body specific gravity (WBSG)
    D. The whole-body specific absorption rate (SAR)

ANSWER D: Maximum permissible exposure limits are based on our whole-body specific absorption rate. You can remember "SAR" as "Soon About to Roast".

T0B RF safety rules and guidelines

T0B01 Where will you find the applicable FCC RF radiation maximum permissible exposure (MPE) limits defined?

    A. FCC Part 97 Amateur Service Rules and Regulations
    B. FCC Part 15 Radiation Exposure Rules and Regulations

C. FCC Part 1 and Office of Engineering and Technology (OET) Bulletin 65

D. Environmental Protection Agency Regulation 65

ANSWER C: The Federal Communications Commission defines the maximum permissible exposure (MPE) limits in its Part 1 Rules and Regulations. The limits are also found in the Office of Engineering and Technology (OET) Bulletin Number 65, a half-inch-thick document that provides a detailed analysis of how close we can safely get to our own antennas on transmit (controlled environment), and how far away we must keep our antennas from our neighbors and others around us (uncontrolled environment).

T0B02 What factors must you consider if your repeater station antenna will be located at a site that is occupied by antennas for transmitters in other services?

A. Your radiated signal must be considered as part of the total RF radiation from the site when determining RF radiation exposure levels

B. Each individual transmitting station at a multiple transmitter site must meet the RF radiation exposure levels

C. Each station at a multiple-transmitter site may add no more than 1% of the maximum permissible exposure (MPE) for that site

D. Amateur stations are categorically excluded from RF radiation exposure evaluation at multiple-transmitter sites

ANSWER A: Now here is an interesting situation — you will be putting up a repeater station and antenna system on top of a building where the maximum permissible exposure (MPE) is just barely within the legal limit. You now turn on your system, and when your station is transmitting the collective signals may exceed MPE limits. Do they judge your system all by itself, or collectively? That's right, collectively as part of the total RF radiation from the transmitter site.

T0B03 To determine compliance with the maximum permitted exposure (MPE) levels, safe exposure levels for RF energy are averaged for an "uncontrolled" RF environment over what time period?

A. 6 minutes

B. 10 minutes

C. 15 minutes

D. 30 minutes

ANSWER D: The term "uncontrolled RF environment" deals with your unsuspecting neighbors who may live a house or 2 away receiving a little bit of your transmitted radio frequency energy. Since they are normally further away than right under your transmitting antenna, we take a 30-minute average to determine safe exposure levels of RF energy. Remember, 30 minutes for the uncontrolled neighbors.

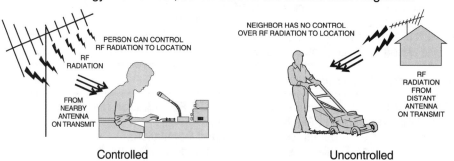

Controlled   Uncontrolled

RF Radiation Exposure Environments

T0B04 To determine compliance with the maximum permitted exposure (MPE) levels, safe exposure levels for RF energy are averaged for a "controlled" RF environment over what time period?
A. 6 minutes
B. 10 minutes
C. 15 minutes
D. 30 minutes

ANSWER A: Everyone at your household is probably right underneath your transmitting antenna system, and they probably know that you took the plunge to become a licensed amateur operator and will be regularly beaming them up with traces of RF energy. Since they are very close to your antenna system and know that you are sending out radio waves, our time limit measurements would be 6 minutes. So keep this in mind — 30 minutes for uncontrolled neighbors, and 6-minute measurements for you and your family right under the antenna system.

T0B05 Which of the following categories describes most common amateur use of a hand-held transceiver?
A. Mobile devices
B. Portable devices
C. Fixed devices
D. None of these choices is correct

ANSWER B: Your handheld transceiver is considered a portable device.

T0B06 How does an Amateur Radio operator demonstrate that he or she has read and understood the FCC rules about RF-radiation exposure?
A. By indicating his or her understanding of this requirement on an amateur license application form at the time of application
B. By posting a copy of Part 97 at the station
C. By completing an FCC Environmental Assessment Form
D. By completing an FCC Environmental Impact Statement

ANSWER A: All amateur radio operators must know and understand the FCC rules about RF-radiation exposure to both controlled and uncontrolled environments. When you fill out your amateur license application form, you will be signing the form that will include a statement that you understand the rules about RF-radiation exposure. And the best plan when you get on the air is to always caution people to stay away from your antenna when you are transmitting, and transmit only with enough power to easily make the circuit without having to switch to excessive amounts of power output.

T0B07 What amateur stations must comply with the requirements for RF radiation exposure spelled out in Part 97?
A. Stations with antennas that exceed 10 dBi of gain.
B. Stations that have a duty cycle greater than 50 percent.
C. Stations that run more than 50 watts peak envelope power (PEP)
D. All amateur stations regardless of power

ANSWER D: All amateur stations regardless of RF power must review their RF radiation evaluation to ensure there is no excessive RF exposure and the licensee must take action to prevent such an occurrence. [97.13c, 1.1307 (6)(1)]

T0B08 Who is responsible for ensuring that an amateur station complies with FCC Rules about RF radiation exposure?
A. The Federal Communications Commission
B. The Environmental Protection Agency
C. The licensee of the amateur station
D. The Food and Drug Administration

ANSWER C: When you pass your Amateur Radio examination, you are the amateur licensee of the amateur station, and you are the person responsible for insuring that your station complies with the FCC rules about RF radiation exposure.

T0B09 Why do exposure limits vary with frequency?
A. Lower-frequency RF fields have more energy than higher-frequency fields
B. Lower-frequency RF fields penetrate deeper into the body than higher-frequency fields
C. The body's ability to absorb RF energy varies with frequency
D. It is impossible to measure specific absorption rates at some frequencies

ANSWER C: The human body becomes nice and resonant for roasting between 30 MHz and 300 MHz. This puts us right in the middle of the dangerous portion of the band when we run high power on the 2-meter band at 144 MHz.

T0B10 Why is the concept of "duty cycle" one factor used to determine safe RF radiation exposure levels?
A. It takes into account the amount of time the transmitter is operating at full power during a single transmission
B. It takes into account the transmitter power supply rating
C. It takes into account the antenna feed line loss
D. It takes into account the thermal effects of the final amplifier

ANSWER A: Radiofrequency emissions from your new ham radio station will vary in "duty cycle" depending on what type of emission you are using. On FM, every time you key your microphone, your transmitter is working at full tilt. On single sideband, every time you pause between words and syllables, transmitter output drops to almost zero, decreasing the overall duty cycle. When sending CW, your dots and dashes will be active energy, with the spaces in between as no energy.

The averaging time period for controlled exposure is six minutes. The averaging time for uncontrolled exposure is 30 minutes. Here are examples of equivalent exposure:

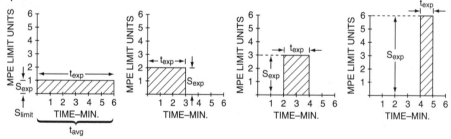

The general equation for time averaging exposure equivalence is:

$$S_{exp}\, t_{exp} \;=\; S_{limit}\, t_{avg}$$

The duty cycle is:
$$\text{DC (in \%)} \;=\; \frac{t_{exp}}{t_{avg}} \times 100$$

T0B11 From an RF safety standpoint, what impact does the duty cycle have on the minimum safe distance separating an antenna and the neighboring environment?
- A. The lower the duty cycle, the shorter the compliance distance
- B. The compliance distance is increased with an increase in the duty cycle
- C. Lower duty cycles subject the environment to lower radio-frequency radiation cycles
- D. All of these answers are correct

ANSWER D: The less you transmit, the lower the duty cycle, and the shorter the distance separation required between you and your neighbors. The more you talk, the further away your antenna must be from your neighbor to be within compliance. Lower duty cycle subjects the environment to lower radiofrequency radiation cycles — and this is good.

T0C Routine station evaluation (Practical applications for VHF/UHF and above operations)

T0C01 If you do not have the equipment to measure the RF power densities present at your station, what might you do to ensure compliance with the FCC RF radiation exposure limits?
- A. Use one or more of the methods included in the amateur supplement to FCC OET Bulletin 65
- B. Call an FCC-Certified Test Technician to perform the measurements for you
- C. Reduce power from 200 watts PEP to 100 watts PEP
- D. Operate only low-duty-cycle modes such as FM

ANSWER A: Bulletin 65 from OET lists the elaborate formulas to calculate power densities on specific frequencies, different types of antennas, ground reflections and a host of other variables.

T0C02 Is it necessary for you to perform mathematical calculations of the RF radiation exposure if your station transmits with more than 50 watts peak envelope power (PEP)?
- A. Yes, calculations are always required to ensure greatest accuracy
- B. Calculations are required if your station is located in a densely populated neighborhood
- C. No, calculations may not give accurate results, so measurements are always required
- D. No, there are alternate means to determine if your station meets the RF radiation exposure limits

ANSWER D: The W5YI RF Safety Tables and Figures on pages 176 are one source to determine RF radiation exposure limits. This will save you hours on your calculator trying to work out the complicated math calculations!

T0C03 Why should you make sure the antenna of a hand-held transceiver is not too close to your head when transmitting?
- A. To help the antenna radiate energy equally in all directions
- B. To reduce your exposure to the radio-frequency energy
- C. To use your body to reflect the signal in one direction
- D. To keep electrostatic charges from harming the operator

ANSWER B: One good way to prevent unwanted RF radiation when transmitting is to position the antenna as far away from your head and eyes as possible. This

---

reduces your exposure to the radiofrequency energy coming off of that little rubber-duck antenna.

T0C04 What should you do for safety if you put up a UHF transmitting antenna?
    A. Make sure the antenna will be in a place where no one can get near it when you are transmitting
    B. Make sure that RF field screens are in place
    C. Make sure the antenna is near the ground to keep its RF energy pointing in the correct direction
    D. Make sure you connect an RF leakage filter at the antenna feed point
ANSWER A: When you're planning your new ham radio station, pay particular attention to where your UHF antenna is placed. Make sure it will be in an area where no one can get near it or touch it when you are transmitting.

T0C05 How should you position the antenna of a hand-held transceiver while you are transmitting?
    A. Away from your head and away from others
    B. Towards the station you are contacting
    C. Away from the station you are contacting
    D. Down to bounce the signal off the ground
ANSWER A: When transmitting on a 2-meter or other VHF/UHF radio, keep that little rubber antenna away from your head and eyes, and also keep it well away from others standing near you.

T0C06 Why should your antennas be located so that no one can touch them while you are transmitting?
    A. Touching the antenna might cause television interference
    B. Touching the antenna might cause RF burns
    C. Touching the antenna might cause it to radiate harmonics
    D. Touching the antenna might cause it to go into self-oscillation
ANSWER B: Keep everyone from touching your antenna because it could cause them to sustain a nasty RF burn. Also, keep them from standing in front of it.

T0C07 For the lowest RF radiation exposure to passengers, where would you mount your mobile antenna?
    A. On the trunk lid
    B. On the roof
    C. On a front fender opposite the broadcast radio antenna
    D. On one side of the rear bumper
ANSWER B: Put your mobile antenna on the roof of your vehicle to minimize RF radiation exposure to everyone inside. The metal roof will act as a barrier to the radio waves.

T0C08 What should you do for safety before removing the shielding on a UHF power amplifier?
    A. Make sure all RF screens are in place at the antenna feed line
    B. Make sure the antenna feed line is properly grounded
    C. Make sure the amplifier cannot accidentally be turned on
    D. Make sure that RF leakage filters are connected
ANSWER C: If you are doing some maintenance on that mobile or base station amplifier, make absolutely sure no one can accidentally turn it on when you are just

a few inches away from the power output transistors. Would you ever work on your mom's microwave oven with the door open and the metal top and sides removed, with the oven actually turned on? Heck no!

T0C09 Why might mobile transceivers produce less RF radiation exposure than hand-held transceivers in mobile operations?
A. They do not produce less exposure because they usually have higher power levels.
B. They have a higher duty cycle
C. When mounted on a metal vehicle roof, mobile antennas are generally well shielded from vehicle occupants
D. Larger transmitters dissipate heat and energy more readily

ANSWER C: Never transmit with your handheld using the little rubber antenna inside the vehicle. You could actually generate more damaging RF exposure that way than you could with a more powerful output using an antenna on the metal roof. You can buy adaptors that will let a roof-mounted antenna work quite nicely on your mobile handheld. This is the safe way to go!

T0C10 What are some reasons you should never operate a power amplifier unless its covers are in place?
A. To maintain the required high operating temperatures of the equipment and reduce RF radiation exposure
B. To reduce the risk of shock from high voltages and reduce RF radiation exposure
C. To ensure that the amplifier will go into self oscillation and to minimize the effects of stray capacitance
D. To minimize the effects of stray inductance and to reduce the risk of shock from high voltages

ANSWER B: You've been told several times, don't run any type of power amplifier when it has been opened up for service and the metal covers are not in place. If you do, you could get a shock from the high voltage, and the RF radiation exposure could ultimately affect your eyesight.

Well, you've made it through the question pool. Now it's time to go back page 34 and begin reviewing your new-found knowledge. Work the book!

4

Learning Morse Code

ABOUT THIS CHAPTER

As of April 15, 2000, the Federal Communications Commission dropped the 20- and 13-wpm Morse code requirements, leaving 5-wpm as the only Morse code requirement for ham radio licensing in the U.S. 5-wpm code speed is so slow that your brain has plenty of time to hear the sound of the code, recall what letter or number it is, and transfer that message to your hand where you write it down and then wait patiently for the next sound group.

In this chapter, we provide you with a look at the code, and lots of helpful hints for learning the code. However, learning the code *by ear* is by far the best way to go, but adding some visual learning will help.

So begin memorizing the alphabet, and then see how easy it is to get the pattern down of the numerals. On the special signals and punctuation, all your 5-wpm Element 1 code test will have is the period, the comma, the question mark, the slant bar, break or pause and, at the final end of the test, the AR for "end of message," and SK for "end of work," pro signs.

LOOKING AT MORSE CODE

The International Morse code, originally developed as the American Morse code by Samuel Morse, is truly international — all countries use it, and most commercial worldwide services employ operators who can recognize it. It is made up of short and long duration sounds. Long sounds, called "dahs," are three times longer than short sounds, called "dits." *Figure 4-1* shows the time intervals for Morse code sounds and spaces. *Figure 4-2* indicates the sounds for the characters and symbols.

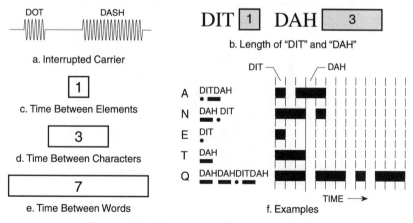

Figure 4-1. Time Intervals for Morse Code

Learning Morse Code

a. Alphabet

LETTER	Composed of:	Sounds like:	LETTER	Composed of:	Sounds like:
A	▪ —	didah	N	— ▪	dahdit
B	— ▪ ▪ ▪	dahdididit	O	— — —	dahdahdah
C	— ▪ — ▪	dahdidahdit	P	▪ — — ▪	didahdahdit
D	— ▪ ▪	dahdidit	Q	— — ▪ —	dahdahdidah
E	▪	dit	R	▪ — ▪	didahdit
F	▪ ▪ — ▪	dididahdit	S	▪ ▪ ▪	dididit
G	— — ▪	dahdahdit	T	—	dah
H	▪ ▪ ▪ ▪	didididit	U	▪ ▪ —	dididah
I	▪ ▪	didit	V	▪ ▪ ▪ —	didididah
J	▪ — — —	didahdahdah	W	▪ — —	ditdahdah
K	— ▪ —	dahdidah	X	— ▪ ▪ —	dahdididah
L	▪ — ▪ ▪	didahdidit	Y	— ▪ — —	dahdidahdah
M	— —	dahdah	Z	— — ▪ ▪	dahdahdidit

b. Special Signals and Punctuation

CHARACTER	Meaning:	Composed of:	Sounds like:
A̅R̅	(end of message)	▪ — ▪ — ▪	didahdidahdit
K	invitation to transmit (go ahead)	— ▪ —	dahdidah
S̅K̅	End of work	▪ ▪ ▪ — ▪ —	didididahdidah
S̅O̅S̅	International distress call	▪ ▪ ▪ — — — ▪ ▪ ▪	dididahdahdahdididit
V	Test letter (V)	▪ ▪ ▪ —	didididah
R	Received, OK	▪ — ▪	didahdit
B̅T̅	Break or Pause	— ▪ ▪ ▪ —	dahdidididah
D̅N̅	Slant Bar	— ▪ ▪ — ▪	dahdididahdit
K̅N̅	Back to You Only	— ▪ — — ▪	dahdidahdahdit
Period		▪ — ▪ — ▪ —	didahdidahdidah
Comma		— — ▪ ▪ — —	dahdahdididahdah
Question mark		▪ ▪ — — ▪ ▪	dididahdahdidit

c. Numerals

NUMBER	Composed of:	Sounds like:
1	▪ — — — —	didahdahdahdah
2	▪ ▪ — — —	dididahdahdah
3	▪ ▪ ▪ — —	didididahdah
4	▪ ▪ ▪ ▪ —	dididididah
5	▪ ▪ ▪ ▪ ▪	didididit
6	— ▪ ▪ ▪ ▪	dahdidididit
7	— — ▪ ▪ ▪	dahdahdididit
8	— — — ▪ ▪	dahdahdahdidit
9	— — — — ▪	dahdahdahdahdit
Ø	— — — — —	dahdahdahdahdah

Figure 4-2. Morse Code and Its Sound

CODE KEY

Morse code is usually sent by using a code key. A typical one is shown in *Figure 4-3a*. Normally it is mounted on a thin piece of wood or plexiglass. You can use wood screws, or simply glue the key in place. Make sure that what you mount it on is thin; if the key is raised too high, it will be uncomfortable to the wrist. The correct sending position for the hand is shown in *Figure 4-3b*.

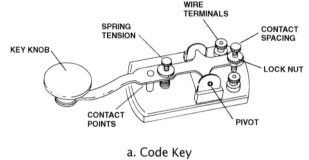

a. Code Key

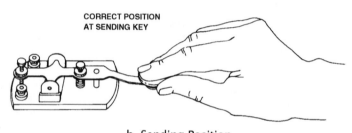

b. Sending Position

Figure 4-3. Code Key for Sending Code

LEARNING MORSE CODE

The reason you are learning the Morse code is to be able to operate on the worldwide bands. Here are five suggestions (four serious ones) on how to learn the code:

1. Memorize the code from the code charts in this book.
2. Use the author's fun cassette tapes available at all ham radio stores, including RadioShack.
3. Go out and spend $1,000 and buy a worldwide radio, and listen to the code live and on the air You don't need to spend that much, but you can listen to Morse code practice on the air, as shown in *Table 4-1*.
4. Use a code key and oscillator to practice sending the code. Believe it or not, someday you're actually going to do code over the live airwaves, using this same code key hooked up to your new megabuck transceiver.
5. Play with code programs on your computer, and *have fun!*

Table 4-1. Radio Frequencies for Code Reception

Pacific	Mountain	Central	Eastern	Mon.	Tue.	Wed.	Thu.	Fri.
6 a.m.	7 a.m.	8 a.m.	9 a.m.		Fast Code	Slow Code	Fast Code	Slow Code
7 a.m. – 9 a.m. 10 a.m. – 12:45 p.m.	8 a.m. – 10 a.m. 11 a.m. – 1:45 p.m.	9 a.m. – 11 a.m. 12 p.m. – 2:45 p.m.	10 a.m. – 12 p.m. 1 p.m. – 3:45 p.m.	**VISITING OPERATOR TIME**				
1 p.m.	2 p.m.	3 p.m.	4 p.m.	Fast Code	Slow Code	Fast Code	Slow Code	Fast Code
2 p.m.	3 p.m.	4 p.m.	5 p.m.	Code Bulletin				
3 p.m.	4 p.m.	5 p.m.	6 p.m.	Teleprinter Bulletin				
4 p.m.	5 p.m.	6 p.m.	7 p.m.	Slow Code	Fast Code	Slow Code	Fast Code	Slow Code
5 p.m.	6 p.m.	7 p.m.	8 p.m.	Code Bulletin				
6 p.m.	7 p.m.	8 p.m.	9 p.m.	Teleprinter Bulletin				
6:45 p.m.	7:45 p.m.	8:45 p.m.	9:45 p.m.	Voice Bulletin				
7 p.m.	8 p.m.	9 p.m.	10 p.m.	Fast Code	Slow Code	Fast Code	Slow Code	Fast Code
8 p.m.	9 p.m.	10 p.m.	11 p.m.	Code Bulletin				

CW is broadcast on the following MHz frequencies: 1.818, 3.5815, 7.0475, 14.0475, 18.0975, 21.0675, 28.0675, and 147.555 (local).

CODE REQUIREMENTS FOR AMATEUR RADIO LICENSES

Morse code is not required for a Technician Class license, but passing the 5-wpm Element 1 code test will give you additional privileges, as explained in Chapter 2. In order to upgrade to General Class, and in order to hold the top Extra Class ticket, you must pass the Element 1 test. *Table 4-2* summarizes the code requirements for all three amateur radio license classes.

Table 4-2. Amateur Radio Morse Code Requirements

License Class	Code Requirement
Technician	No code test required. Optional 5-wpm code test provides permanent operating privileges on HF worldwide frequencies. Exam credit for upgrade to General Class good for 365-days.
General	5 wpm, receiving plain language text
Extra	5 wpm, receiving plain language text

You don't need to take the code test again when you upgrade from General to Extra. If you upgrade from Technician to General, the 5-wpm code test certificate (CSCE) is valid for 365 days. If it expires prior to taking and passing the General Class Element 3 written examination, you will be required to re-take and re-pass the Element 1 code test. Once you achieve General or Extra class levels, keeping your license current means never having to repeat the code test or written exams again.

WHY MORSE CODE?

Learning the code to obtain an amateur operator/primary station license is an old tradition. Actually, back in the early 1900's, code was the only form of radio transmission, since microphones didn't come along until the '20s and '30s.

In the '80s, international radio regulations were changed so that a telegraph test was no longer required for those worldwide operators transmitting on frequencies above 30 MHz. And 10 years later, in 1991, the Technician "no-code" class of license was created. For the next nine years, the U.S. code requirements for worldwide frequencies were 5-wpm for Novice CW sub-band operation; 13-wpm for General Class voice, data, and code on the worldwide bands; and 20-wpm for Extra Class code where the Extra Class operator could enjoy any and all worldwide frequencies.

In its December 30, 1999, Report & Order restructuring amateur radio licensing requirements, the Federal Communications Commission found that many amateurs believed that the then-current licensing structure over-emphasized the importance of manual telegraphy. The FCC received many comments that Morse code proficiency is not relevant to modern communications practices and technologies. The FCC said it was *"not persuaded by the arguments of those opposing reduction or elimination of the emphasis on telegraphy proficiency as a license requirement in the amateur service."*

International regulations still require that all amateurs operating on the worldwide frequencies below 30 MHz know the Morse code — but not necessarily at 20- or 13-wpm. Knowing the code at 5 wpm satisfies the international regulations.

So the FCC concluded that the required speed for a single telegraphy examination for all grades of worldwide operation should be 5 wpm, stating: *"We know that this is the minimum telegraphy speed that has been required for the Novice class operator license since 1951, and is the minimum telegraphy proficiency that must be demonstrated by a Technician Class licensee to be authorized high-frequency privileges. Because both of these classes of operator licenses authorizes HF privileges, 5 wpm is the speed that the Commission has found sufficient to meet the requirement of the International Radio Regulations, and the slowest telegraphy speed in the amateur service examination system. We believe that, consistent with our decision to reduce the number of telegraphy elements from three to one, we also should use the lease burdensome requirement, the 5 wpm requirement, as the standard for that element."*

As a Technician Class operator, if all you want are privileges on the VHF and UHF frequency bands, you can skip the code and never learn a dot or dash. But if you want access to all of the worldwide excitement from ionospheric skywave skip communications, knuckle down and learn the code so you can pass that 5-wpm test. When you upgrade to General within 365 days of passing the 5-wpm test during your Tech test, you will be awarded the General Class license on successful completion of the Element 3 examination!

Cassette Tapes

Five words per minute is so slow, and so easy, that many ham radio applicants learn it completely in a single week! You can do it, too, by using the code tapes mentioned above.

Code cassettes personally recorded by your author make code learning *fun*. They will train you to send and receive the International Morse code in just a few short weeks. They are narrated and parallel the instructions in this book. The available cassette tapes mentioned have code characters generated at a 17-wpm character rate, spaced out to a 5-wpm word rate. This is known as Farnsworth spacing.

Getting Started

The hardest part of learning the code is taking the first cassette out of the case, putting it in your cassette player, and pushing the play button! Try it, and you will be over your biggest hurdle. After that, the tapes will talk you through the code in no time at all.

The cassette tapes make code learning *fun*. You'll hear how humor has been added to the learning process to keep your interest high. Since ham radio is a hobby, there's no reason we can't poke ourselves in the ribs and have a little fun learning the code as part of this hobby experience. Okay, you're still not convinced — you probably have already made up your mind that trying to learn the code will be the hardest part of getting your ham license. It will not. Give yourself a fair chance. Don't get discouraged. Have patience and remember these important reminders when practicing to learn the Morse code:

- Learn the code by sound. Don't stare at the tiny dots and dashes that we have here in the book — the dit and dah sounds on the cassette and on the air and with your practice keyer will ultimately create an instant letter at your fingertips and into the pencil.
- *Never* scribble down dots or dashes if you forget a letter. Just put a small dash on your paper for a missed letter. You can go back and figure out what the word is by the letters you did copy!
- Practice only with fast code characters; 17-wpm character speed, spaced down to 5-wpm speed, is ideal. The FCC recommendations are quite clear about the rate that code characters are generated for the code examination. You will find the code speed, character speed, and actual tone (1000 Hz) on cassette courses identical to cassettes used by most hams who give code tests.
- Practice the code by writing it down whenever possible. This further trains your brain and hand to work together in a subconscious response to the sounds you hear. (Remember Pavlov and his dog "Spot"?)
- Practice only for 15 minutes at a time. The tapes will tell you when to start and when to stop. Your brain and hand will lose that sharp edge once you go beyond 16 minutes of continuous code copy. You will learn much faster with five 15-minute practices per day than a one-hour marathon at night.
- Stay on course with the cassette instructions. Learn the letters, numbers, punctuation marks, and operating signals in the order they are presented here. Your author's code teaching system parallels that of the American Radio Relay League, Boy Scouts of America, the Armed Forces, and has worked for thousands in actual classroom instruction.

It was no accident that Samuel Morse gave the single dit for the letter "E" which occurs most often in the English language. He determined the most used letters in the alphabet by counting letters in a printer's type case. He reasoned a printer would have more of the most commonly-used letters. It worked! With just the first lesson, you will be creating simple words and simple sentences with no previous background.

Table 4-3 shows the sequence of letters, punctuation marks, operating signals, and numbers covered in six lessons on the cassettes recorded by your author.

Table 4-3. Sequence of Lessons on Cassettes

▪ Lesson 1	E T M A N I S O $\overline{SK}$ Period
▪ Lesson 2	R U D C 5 Ø $\overline{AR}$ Question Mark
▪ Lesson 3	K P B G W F H $\overline{BT}$ Comma
▪ Lesson 4	Q L Y J X V Z $\overline{DN}$ 1 2 3 4 6 7 8 9
▪ Lesson 5	Random code with narrated answers
▪ Lesson 6	A typical 5-wpm code test

Code Key and Oscillator — Ham Receiver

All worldwide ham transceivers have provisions for a code key to be plugged in for both CW practice off the air as well as CW operating on the air. If you already own a worldwide set, chances are all you will need is a code key for some additional code-sending practice.

Read over your worldwide radio instruction manual where it talks about hooking up the code key. For code practice, read the notes about operating with a "side tone" but not actually going on the air. This "side tone" capability of most worldwide radios will eliminate your need for a separate code oscillator.

Code Key and Oscillator — Separate Unit

Many students may wish to simply buy a complete code key and oscillator set. They are available from local electronic outlets or through advertisements in the ham magazines.

Look again at the code key in *Figure 4-3a.* Note the terminals for the wires. Connect wires to these terminals and tighten the terminals so the wires won't come loose. The two wires will go either to a code oscillator set or to a plug that connects into your ham transceiver. Hook up the wires to the plug as described in your ham transceiver instruction book or the code oscillator set instruction book.

Mount the key firmly, as previously described, then adjust the gap between the contact points. With most new telegraph keys, you will need a pair of pliers to loosen the contact adjustment knob. It's located on the very end of your keyer. First loosen the lock nut, then screw down the adjustment until you get a gap no wider than the thickness of a business card. You want as little space as possible between the points. The contact points are located close to the sending plastic knob.

Now turn on your set or oscillator and listen. If your hear a constant tone, check that the right-hand movable shorting bar is not closed. If it is, swing it open. Adjust the spring tension adjustment screw so that you get a good "feel" each time you push down on the key knob. Adjust it tight enough to keep the contacts from closing while your fingers are resting on the key knob.

Pick up the key by the knob! This is the exact position your fingers should grasp the knob—one or two on top, and one or two on the side of it. Poking at the knob with one finger is unacceptable. Letting your fingers fly off the knob between dots and dashes (dits and dahs) also is not correct. As you are sending, you should be able to instantly pick up the whole key assembly to verify proper finger position.

Your arm and wrist should barely move as you send CW. All the action is in your hand — and it should be almost effortless. Give it a try, and look at *Figure 4-3b* again to double-check your hand position.

Letting someone else use the key to send CW to you will also help you learn the code.

Morse Code Computer Software

The newest way to learn Morse code is through computer-aided instruction. There are many good PC programs on the market that not only teach you the characters, but build speed and allow you to take actual telegraphy examinations, which the computer constructs. Personal computer programs are also often used to make audio tapes on your tape recorder so you can listen to them on the cassette player in your car.

A big advantage of computer-aided Morse code learning is that you can easily customize the program to fit your own needs! You can select the sending speed, Farnsworth character-spacing speed, duration of transmission, number of characters in a random group, tone frequency — and more!

Some have built-in "weighting." That means the software will determine your weaknesses and automatically adjust future sending to give you more study on your problem characters! All Morse code software programs transmit the tone by keying the PC's internal speaker. Some generate a clearer audio tone through the use of external oscillators or internal computer sound cards.

THE ACTUAL CODE TEST

Now that 5 wpm is the only speed that a code test may be generated at, you need to know a little bit more about what 5 wpm sounds like. The actual character rate is around 15- to 17-wpm. This is called Farnsworth method where you hear the code sounds as a "package," and can much more easily recall what the letter is by their group sound. Code tests are no longer strung-out with extremely slow dots and dashes.

The pitch of the tone will be between 800 Hz to 1,000 Hz. The rate and tone are identical to the author's code training cassettes and CDs. Again, these should be available at the same place where you purchased this book.

The actual code test will be administered by your accredited test team. They usually generate the code from pre-recorded audio cassettes supplied to them by their Volunteer Examiner Coordinator. These are played over a boom box, and some teams may even offer headsets to decrease the echoes found in a larger room. If you aren't given a headset, sit as close to the audio system speaker as possible.

The code test is preceded with a 1-minute warm-up message sent in Morse code, such as this: THIS IS A TEST. ONE TWO THREE. COPY? Your examiner team will then ask if everyone can hear the code okay and does anyone need to change seats to minimize echoes in the room.

Then the code test begins, usually preceded with a series of 6 Vs. Some examiners will use a typical communication from one ham to another as the 5 to 6 minute test. *Figure 4-4* is an example of what may be sent on your 5-wpm code test:

VVV VVV W2ZE DE K9QY HI CINDY, NAME IS JOE. UR RST 589 BT 589. RIG IS ICOM 746 AND ANTENNA IS BEAM UP 130 FEET. WX VERY COLD / RAIN. I AM A TEACHER. MUST QRT FOR LUNCH, HOW COPY? W2ZE DE K9QY AR SK

Figure 4-4. A Typical Element 1 Code Test

Your examination team will send a plain text message. You won't need to copy random, military-style code groups. The plain text may contain some abbreviations, and you will find some of the more popular ham abbreviations in the back of this book.

By FCC order, the code test must contain every number, every letter of the alphabet, and the procedural signals. At 5 wpm, it is sometimes tough to use up all of the letters and numbers, so many times they may have a statement, "I still have problems copying…," and they stuff in the numbers and letters they couldn't figure out how to use in the text. So you could get some random numbers and characters in the last part of the test.

After the test is over and you hear the final AR SK, your examination team will smile and ask how you did, and then give you instructions for preparing your code copy for their review. If you did really well, look for 1 minute of solid copy, and underline it. This will easily meet the FCC rules. That's 25 letters in a row. And yes, you can go back and correct any errors in your code copy. Watch for spelling errors – your examiners will not intentionally misspell words, so perhaps you copied them down wrong, and this is a good time to correct them for that 1 minute of solid copy.

An alternate way of passing the 5-wpm Element 1 code test is by answering 7 out of 10 questions about the text correctly. Referring to the sample test transmission shown in *Figure 4-4,* here is an example of a "fill in the blank" code test:

1. Call sign of sending station?
   Answer: K9QY
2. Call sign of receiving station?
   Answer: W2ZE
3. Name of sender?
   Answer: Joe
4. RST Report?
   Answer: 589
5. Type of radio?
   Answer: ICOM
6. Type of antenna?
   Answer: Beam
7. Antenna height?
   Answer: 130 feet
8. Weather?
   Answer: Cold/rain
9. Occupation of sender?
   Answer: Teacher
10. Why is sender signing off?
    Answer: Lunch

Trying to squeeze a logical, typical CW exchange into 5 or 6 minutes is tough. It's even more difficult when the Volunteer Exam Coordinators need to come up with 10 questions about the copy. But if you write down every single letter you hear, chances are you'll do just fine.

The author's audio code course has many tips on how to identify correct answers on the code test. For instance, the call sign of the sender is always preceded by the letters "DE," "FROM." The call sign of the receiver usually comes first, right after the series of Vs. Both call signs are repeated a second time, but just don't get them backwards!

Some code tests may say "handle" instead of "name" for the sending or receiving operator. A "rig" is a type of transceiver. Antenna height might be listed in feet or — be careful — sometimes in meters. On weather reports, they sometimes slip the slant bar in between the 2 weather conditions. The term "QRT" is a name for why the operator is having to sign off. All of this is explained on the audio code cassette and CD courses.

Taking the Test

To take the actual test, your examiners will have a separate station for your code test, different from the written examination. The examiners will send a typical transmission from one ham to another. This will consist of an exchange of call signs, names, signal reports, the local weather, the type of rig or antenna the operators are using, occupation, and anything else that normally takes place in a ham radio conversation. You write down as much as you can, without worrying about missing a letter here or there.

After the Test

After the test is over, you can go back and work on your copy to fill in where you missed a letter. Since they were using plain language, it's easy to spot letters you accidentally copied wrong, or misspellings because you accidentally wrote an "A" instead of an "N".

When you think you have done the best to correct your material, the examiners will look for one minute of perfect copy, or may ask you ten simple questions about what you copied. These questions might have fill-in-the-blank answers, or better yet, multiple-choice answers. Seven out of ten is usually a passing score. They might also send another code transmission if you need a second chance — there is no longer a required waiting time between missed examination elements.

At 5 wpm, we have seen some students write down individual dots and dashes for the code received, and then translate them like a cryptogram into letters and numbers after the code test has been completed. This is one way to pass the test, but you'll find it easier just to memorize the characters and recognize them by their sound.

SENDING CODE AS AN ALTERNATIVE

Is your hearing shot from playing your boom box into the headphones too loud a few years ago? If you truly have a hearing disability, your examiners may allow you to take a code test by sending to them a predetermined text. Although the Federal Communications Commission rules mention sending as part of the code test, most examiners will usually do the code test as a receiving test.

Hey, sending is easier than receiving; and if you really do have a hearing disability, opt for the sending test. But I suggest you get a note from your doctor to back up the fact that your ear drums are no longer what they should be. This will allow the examiners to work with you on performing a sending code test, rather than a receiving code test.

ALL YOU NEED IS 5!

There no longer is a 20-wpm code test for Extra. There no longer is a 13-wpm rate for General. Now the only code speed you need for General or Extra — the top ham license — is 5 wpm.

And you don't need to take any code test for Technician Class, but you should — because that gets the code test out of the way and gives you permanent operating privileges of 10-meter phone and code excitement, plus 10-, 15-, 40-, and 80-meters CW. And you'll have 365 days of exam credit to get ready to take your General Class Element 3 written exam for your upgrade.

For heaven sake, don't lose that certificate showing you passed the 5-wpm code test. You'll need it when you upgrade to General Class. DON'T LOSE THAT CODE-PASSING CERTIFICATE! This is your proof that you don't have to go through the code test again when you upgrade to General.

NOW WE'RE READY

Obtain the code practice materials that will best suit your listening pleasure and learning needs. If you regularly work with computers, we've mentioned the excellent computer programs for learning code. If you regularly listen to tape cassettes in your automobile, we've mentioned the code learning cassettes developed and recorded by your author. Both of these products are available in the amateur radio marketplace.

You might also consider purchasing your high frequency equipment ahead of time, in preparation for your privileges on 10 meters, 15 meters, 40 meters, and 80 meters. You don't need a license to buy ham equipment; however, don't transmit until your license is granted by the FCC. Listen to the code practice on 80 and 40 meters at night, and at 15 and 10 meters during the day. This is another great way to prepare yourself for the 5-wpm Element 1 code test.

TAKING THE LICENSE EXAMINATION & RECEIVING YOUR FIRST LICENSE

ABOUT THIS CHAPTER

This chapter tells you when and where to test, how the examination will be given, who is qualified to give the Element 2 exam, and what happens after you complete it. There's also some good tips on finding a Volunteer Examiner team near you, and what to look for when asking questions about how they might conduct their Morse code test.

EXAMINATION ADMINISTRATION

All amateur radio service examinations are conducted by licensed amateur operators who volunteer and who are accredited by a Volunteer Examiner Coordinator (VEC). Each exam session is coordinated by national or regional VEC. Licensed amateurs who hold a General Class or higher class license may be accredit by a VEC to administer the Element 2 Technician Class examination, and the Element 1 Morse code test. Advanced Class VEs may administer Elements 1, 2, and 3 only. Extra Class VEs may administer all examinations, including Element 4.

A team of 3 officially-accredited Volunteer Examiners (VEs) are required to form an examination session. No one-on-one or one-on-two. Three examiners must be present for the exam session to be valid.

The VEs who will conduct your exam session are your fellow hams, and as volunteers don't get a penny for their time and skills. However, they are permitted to charge you a fee for certain reimbursable expenses incurred in preparing, administering, and processing the examination. The Federal Communications Commission adjusts the fee annually based on inflation. The current fee is still less than $7.00.

HOW TO FIND AN EXAM SITE

Exam sessions are held regularly at sites throughout the country to serve their local communities. The exam site could be a public library, a fire house, someone's office, in a warehouse, and maybe even in someone's private home. Each examination team may regularly post their examination locations down at the local ham radio store. They also inform their VEC when and where they regularly hold test sessions. So the easiest way for you to find an exam session that is near you and at a convenient time is to call the VEC.

A complete list of VECs is located on page 175 in the Appendix of this book. The W5YI VEC and the ARRL VEC are the 2 largest examination groups in the country, and they test in all 50 states. Their 3-member, accredited examination teams are just about *everywhere.* So when you call the W5YI-VEC in Texas, or the ARRL-VEC in Connecticut, be assured they probably have an examination team only a few miles from where you are reading this book right now!

Want to find a test site fast?
Visit the W5YI-VEC website at www.w5yi.org, or call them at 817-461-6443.

Any of the VECs listed will provide you with the phone number of a local Volunteer Examiner team leader who can tell you the schedule of upcoming exam sessions near you. Go ahead — give them a call now and let them know you are studying my book. Select a session you wish to attend, and make a reservation so the VEs know to expect you. Don't be a "no-show" and don't be a "surprise-show." Make a reservation. And don't hesitate to tell them how much we all appreciate their efforts in supporting ham radio testing.

Ask them ahead of time what you will need to bring to the examination session. And ask them how much the current fee is for your exam session.

Remember, your volunteer examiners don't get paid for their time, so anything that you can do to help out during the exam session will be appreciated. Maybe stick around after the exam session to help the VEs put away the tables and chairs. Someday *you* may be a volunteer examiner, and you will appreciate the help!

WHAT TO BRING TO THE EXAM

Here's what you'll need to bring with you for your Technician Class, Element 2 written examination and/or optional Element 1 Morse code test:
1. Examination fee of approximately $7.00 in cash.
2. Personal identification with a photo.
3. Any Certificates of Successful Completion of Examinations (CSCEs) issued within the last 365 days prior to this test session date. Bring the originals, plus two copies of everything.
4. Some sharp pencils and fine-tip pens. Bring a backup!
5. Calculators may be used, so bring your calculator.
6. Any other item that the VE team asks you to bring. Remember, these volunteer examiners receive no pay for their work.

EXAM CONTENT

Years ago, the FCC staff administered amateur radio exams, and the questions and answers were *secret.* The FCC developed their secret questions, their secret multiple-choice answers, and they had all sorts of secret subjects that you never knew about until after you took the exam for the first time.

In the 80's, things improved when President Ronald Reagan signed legislation providing for volunteer amateur operator examinations, allowing the Federal Communications Commission to transfer testing responsibilities over to the amateur community. This included making up the examination questions and answers, which would then be available in the public domain. It is the role of Volunteer Exam

Coordinators — specifically the Question Pool Committee — to review the questions in each of the three pools for the various amateur operator licenses. This procedure has been in effect for years for FAA airplane pilot testing. The amateur radio exam process has been privatized, and has worked out very well.

So, there won't be any surprises on you upcoming Element 2 written examination. Again, every one of the 35 questions on your exam will be taken from the 384 question pool in this book. The wording of the questions, answer, and distracters will be exactly as they appear here. The only change that the VECs are allowed to make is in the order of the A B C D answers.

TAKING THE EXAMINATION

Get a good night's sleep before exam day. Continue to study theory Q&A up to the moment you go into the room. Make a list of questions you have the most difficulty answering. Memorize the answers, and review them as you go to the examination. If someone is going with you to the examination, have them ask you the questions on the way, so that you can practice answering them. Listen to the *Learning Morse Code* tapes available from RadioShack in your car as you drive to the examination session if you are going to take a code test.

Check and Double-Check

When the examiners hand out the examination material, put your name, date, and test number on the answer sheet. *Make no marks on the multiple-choice question sheet.* Only write on the answer sheets.

Read over the examination questions carefully. Take your time in looking for the correct answer. Some answers start out looking correct, but end up wrong. Don't speed read the test.

When you are finished with the examination, go back over every question and double-check your answers. Try a game where you read what you have selected as the correct answer, and see if it agrees with the question.

When you are finished with the exam, turn in all of your paperwork. Tell the examiners how much you appreciate their efforts to help promote ham radio participation. If you are the last one in the room, volunteer to help them take down the testing location. The VE team will appreciate your offer.

And now, wait patiently outside for the examiners to announce you have passed your examination. Chances are they will greet you with a smile and your Certificate of Successful Completion of Examination. Make sure to immediately sign this certificate when it is handed to you.

COMPLETING NCVEC FORM 605

When you arrive at the examination site, one of the first things you will do is complete the NCVEC Form 605. This form is retained by the Volunteer Exam Coordinator who transfers your printed information to an electronic file and sends it to the FCC for your new license, or upgrade. Your application may be delayed or kicked-back to you if the VEC can't read your writing. Make absolutely sure you print as legibly as you can, and carefully follow the instructions on the form.

NCVEC QUICK-FORM 605 APPLICATION FOR
AMATEUR OPERATOR/PRIMARY STATION LICENSE

SECTION 1 - TO BE COMPLETED BY APPLICANT

PRINT LAST NAME	SUFFIX	FIRST NAME	INITIAL	STATION CALL SIGN (IF ANY)
MARCONI		JOE	G	

MAILING ADDRESS (Number and Street or P.O. Box)	SOCIAL SECURITY NUMBER / TIN (OR LICENSEE ID)
7101 RECTIFIER ROAD	090 - 909 - 090

CITY	STATE CODE	ZIP CODE (5 or 9 Numbers)	E-MAIL ADDRESS (OPTIONAL)
INDUCTOR	IL	60777	SPARKS@MSN.COM

DAYTIME TELEPHONE NUMBER (Include Area Code) OPTIONAL	FAX NUMBER (Include Area Code) OPTIONAL	ENTITY NAME (IF CLUB, MILITARY RECREATION, RACES)

Type of Applicant: [X] Individual [ ] Amateur Club [ ] Military Recreation [ ] RACES (Renewal Only)

TRUSTEE OR CUSTODIAN CALL SIGN

I HEREBY APPLY FOR (Make an X in the appropriate box(es))

SIGNATURE OF RESPONSIBLE CLUB OFFICIAL

[X] EXAMINATION for a **new** license grant

[ ] CHANGE my mailing address to **above** address

[ ] EXAMINATION for **upgrade** of my license class

[ ] CHANGE my station **call sign** systematically

[ ] CHANGE my **name** on my license to my new name

Applicant's Initials: _____

Former Name: _____
(Last name) (Suffix) (First name) (MI)

[ ] RENEWAL of my license grant.

Do you have another license application on file with the FCC which has not been acted upon?	PURPOSE OF OTHER APPLICATION	PENDING FILE NUMBER (FOR VEC USE ONLY)

I certify that:
* I waive any claim to the use of any particular frequency regardless of prior use by license or otherwise;
* All statements and attachments are true, complete and correct to the best of my knowledge and belief and are made in good faith;
* I am not a representative of a foreign government;
* I am not subject to a denial of Federal benefits pursuant to Section 5301 of the Anti-Drug Abuse Act of 1988, 21 U.S.C. § 862;
* The construction of my station will NOT be an action which is likely to have a significant environmental effect (See 47 CFR Sections 1.301-1.319 and Section 97.13(a));
* I have read and WILL COMPLY with Section 97.13(c) of the Commission's Rules regarding RADIOFREQUENCY (RF) RADIATION SAFETY and the amateur service section of OST/OET Bulletin Number 65.

Signature of applicant (Do not print, type, or stamp. Must match applicant's name above.)

X   Jos G Marconi   Date Signed: 4-15-00

NCVEC Form 605

Name

This isn't a tough one — your last name, first name, middle initial, and suffix such as junior or senior. You must stay absolutely consistent with your name on any future Form 605s for upgrades or changes of address. If you start out as "Jack" and end up "John," the computer will throw out your next application. If you don't list a middle initial the first time, but do the second time, the computer will again hiccup. If you decide to use a nickname, this is okay — but down the line when you visit a foreign country, they may ask you for your personal identification that needs to illustrate this same nickname. It is best to stick with the name that is on most of your personal pictured IDs, such as your Driver's License.

Date of Birth

The biggest problem here is, without thinking, putting down this year's date rather than the year in which you were born. One out of twenty make this mistake.

Social Security Number

Put in your Social Security Number in the designated box. If you are a citizen of another country, put down the country name in this box. If you are a U.S. citizen and prefer not to disclose your Social Security Number on this application, you will want to check with the VEC ahead of time and follow their detailed instructions on how to secure a Federal Communications Commission "Licensee ID" number to use in lieu of your SSN. Take our word for it — just give them your SSN, and you will avoid a lot of grief.

Address

Where do you want your paper license mailed? If you move around frequently, you will need to be contacting the FCC regularly for a change of address. Use a mailing address that you plan to keep as permanent as possible.

e-mail Address

This is optional, but it's a good idea because the amateur radio service is now under the FCC's Universal Licensing System. Once you get your new call sign, you will be able to work with the Federal Communications Commission directly via computer, including change of address, change of name, and license renewals without having to do any paperwork. There's more information about the ULS system in our *General Class* book.

Phone Numbers

There are two boxes for phone numbers — one for a daytime contact, and the other for your FAX number. These are optional, but it's a good idea to put these numbers down just in case the VEC or VE team need to re-contact you because they can't read your writing.

Signature

When you sign your name, make sure to include all of the letters that you printed as your name at the top of the form. Don't just put down a squiggle or an initial. You need to sign your name all the way out, including all of the letters that were in your printed name.

Final Check

Finally, double-check that your handwriting is legible. If a single letter in your name can't be read clearly and is misinterpreted, subsequent electronic filings may get returned as no action. Make sure your NCVEC Form 605 is as clear as a bell to your Volunteer Examination team, who will then forward it to their VEC. Stay away from red ink, too.

Your Examiners' Portion

The Volunteer Examination Team will carefully review your NCVEC Form 605 to ensure that they can read your handwriting and that everything looks okay. They will then enter this information into their computer database, and will more than likely file your test passing results electronically to their Volunteer Examiner Coordinator. The VEC will then electronically file your results with the Federal Communications Commission.

CONGRATULATIONS! YOU PASSED!

After you pass the examination, congratulations and a big welcome to Technician Class privileges are in order! The world of microwave and VHF/UHF operating awaits you. And, if you also passed the code test, welcome to the additional HF privileges and the world of long-range, high-frequency operation that you earned.

You can begin operating as soon as you obtain your official FCC call sign. This means you do not have to wait for the hard copy of your license to arrive at the address listed on your NCVEC 605.

Ask your examining team how you might determine your new call sign before the actual license document arrives. As mentioned previously, the FCC has a system that provide public access its amateur service license data base over the Internet. Visit www.w5yi.org for links to the FCC website. The FCC will also provide your call sign if you call them at 1-888-225-5322 between the hours of 8:30 A.M. and 4:30 P.M. EST, Monday through Friday. And W5YI VEC (1-817-548-8200) also provide this service to its applicants.

GETTING YOUR FIRST CALL SIGN

Once the VE team scores your test, and you've passed, the process of getting your official FCC Amateur Radio License will begin — usually that same day.

Electronic Filing

After you pass your Technician Class examination, your VE team will probably submit your amateur license application results electronically to their Volunteer Examiner Coordinator (VEC). The VEC will then electronically file for your license grant, and within days of passing your test your call sign is granted and you are permitted to go on the air immediately!

The system of electronic filing has been working so well that most new applicants who pass their exam over the weekend are able to go on the air that following Wednesday or Thursday once they have seen their new call letters appear on the FCC database. If you are on the Internet, you can regularly log in with several different FCC database servers, look for your name, and then spot your new call sign. Recent rule changes now allow you to instantly go on the air with those call letters, as an FCC grant, even though you don't actually have the official FCC paper license in your possession. It takes about two weeks to receive that official FCC license, which you may wish to frame, or cut off the top portion to keep in your wallet.

Occasionally, an applicant may test with a VE team that meets the same evening with their Volunteer Examiner Coordinator and sends in the electronic file that evening. As a result, call letters are issued the very next day! A 24-hour turnaround time is just about as close to an "instant license" as possible, but a 72-hour turnaround time is more common with electronic filing.

Ask your Volunteer Examination team when they will electronically file your test results. They can then give you an approximate date to check the FCC database to find out your new call sign.

Many years ago, before electronic filing, it was a 60-day wait for your call letters. Then there was a period that call signs took up to 90 days to be issued. But all this changed in 1996 when electronic filing of applications was implemented, making it possible for brand new ham operators to receive call letters within hours of successfully passing the exam!

Amateur Call Signs

As an aid to enforcement of the radio rules, transmitting stations throughout the world are required to identify themselves at regular intervals when they are in operation. That's the primary purpose of your call sign. A call sign is a very important matter to a ham — sometimes more personal than his or her name!

By international agreement, the prefix letters of a station's call sign indicates the country in which that station is authorized to operate. The national prefixes allocated to the United States are AA through AL, KA through KZ, NA through NZ, and WA through WZ. In addition, U.S. amateur stations with call signs that start with AA-AL, K, N or W are followed by a number indicating their location in a specific U.S. geographic area. *Table 5-1* details these geographical areas. On the DX airwaves,

Table 5-1. Call Sign Area for U.S. Geographical Areas

Call Sign Area No.	Geographical Area
1	Maine, New Hampshire, Vermont, Massachusetts, Rhode Island, Connecticut
2	New York, New Jersey, Guam and the U.S. Virgin Islands
3	Pennsylvania, Delaware, Maryland, District of Columbia
4	Virginia, North and South Carolina, Georgia, Florida, Alabama, Tennessee, Kentucky, Midway Island, Puerto Rico[1]
5	Mississippi, Louisiana, Arkansas, Oklahoma, Texas, New Mexico
6	California, Hawaii[2]
7	Oregon, Washington, Idaho, Montana, Wyoming, Arizona, Nevada, Utah, Alaska[3]
8	Michigan, Ohio, West Virginia, American Samoa
9	Wisconsin, Illinois, Indiana
0	Colorado, Nebraska, North and South Dakota, Kansas, Minnesota, Iowa, Missouri, Northern Mariana Island

[1] Puerto Rico also issued Area #3.
[2] Hawaii also issued Area #7.
[3] Alaska also issued Areas #1 through #0.

Figure 5-1. U.S. Call Sign Areas

hams can readily identify the national origin of the ham signal they hear by its call sign prefix. The suffix letters indicate a specific amateur station.

The Amateur Operator/Primary Station call sign is issued by the FCC's licensing facility in Gettysburg, Pennsylvania, on a systematic basis after it receives your application information from the VEC. There are four call sign groupings, A, B, C, and D. Tables showing the call sign groups and formats for operator/station licenses within and outside the contiguous U.S. are shown in the Appendix.

- Group A call signs are issued to Extra Class licensees, and have a 1-by2, 2-by-1, or 2-by-2 format that begins with the letter A. W9MU is an example.
- Group B call signs are issued to grandfathered Advanced Class licensees, and have a 2-by-2 format that begins with K, N, or W. WA6PT is an example.
- Group C call signs are issued to General, grandfathered Technician-Plus, and Technician Class licensees, and have a 1-by-3 format. N7LAT is an example. (However, because of the large number of Technician licenses that have been issued since the inception of the "no-code" license in 1991, there are no Group C call signs available. Thus, in accordance with FCC rules, new General and Technician Class operators are issued a Group D call sign.)
- Group D call signs are issued to new Technician and General Class operators, and to grandfathered Novice Class operators. They have a 2-by-3 format. KB9SMG is an example.

Once assigned, a call sign is never changed unless the licensee specifically requests the change — even if they move out of the continental United States. FCC licensees residing in foreign countries must show a U.S. mailing address on their applications. You may change your call sign to a new group when you upgrade your amateur license.

Of course, if you get a real neat call sign as your first issued call sign, you can elect to hold onto it all the way to the top. Your author's very first call sign was WB6NOA, and he has retained this same call sign all the way up to his current Extra Class license.

So what does all this mean? You can no longer easily tell what grade of license someone has by how many letters and single number in their call sign. But you're just a few keystrokes away from finding out on your computer by visiting www.qrz.com on the worldwide web. This website contains a data base of call signs that you can scan. Prior FCC licensing records also can be looked up, for a fee, through ITS, Inc. Visit www.itsdocs.com. You also can look up call signs on the FCC's ULS database located at: www.fcc.gov/wtb/uls.

The W5YI Group also offers several call sign services to amateurs. As a VEC, it has direct access to the FCC licensing computer and can handle address changes and license renewals for you. In addition, it can obtain a "Vanity" call sign for you, request a one-by-one call sign for your special event, or do the research and provide evidence that you were licensed prior to March 21, 1987 and therefore qualify for a General Class ticket without further examination. Check their website at www.w5yi.org for more information on these and other services it offers, or call 817-461-6443 during regular business hours.

Vanity Call Signs

Once you receive your first "no-choice," computer-assigned call letters, you may be eligible to replace them with a vanity call sign of your choosing. This call sign could be made up of your initials, or represent your love of animals (K9DOG) or could be call letters that your late mom or dad had when they got started in ham radio years ago.

General and Technician Class amateur operators may request a vanity call sign from Group D or Group C. However, since Group C call signs beginning with the letter N are completely used up, only Group D call signs are available. These call signs have two letters, a number, and three letters (such as KA5GMO).

You also may request a call sign that was previously assigned to you that may have expired years ago, as well as a call sign of a close relative or former holder who is now deceased. This call sign can be from any group.

There is an additional fee for a vanity call sign. You must complete FCC Form 605 and Form 159, and attach your check payable to the Federal Communications Commission to Form 159. Both forms are available on the FCC Internet site: www.fcc.gov/wtb/amateur.

You can file Form 605 electronically, and then mail in the Form 159 with your check attached. Electronically-filed Forms for which the filing fee and Form 159 have been received will be processed first. Instructions for electronic filing are included on the FCC website. Mail the required paperwork and fee to: FCC, PO Box 358994, Pittsburgh, PA 15251-5994. The Form 159 and the fee must be received within 10 days of electronically filing your Form 605 or your application will be dismissed.

To make it easier for you to select a vanity call sign, you may wish to contact the W5YI Group at 817/461-6443 and ask for their vanity call sign application package. The W5YI Group can help you to file electronically so you end up with exact call sign of your choice.

As for me, I'm staying with my original-issue WB6NOA call sign. If I changed it, I would be breaking a 30-year tradition!

THANK YOUR VE TEAM!

Your Volunteer Examination team is made up of men and women who are volunteering their time to provide you with an examination opportunity. Your VE team typically spends three additional hours for every one hour at the actual examination site. Since most exam sessions last for three hours, your three examiners may be spending as much as nine additional hours in electronic processing of your paperwork, handling the paperwork, sending the results to their Volunteer Examiner Coordinators, paying for the examination room, and all of the other chores that go along with conducting a volunteer exam session.

Work closely with your VE team and follow their instructions specifically. They are the absolute boss at the exam session, and you must follow their instructions to the letter.

Keep in mind that the volunteers are not paid. The fee that you are charged to take the exams is used to pay expenses. Your Volunteer Examiners don't keep any part of this fee to pay for their time in volunteering their services. So let them know you are grateful that they have given up their weekend or evening to provide you with an examination opportunity.

When you achieve the General Class level, or higher, it's time for you to become a Volunteer Examiner. Ask the Volunteer Examination team how you can sign up when you make General Class, and higher.

Finally, please tell your Volunteer Examination Team how much Gordon West Radio School appreciates their testing efforts. Show them these comments in this book. Tell them that Gordon West sincerely appreciates all of the hard work they are putting in to help the amateur service grow.

YOUR NEXT STEP

Did you pass the code test? If not, get the author's tapes, computer course, and CDs and learn the code at 5 wpm. Remember, 5-wpm is all that is necessary for General Class and Extra Class after you have passed the next 2 written exams, Element 3 for General Class, and Element 4 for Extra Class. Study materials for these two exams are contain in our *General Class* and *Extra Class* books.

SUMMARY

Welcome to the new, improved and simplified Amateur Radio service. One 5 wpm code test for all classes of license. Restructured and simplified Element 2, Technician. Straight-forward Element 3, General Class. And for you high-techies, Element 4, the Extra Class.

Learn the code. Never in the history of ham radio has 5 wpm given you so many operating privileges on the worldwide bands as the new General Class license.

Become an *active* amateur, and help establish new radio clubs and volunteer examination programs near where you live. Introduce ham radio to kids, and let's keep our service growing!

FREE PASSING CERTIFICATE

When you pass your exams and code test, I want to know about it! I have a very nice certificate available to you, suitable for framing. All I need is a large, self-addressed envelope with 10 first-class stamps on the inside to cover postage and handling and I'll send one your way. Write me at:

Gordon West Radio School
2414 College Drive
Costa Mesa, California 92626

Listen for me on the airwaves as WB6NOA. Say "hi" at many of the hamfests that I attend throughout the country every year. And if ever you would just like to speak with me, call me Monday through Friday, 10 am to 4 pm (California time), 714-549-5000.

Welcome to ham radio! It's been FUN teaching you the Technician Class.

Gordon West, WB6NOA

U.S. VOLUNTEER EXAMINER COORDINATORS IN THE AMATEUR SERVICE

Anchorage Amateur Radio Club
HC01 Box 6139-C
Palmer, AK 99645-9604
907/746-3996
worcester@alaska.com

ARRL/VEC
225 Main Street
Newington, CT 06111-1494
860/594-0300
860/594-0339 (fax)
e-mail: vec@arrl.org
Internet: www.arrl.org

Central America VEC, Inc.
1215 Dale Drive SE
Huntsville, AL 35801-2031
256/536-3904
256/534-5557 (fax)
e-mail: dtunstil@hiwaay.net

Golden Empire Amateur Radio Society
P.O. Box 508
Chico, CA 95927-0508
530/345-3515
wa6zrt@aol.com

Greater Los Angeles Amateur Radio Group
9737 Noble Avenue
North Hills, CA 91343-2403
818/892-2068
818/892-9855 (fax)
e-mail: gla.arg@gte.net

Jefferson Amateur Radio Club
P.O. Box 24368
New Orleans, LA 70184-4368
e-mail: doug@bellsouth.net

Laurel Amateur Radio Club, Inc.
P.O. Box 3039
Laurel, MD 20709-3039
301/317-7819
301/572-5124 (6-9 PM)
e-mail: rbusch@erols.com

The Milwaukee Radio Amateurs Club, Inc.
P.O. Box 25707
Milwaukee, WI 53225-0707
262/797-6722
e-mail: tfuszard@aero.net

MO-KAN/VEC
P.O. Box 11
Liberty, MO 64068-0011
816/781-7313
913/375-1177 (back-up)
wa0kuh@juno.com

SANDARC-VEC
P.O. Box 2446
La Mesa, CA 91943-2446
619/697-1475
e-mail: n6nyx@primenet.com

Sunnyvale VEC Amateur Radio Club, Inc.
P.O. Box 60307
Sunnyvale, CA 94088-0307
408/255-9000 (exam info 24 hours)
e-mail: vec@amateur-radio.org
Internet: www.amateur-radio.org

W4VEC
3504 Stonehurst Place
High Point, NC 27265-2106
336/841-7576
e-mail: w4vec@aol.com

Western Carolina Amateur Radio Society/
  VEC, Inc.
6702 Matterhorn Ct.
Knoxville, TN 37918-6314
865/687-5410
e-mail: wcars@korrnet.org
Internet: www.korrnet.org/wcars

W5YI-VEC
P.O. Box 565101
Dallas, TX 75356-5101
817/461-6443
817/548-9594 (fax)
e-mail: w5yi-vec@w5yi.org
Internet: www.w5yi.org

THE W5YI RF SAFETY TABLES

(Developed by Fred Maia, W5YI Group, working in cooperation with the ARRL.)

There are two ways to determine whether your station's radio frequency signal radiation is within the MPE (Maximum Permissible Exposure) guidelines established by the FCC for *"controlled"* and *"uncontrolled"* environments. One way is direct *"measurement"* of the RF fields. The second way is through *"prediction"* using various antenna modeling, equations and calculation methods described in the FCC's *OET Bulletin 65* and *Supplement B.*

In general, most amateurs will not have access to the appropriate calibrated equipment to make precise field strength/power density measurements. The field-strength meters in common use by amateur operators and inexpensive, hand-held field strength meters do not provide the accuracy necessary for reliable measurements, especially when different frequencies may be encountered at a given measurement location. It is more practical for amateurs to determine their PEP output power at the antenna and then look up the required distances to the controlled/uncontrolled environments using the following tables, which were developed using the prediction equations supplied by the FCC.

The FCC has determined that radio operators and their families are in the "controlled" environment and your neighbors and passers-by are in the "uncontrolled" environment. The estimated minimum compliance distances are in meters from the transmitting antenna to either the occupational/controlled exposure environment ("Con") or the general population/uncontrolled exposure environment ("Unc") using typical antenna gains for the amateur service and assuming 100% duty cycle and maximum surface reflection. Therefore, these charts represent the worst case scenario. They do not take into consideration compliance distance reductions that would be caused by:

(1) Feed line losses, which reduce power output at the antenna especially at the VHF and higher frequency levels.

(2) Duty cycle caused by the emission type. The emission type factor accounts for the fact that, for some modulated emission types that have a non-constant envelope, the PEP can be considerably larger than the average power. Multiply the distances by 0.4 if you are using CW Morse telegraphy, and by 0.2 for two-way SSB (single sideband) voice. There is no reduction for FM.

(3) Duty cycle caused by on/off time or "time-averaging." The RF safety guidelines permit RF exposures to be averaged over certain periods of time with the average not to exceed the limit for continuous exposure. The averaging time for occupational/controlled exposures is 6 minutes, while the averaging time for general population/uncontrolled exposures is 30 minutes. For example, if the relevant time interval for time-averaging is 6 minutes, an amateur could be exposed to two times the applicable power density limit for three minutes as long as he or she were not exposed at all for the preceding or following three minutes.

A routine evaluation is not required for vehicular mobile or hand-held transceiver stations. Amateur Radio operators should be aware, however, of the potential for exposure to RF electromagnetic fields from these stations, and take measures (such as reducing transmitting power to the minimum necessary, positioning the radiating antenna as far from humans as practical, and limiting continuous transmitting time) to protect themselves and the occupants of their vehicles.

Amateur Radio operators should also be aware that the new FCC radio-frequency safety regulations address exposure to people — and not the strength of the signal. Amateurs may exceed the Maximum Permissible Exposure (MPE) limits as long as no one is exposed to the radiation.

How to read the chart: If you are radiating 500 watts from your 10 meter dipole (about a 3 dB gain), there must be at least 4.5 meters (about 15 feet) between you (and your family) and the antenna — and a distance of 10 meters (about 33 feet) between the antenna and your neighbors.

Medium and High Frequency Amateur Bands

All distances are in meters

Freq. (MF/HF) (MHz/Band)	Antenna Gain (dBi)	Peak Envelope Power (watts)							
		100 watts		500 watts		1000 watts		1500 watts	
		Con.	Unc.	Con.	Unc.	Con.	Unc.	Con.	Unc.
2.0 (160m)	0	0.1	0.2	0.3	0.5	0.5	0.7	0.6	0.8
2.0 (160m)	3	0.2	0.3	0.5	0.7	0.6	1.06	0.8	1.2
4.0 (75/80m)	0	0.2	0.4	0.4	1.0	0.6	1.3	0.7	1.6
4.0 (75/80m)	3	0.3	0.6	0.6	1.3	0.9	1.9	1.0	2.3
7.3 (40m)	0	0.3	0.8	0.8	1.7	1.1	2.5	1.3	3.0
7.3 (40m)	3	0.5	1.1	1.1	2.5	1.6	3.5	1.9	4.2
7.3 (40m)	6	0.7	1.5	1.5	3.5	2.2	4.9	2.7	6.0
10.15 (30m)	0	0.5	1.1	1.1	2.4	1.5	3.4	1.9	4.2
10.15 (30m)	3	0.7	1.5	1.5	3.4	2.2	4.8	2.6	5.9
10.15 (30m)	6	1.0	2.2	2.2	4.8	3.0	6.8	3.7	8.3
14.35 (20m)	0	0.7	1.5	1.5	3.4	2.2	4.8	2.6	5.9
14.35 (20m)	3	1.0	2.2	2.2	4.8	3.0	6.8	3.7	8.4
14.35 (20m)	6	1.4	3.0	3.0	6.8	4.3	9.6	5.3	11.8
14.35 (20m)	9	1.9	4.3	4.3	9.6	6.1	13.6	7.5	16.7
18.168 (17m)	0	0.9	1.9	1.9	4.3	2.7	6.1	3.3	7.5
18.168 (17m)	3	1.2	2.7	2.7	6.1	3.9	8.6	4.7	10.6
18.168 (17m)	6	1.7	3.9	3.9	8.6	5.5	12.2	6.7	14.9
18.168 (17m)	9	2.4	5.4	5.4	12.2	7.7	17.2	9.4	21.1
21.145 (15m)	0	1.0	2.3	2.3	5.1	3.2	7.2	4.0	8.8
21.145 (15m)	3	1.4	3.2	3.2	7.2	4.6	10.2	5.6	12.5
21.145 (15m)	6	2.0	4.6	4.6	10.2	6.4	14.4	7.9	17.6
21.145 (15m)	9	2.9	6.4	6.4	14.4	9.1	20.3	11.1	24.9
24.99 (12m)	0	1.2	2.7	2.7	5.9	3.8	8.4	4.6	10.3
24.99 (12m)	3	1.7	3.8	3.8	8.4	5.3	11.9	6.5	14.5
24.99 (12m)	6	2.4	5.3	5.3	11.9	7.5	16.8	9.2	20.5
24.99 (12m)	9	3.4	7.5	7.5	16.8	10.6	23.7	13.0	29.0
29.7 (10m)	0	1.4	3.2	3.2	7.1	4.5	10.0	5.5	12.2
29.7 (10m)	3	2.0	4.5	4.5	10.0	6.3	14.1	7.7	17.3
29.7 (10m)	6	2.8	6.3	6.3	14.1	8.9	19.9	10.9	24.4
29.7 (10m)	9	4.0	8.9	8.9	19.9	12.6	28.2	15.4	34.5

VHF/UHF Amateur Bands
All distances are in meters

Freq. (MF/HF) (MHz/Band)	Antenna Gain (dBi)	Peak Envelope Power (watts)							
		50 watts		100 watts		500 watts		1000 watts	
		Con.	Unc.	Con.	Unc.	Con.	Unc.	Con.	Unc.
50 (6m)	0	1.0	2.3	1.4	3.2	3.2	7.1	4.5	10.1
50 (6m)	3	1.4	3.2	2.0	4.5	4.5	10.1	6.4	14.3
50 (6m)	6	2.0	4.5	2.8	6.4	6.4	14.2	9.0	20.1
50 (6m)	9	2.8	6.4	4.0	9.0	9.0	20.1	12.7	28.4
50 (6m)	12	4.0	9.0	5.7	12.7	12.7	28.4	18.0	40.2
50 (6m)	15	5.7	12.7	8.0	18.0	18.0	40.2	25.4	56.8
144 (2m)	0	1.0	2.3	1.4	3.2	3.2	7.1	4.5	10.1
144 (2m)	3	1.4	3.2	2.0	4.5	4.5	10.1	6.4	14.3
144 (2m)	6	2.0	4.5	2.8	6.4	6.4	14.2	9.0	20.1
144 (2m)	9	2.8	6.4	4.0	9.0	9.0	20.1	12.7	28.4
144 (2m)	12	4.0	9.0	5.7	12.7	12.7	28.4	18.0	40.2
144 (2m)	15	5.7	12.7	8.0	18.0	18.0	40.2	25.4	56.8
144 (2m)	20	10.1	22.6	14.3	32.0	32.0	71.4	45.1	101.0
222 (1.25m)	0	1.0	2.3	1.4	3.2	3.2	7.1	4.5	10.1
222 (1.25m)	3	1.4	3.2	2.0	4.5	4.5	10.1	6.4	14.3
222 (1.25m)	6	2.0	4.5	2.8	6.4	6.4	14.2	9.0	20.1
222 (1.25m)	9	2.8	6.4	4.0	9.0	9.0	20.1	12.7	28.4
222 (1.25m)	12	4.0	9.0	5.7	12.7	12.7	28.4	18.0	40.2
222 (1.25m)	15	5.7	12.7	8.0	18.0	18.0	40.2	25.4	56.8
450 (70cm)	0	0.8	1.8	1.2	2.6	2.6	5.8	3.7	8.2
450 (70cm)	3	1.2	2.6	1.6	3.7	3.7	8.2	5.2	11.6
450 (70cm)	6	1.6	3.7	2.3	5.2	5.2	11.6	7.4	16.4
450 (70cm)	9	2.3	5.2	3.3	7.3	7.3	16.4	10.4	23.2
450 (70cm)	12	3.3	7.3	4.6	10.4	10.4	23.2	14.7	32.8
902 (33cm)	0	0.6	1.3	0.8	1.8	1.8	4.1	2.6	5.8
902 (33cm)	3	0.8	1.8	1.2	2.6	2.6	5.8	3.7	8.2
902 (33cm)	6	1.2	2.6	1.6	3.7	3.7	8.2	5.2	11.6
902 (33cm)	9	1.6	3.7	2.3	5.2	5.2	11.6	7.3	16.4
902 (33cm)	12	2.3	5.2	3.3	7.3	7.3	16.4	10.4	23.2
1240 (23cm)	0	0.5	1.1	0.7	1.6	1.6	3.5	2.2	5.0
1240 (23cm)	3	0.7	1.6	1.0	2.2	2.2	5.0	3.1	7.0
1240 (23cm)	6	1.0	2.2	1.4	3.1	3.1	7.0	4.4	9.9
1240 (23cm)	9	1.4	3.1	2.0	4.4	4.4	9.9	6.3	14.0
1240 (23cm)	12	2.0	4.4	2.8	6.2	6.2	14.0	8.8	19.8

All distances are in meters. To convert from meters to feet multiply meters by 3.28. Distance indicated is shortest line-of-sight distance to point where MPE limit for appropriate exposure tier is predicted to occur.

AUTHORIZED FREQUENCY BANDS – AMATEUR SERVICE (for U.S. Amateur Stations operating from ITU-Region 2–North and South America)

Current License Class[1] Grandfathered[2]	Novice	Technician Technician	Tech. w/Code Technician Plus	General General	Advanced Advanced	Extra Class Extra Class
160				1800-2000 kHz/All	1800-2000 kHz/All	1800-2000 kHz/All
80	3675-3725 kHz/CW		3675-3725 kHz/CW	3525-3750 kHz/CW 3850-4000 kHz/Ph	3525-3750 kHz/CW 3775-4000 kHz/Ph	3500-4000 kHz/CW 3750-4000 kHz/Ph
40	7100-7150 kHz/CW		7100-7150 kHz/CW	7025-7150 kHz/CW 7225-7300 kHz/Ph	7025-7300 kHz/CW 7150-7300 kHz/Ph	7000-7300 kHz/CW 7150-7300 kHz/Ph
30				10.1-10.15 MHz/CW	10.1-10.15 MHz/CW	10.1-10.15 MHz/CW
20				14.025-14.15 MHz/CW 14.225-14.35 MHz/Ph	14.025-14.15 MHz/CW 14.175-14.35 MHz/Ph	14.0-14.35 MHz/CW 14.15-14.35 MHz/Ph
17				18.068-18.11 MHz/CW 18.11-18.168 MHz/Ph	18.068-18.11 MHz/CW 18.11-18.168 MHz/Ph	18.068-18.11 MHz/CW 18.11-18.168 MHz/Ph
15	21.1-21.2 MHz/CW		21.1-21.2 MHz/CW	21.025-21.2 MHz/CW 21.3-21.45 MHz/Ph	21.025-21.2 MHz/CW 21.225-21.45 MHz/Ph	21.0-21.45 MHz/CW 21.2-21.45 MHz/Ph
12				24.89-24.99 MHz/CW 24.93-24.99 MHz/Ph	24.89-24.99 MHz/CW 24.93-24.99 MHz/Ph	24.89-24.99 MHz/CW 24.93-24.99 MHz/Ph
10	28.1-28.5 MHz/CW 28.3-28.5 MHz/Ph		28.1-28.5 MHz/CW 28.3-28.5 MHz/Ph	28.0-29.7 MHz/CW 28.3-29.7 MHz/Ph	28.0-29.7 MHz/CW 28.3-29.7 MHz/Ph	28.0-29.7 MHz/CW 28.3-29.7 MHz/Ph
6		50-54 MHz/CW 50.1-54 MHz/Ph	50-54 MHz/CW 50.1-54 MHz/Ph	50-54 MHz/CW 50.1-54 MHz/Ph	50-54 MHz/CW 50.1-54 MHz/Ph	50-54 MHz/CW 50.1-54 MHz/Ph
2		144-148 MHz/CW 144.1-148 MHz/All	144-148 MHz/CW 144.1-148 MHz/All	144-148 MHz/CW 144.1-148 MHz/All	144-148 MHz/CW 144.1-148 MHz/All	144-148 MHz/CW 144.1-148 MHz/All
1.25	222-225 MHz/All	[3]222-225 MHz/All	222-225 MHz/All	222-225 MHz/All	222-225 MHz/All	222-225 MHz/All
0.70		420-450 MHz/All	420-450 MHz/All	420-450 MHz/All	420-450 MHz/All	420-450 MHz/All
0.33		902-928 MHz/All	902-928 MHz/All	902-928 MHz/All	902-928 MHz/All	902-928 MHz/All
0.23	1270-1295 MHz/All	1240-1300 MHz/All	1240-1300 MHz/All	1240-1300 MHz/All	1240-1300 MHz/All	1240-1300 MHz/All

[1] Effective 4-15-00   [2] Prior to 4-15-00   [3] Effective 2/1/944 219-220 MHz is authorized for point-to-point fixed digital message forwarding systems.

Note: Morse code (CW, A1A) may be used on any frequency allocated to the amateur service. Telephony emission (abbreviated Ph above) authorized on certain bands as indicated. Higher class licensees may use slow-scan television and facsimile emissions on the Phone bands; radio teletype/digital on the CW bands. All amateur modes and emissions are authorized above 144.1 MHz. In actual practice, the modes/emissions used are somewhat more complicated than shown above due to the existence of various band plans and "gentlemen's agreements" concerning where certain operations should take place.

ITU Regions

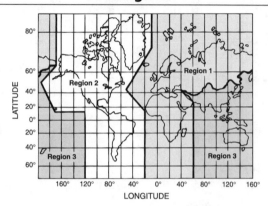

List of Countries Permitting Third-Party Traffic

Country	Call Sign Prefix	Country	Call Sign Prefix	Country	Call Sign Prefix
Antigua and Barbuda	V2	El Salvador	YS	Paraguay	ZP
Argentina	LU	The Gambia	C5	Peru	OA
Australia	VK	Ghana	9G	Philippines	DU
Austria, Vienna	4U1VIC	Grenada	J3	St. Christopher & Nevis	V4
Belize	V3	Guatemala	TG	St. Lucia	J6
Bolivia	CP	Guyana	8R	St. Vincent & Grenadines	J8
Bosnia-Herzegovina	T9	Haiti	HH	Sierra Leone	9L
Brazil	PY	Honduras	HR	South Africa	ZS
Canada	VE, VO, VY	Israel	4X	Swaziland	3D6
Chile	CE	Jamaica	6Y	Trinidad and Tobago	9Y
Colombia	HK	Jordan	JY	Turkey	TA
Comoros	D6	Liberia	EL	United Kingdom	GB*
Costa Rica	TI	Marshall Is	V6	Uruguay	CX
Cuba	CO	Mexico	XE	Venezuela	YV
Dominica	J7	Micronesia	V6	ITU-Geneva	4U1ITU
Dominican Republic	HI	Nicaragua	YN	VIC-Vienna	4U1VIC
Ecuador	HC	Panama	HP		

Countries Holding U.S. Reciprocal Agreements

Antigua, Barbuda	Chile	Greece	Liberia	Seychelles
Argentina	Colombia	Greenland	Luxembourg	Sierra Leone
Australia	Costa Rica	Grenada	Macedonia	Solomon Islands
Austria	Croatia	Guatemala	Marshall Is.	South Africa
Bahamas	Cyprus	Guyana	Mexico	Spain
Barbados	Denmark	Haiti	Micronesia	St. Lucia
Belgium	Dominica	Honduras	Monaco	St. Vincent and
Belize	Dominican Rep.	Iceland	Netherlands	Grenadines
Bolivia	Ecuador	India	Netherlands Ant.	Surinam
Bosnia-	El Salvador	Indonesia	New Zealand	Sweden
Herzegovina	Fiji	Ireland	Nicaragua	Switzerland
Botswana	Finland	Israel	Norway	Thailand
Brazil	France[2]	Italy	Panama	Trinidad, Tobago
Canada[1]	Germany	Jamaica	Paraguay	Turkey
		Japan	Papua New Guinea	Tuvalu
1. Do not need reciprocal permit		Jordan	Peru	United Kingdom[3]
2. Includes all French Territories		Kiribati	Philippines	Uruguay
3. Includes all British Territories		Kuwait	Portugal	Venezuela

Glossary

Amateur communication: Noncommercial radio communication by or among amateur stations solely with a personal aim and without personal or business interest.

Amateur operator/primary station license: An instrument of authorization issued by the FCC comprised of a station license, and also incorporating an operator license indicating the class of privileges.

Amateur operator: A person holding a valid license to operate an amateur station issued by the FCC. Amateur operators are frequently referred to as ham operators.

Amateur Radio services: The amateur service, the amateur-satellite service, and the radio amateur civil emergency service.

Amateur-satellite service: A radiocommunication service using stations on Earth satellites for the same purpose as those of the amateur service.

Amateur service: A radiocommunication service for the purpose of self-training, intercommunication and technical investigations carried out by amateurs; that is, duly authorized persons interested in radio technique solely with a personal aim and without pecuniary interest.

Amateur station: A station licensed in the amateur service embracing necessary apparatus at a particular location used for amateur communication.

AMSAT: Radio Amateur Satellite Corporation, a nonprofit scientific organization. (P.O. Box #27, Washington, DC 20044)

ANSI: American National Standards Institute. A non-government organization that develops recommended standards for a variety of applications.

APRS: Automatic Position Radio System, which takes GPS (Global Positioning System) information and translates it into an automatic packet of digital information.

ARES: Amateur Radio Emergency Service — the emergency division of the American Radio Relay League. Also see RACES

ARRL: American Radio Relay League, national organization of U.S. Amateur Radio operators. (225 Main Street, Newington, CT 06111)

Audio Frequency (AF): The range of frequencies that can be heard by the human ear, generally 20 hertz to 20 kilohertz.

Automatic control: The use of devices and procedures for station control without the control operator being present at the control point when the station is transmitting.

Automatic Volume Control (AVC): A circuit that continually maintains a constant audio output volume in spite of deviations in input signal strength.

Beam or Yagi antenna: An antenna array that receives or transmits RF energy in a particular direction. Usually rotatable.

Block diagram: A simplified outline of an electronic system where circuits or components are shown as boxes.

Broadcasting: Information or programming transmitted by radio means intended for the general public.

Bulletin No. 65: The Office of Engineering & Technology bulletin that provides specified safety guidelines for human exposure to radiofrequency (RF) radiation.

Business communications: Any transmission or communication the purpose of which is to facilitate the regular business or commercial affairs of any party. Business communications are prohibited in the amateur service.

Call Book: A published list of all licensed amateur operators available in North American and Foreign editions.

Call sign: The FCC systematically assigns each amateur station its primary call sign.

Certificate of Successful Completion of Examination (CSCE): A certificate providing examination credit for 365 days. Both written and code credit can be authorized.

Coaxial cable, Coax: A concentric, two-conductor cable in which one conductor surrounds the other, separated by an insulator.

Controlled Environment: Involves people who are aware of and who can exercise control over radiofrequency exposure. Controlled exposure limits apply to both occupational workers and Amateur Radio operators and their immediate households.

Control operator: An amateur operator designated by the licensee of an amateur station to be responsible for the station transmissions.

Coordinated repeater station: An amateur repeater station for which the transmitting and receiving frequencies have been recommended by the recognized repeater coordinator.

Coordinated Universal Time (UTC): (Also Greenwich Mean Time, UCT or Zulu time.) The time at the zero-degree (0°) Meridian which passes through Greenwich, England. A universal time among all amateur operators.

Crystal: A quartz or similar material which has been ground to produce natural vibrations of a specific frequency. Quartz crystals produce a high degree of frequency stability in radio transmitters.

CW: See Morse code.

Dipole antenna: The most common wire antenna. Length is equal to one-half of the wavelength. Fed by coaxial cable.

Dummy antenna: A device or resistor which serves as a transmitter's antenna without radiating radio waves. Generally used to tune up a radio transmitter.

Duplexer: A device that allows a single antenna to be simultaneously used for both reception and transmission.

Duty cycle: As applies to RF safety, the percentage of time that a transmitter is "on" versus "off" in a 6- or 30-minute time period.

Effective Radiated Power (ERP): The product of the transmitter (peak envelope) power, expressed in watts, delivered to the antenna, and the relative gain of an antenna over that of a half-wave dipole antenna.

Electromagnetic radiation: The propagation of radiant energy, including infrared, visible light, ultraviolet, radiofrequency, gamma and X-rays, through space and matter.

Emergency communication: Any amateur communication directly relating to the immediate safety of life of individuals or the immediate protection of property.

Examination Element: The written theory exam or CW test required for various classes of FCC Amateur Radio licenses. Technician must pass Element 2 written theory; General must pass Element 3 written theory plus Element 1 CW; Extra must pass Element 4 written theory.

Far Field: The electromagnetic field located at a great distance from a transmitting antenna. The far field begins at a distance that depends on many factors, including the wavelength and the size of the antenna. Radio signals are normally received in the far field.

FCC Form 605: The FCC application form used to apply for a new amateur operator/primary station license or to renew or modify an existing license.

Federal Communications Commission (FCC): A board of five Commissioners, appointed by the President, having the power to regulate wire and radio telecommunications in the U.S.

Feedline: A system of conductors that connects an antenna to a receiver or transmitter.

Field Day: Annual activity sponsored by the ARRL to demonstrate emergency preparedness of amateur operators.

Field strength: A measure of the intensity of an electric or magnetic field. Electric fields are measured in volts per meter; magnetic fields in amperes per meter.

Filter: A device used to block or reduce alternating currents or signals at certain frequencies while allowing others to pass unimpeded.

Frequency: The number of cycles of alternating current in one second.

Frequency coordinator: An individual or organization which recommends frequencies and other operating and/or technical parameters for amateur repeater operation in order to avoid or minimize potential interferences.

Frequency Modulation (FM): A method of varying a radio carrier wave by causing its frequency to vary in accordance with the information to be conveyed.

Frequency privileges: The transmitting frequency bands available to the various classes of amateur operators. The various Class privileges are listed in Part 97.301 of the FCC rules.

Ground: A connection, accidental or intentional, between a device or circuit and the earth or some common body and the earth or some common body serving as the earth.

Ground wave: A radio wave that is propagated near or at the earth's surface.

Handi-Ham system: Amateur organization dedicated to assisting handicapped amateur operators. (3915 Golden Valley Road, Golden Valley, MN 55422)

Harmful interference: Interference which seriously degrades, obstructs or repeatedly interrupts the operation of a radio communication service.

Harmonic: A radio wave that is a multiple of the fundamental frequency. The second harmonic is twice the fundamental frequency, the third harmonic, three times, etc.

Hertz: One complete alternating cycle per second. Named after Heinrich R. Hertz, a German physicist. The number of hertz is the frequency of the audio or radio wave.

High Frequency (HF): The band of frequencies that lie between 3 and 30 Megahertz. It is from these frequencies that radio waves are returned to earth from the ionosphere.

High-Pass filter: A device that allows passage of high frequency signals but attenuates the lower frequencies. When installed on a television set, a high-pass filter allows TV frequencies to pass while blocking lower-frequency amateur signals.

Inverse Square Law: The physical principle by which power density decreases as you get further away from a transmitting antenna. RF power density decreases by the inverse square of the distance.

Ionization: The process of adding or stripping away electrons from atoms or molecules. Ionization occurs when substances are heated at high temperatures or exposed to high voltages. It can lead to significant genetic damage in biological tissue.

Ionosphere: Outer limits of atmosphere from which HF amateur communications signals are returned to earth.

IRC: International Reply Coupon, a method of prepaying postage for a foreign amateur's QSL card.

Jamming: The intentional, malicious interference with another radio signal.

Key clicks, Chirps: Defective keying of a telegraphy signal sounding like tapping or high varying pitches.

Linear amplifier: A device that accurately reproduces a radio wave in magnified form.

Long wire: A horizontal wire antenna that is one wavelength or longer in length.

Low-Pass filter: Device connected to worldwide transmitters that inhibits passage of higher frequencies that cause television interference but does not affect amateur transmissions.

Machine: A ham slang word for an automatic repeater station.

Malicious interference: See jamming.

MARS: The Military Affiliate Radio System. An organization that coordinates the activities of amateur communications with military radio communications.

Maximum authorized transmitting power: Amateur stations must use no more than the maximum transmitter power necessary to carry out the desired communications. The maximum P.E.P. output power levels authorized Novices are 200 watts in the 80-, 40-, 15- and 10-meter bands, 25 watts in the 222-MHz band, and 5 watts in the 1270-MHz bands.

Maximum Permissible Exposure (MPE): The maximum amount of electric and magnetic RF energy to which a person may safely be exposed.

Maximum usable frequency (MFU): The highest frequency that will be returned to earth from the ionosphere.

Medium frequency (MF): The band of frequencies that lies between 300 and 3,000 kHz (3 MHz).

Microwave: Electromagnetic waves with a frequency of 300 MHz to 300 GHz. Microwaves can cause heating of biological tissue.

Mobile operation: Radio communications conducted while in motion or during halts at unspecified locations.

Mode: Type of transmission such as voice, teletype, code, television, facsimile.

Modulate: To vary the amplitude, frequency, or phase of a radiofrequency wave in accordance with the information to be conveyed.

Morse code: The International Morse code, A1A emission. Interrupted continuous wave communications conducted using a dot-dash code for letters, numbers and operating procedure signs.

Near Field: The electromagnetic field located in the immediate vicinity of the antenna. Energy in the near field depends on the size of the antenna, its wavelength and transmission power.

Nonionizing radiation: Electromagnetic waves, or fields, which do not have the capability to alter the molecular structure of substances. RF energy is nonionizing radiation.

Novice operator: An FCC licensed, entry-level amateur operator in the amateur service.

Occupational exposure: See controlled environment.

OET: Office of Engineering & Technology, a branch of the FCC that has developed the guidelines for radiofrequency (RF) safety.

Ohm's law: The basic electrical law explaining the relationship between voltage, current and resistance. The current (I) in a circuit is equal to the voltage (E) divided by the resistance (R), or $I = E/R$.

OSCAR: "Orbiting Satellite Carrying Amateur Radio." A series of satellites designed and built by amateur operators of several nations.

Oscillator: A device for generating oscillations or vibrations of an audio or radiofrequency signal.

Packet radio: A digital method of communicating computer-to-computer. A terminal-node controller makes up the packet of data and directs it to another packet station.

Peak Envelope Power (PEP): 1. The power during one radiofrequency cycle at the crest of the modulation envelope, taken under normal operating conditions. 2. The maximum power that can be obtained from a transmitter.

Phone patch: Interconnection of amateur radio to the public switched telephone network, and operated by the control operator of the station.

Power density: A measure of the strength of an electromagnetic field at a distance from its source. Usually expressed in milliwatts per square centimeter (mW/cm2). Far-field power density decreases according to the Law of Inverse Squares.

Power supply: A device or circuit that provides the appropriate voltage and current to another device or circuit.

Propagation: The travel of electromagnetic waves or sound waves through a medium.

Public exposure: See "uncontrolled" environment.

Q-signals: International three-letter abbreviations beginning with the letter Q used primarily to convey information using the Morse code.

QSL Bureau: An office that bulk processes QSL (radio confirmation) cards for (or from) foreign amateur operators as a postage-saving mechanism.

RACES (Radio Amateur Civil Emergency Service): A radio service using amateur stations for civil defense communications during periods of local, regional, or national emergencies.

Radiation: Electromagnetic energy, such as radio waves, traveling forth into space from a transmitter.

Radiofrequency (RF): The range of frequencies over 20 kilohertz that can be propagated through space.

Radiofrequency (RF) radiation: Electromagnetic fields or waves having a frequency between 3 kHz and 300 GHz.

Radiofrequency spectrum: The eight electromagnetic bands ranked according to their frequency and wavelength. Specifically, the very-low, low, medium, high, very-high, ultra-high, super-high, and extremely-high frequency bands.

Radio wave: A combination of electric and magnetic fields varying at a radiofrequency and traveling through space at the speed of light.

Repeater operation: Automatic amateur stations that retransmit the signals of other amateur stations.

Routine RF radiation evaluation: The process of determining if the RF energy from a transmitter exceeds the Maximum Permissible Exposure (MPE) limits in a controlled or uncontrolled environment.

RST Report: A telegraphy signal report system of Readability, Strength and Tone.

S-meter: A voltmeter calibrated from 0 to 9 that indicates the relative signal strength of an incoming signal at a radio receiver.

Selectivity: The ability of a circuit (or radio receiver) to separate the desired signal from those not wanted.

Sensitivity: The ability of a circuit (or radio receiver) to detect a specified input signal.

Short circuit: An unintended, low-resistance connection across a voltage source resulting in high current and possible damage.

Shortwave: The high frequencies that lie between 3 and 30 Megahertz that are propagated long distances.

Single-Sideband (SSB): A method of radio transmission in which the RF carrier and one of the sidebands is suppressed and all of the information is carried in the one remaining sideband.

Skip wave, Skip zone: A radio wave reflected back to earth. The distance between the radio transmitter and the site of a radio wave's return to earth.

Sky-wave: A radio wave that is refracted back to earth. Sometimes called an ionospheric wave.

Specific Absorption Rate (SAR): The time rate at which radiofrequency energy is absorbed into the human body.

Spectrum: A series of radiated energies arranged in order of wavelength. The radio spectrum extends from 20 kilohertz upward.

Spurious Emissions: Unwanted radiofrequency signals emitted from a transmitter that sometimes cause interference.

Station license, location: No transmitting station shall be operated in the amateur service without being licensed by the FCC. Each amateur station shall have one land location, the address of which appears in the station license.

Sunspot Cycle: An 11-year cycle of solar disturbances which greatly affects radio wave propagation.

Technician operator: An Amateur Radio operator who has successfully passed Element 2.

Technician-Plus: An amateur operator who has passed a 5-wpm code test in addition to Technician Class requirements.

Telegraphy: Communications transmission and reception using CW, International Morse code.

Telephony: Communications transmission and reception in the voice mode.

Telecommunications: The electrical conversion, switching, transmission and control of audio video and data signals by wire or radio.

Temporary operating authority: Authority to operate your amateur station while awaiting arrival of an upgraded license.

Terrestrial station location: Any location of a radio station on the surface of the earth including the sea.

Thermal effects: As applies to RF radiation, biological tissue damage resulting because of the body's inability to cope with or dissipate excessive heat.

Third-party traffic: Amateur communication by or under the supervision of the control operator at an amateur station to another amateur station on behalf of others.

Time-averaging: As applies to RF safety, the amount of electromagnetic radiation over a given time. The premise of time-averaging is that the human body can tolerate the thermal load caused by high, localized RF exposures for short periods of time.

Transceiver: A combination radio transmitter and receiver.

Transition region: Area where power density decreases inversely with distance from the antenna.

Transmatch: An antenna tuner used to match the impedance of the transmitter output to the transmission line of an antenna.

Transmitter: Equipment used to generate radio waves. Most commonly, this radio carrier signal is amplitude varied or frequency varied (modulated) with information and radiated into space.

Transmitter power: The average peak envelope power (output) present at the antenna terminals of the transmitter. The term "transmitted" includes any external radiofrequency power amplifier which may be used.

Ultra High Frequency (UHF): Ultra high frequency radio waves that are in the range of 300 to 3,000 MHz.

Uncontrolled environment: Applies to those persons who have no control over their exposure to RF energy in the environment. Residences adjacent to ham radio installations are considered to be in an "uncontrolled" environment.

Upper Sideband (USB): The proper operating mode for sideband transmissions made in the new Novice 10-meter voice band. Amateurs generally operate USB at 20 meters and higher frequencies; lower sideband (LSB) at 40 meters and lower frequencies.

Very High Frequency (VHF): Very high frequency radio waves that are in the range of 30 to 300 MHz.

Volunteer Examiner: An amateur operator of at least a General Class level who prepares and administers amateur operator license examinations.

Volunteer Examiner Coordinator (VEC): A member of an organization which has entered into an agreement with the FCC to coordinate the efforts of volunteer examiners in preparing and administering examinations for amateur operator licenses.

Index